LAND HUNGER

New Approaches to Midwestern Studies

Series editors: Brian Schoen and Jon K. Lauck

Nikki M. Taylor, *Driven toward Madness: The Fugitive Slave Margaret Garner and Tragedy on the Ohio*

Jenny Bourne, *In Essentials, Unity: An Economic History of the Grange Movement*

David Andrew Nichols, *Peoples of the Inland Sea: Native Americans and Newcomers in the Great Lakes Region, 1600–1870*

James Simeone, *The Saints and the State: The Mormon Troubles in Illinois*

Timothy Anderson and Brian Schoen, eds., *Settling Ohio: First Peoples and Beyond*

Mansel G. Blackford, *Land Hunger: Ohio and the Western Frontiers*

LAND HUNGER

Ohio and the Western Frontiers

Mansel G. Blackford

OHIO UNIVERSITY PRESS
ATHENS

Ohio University Press, Athens, Ohio 45701
ohioswallow.com

Printed in the United States of America
Ohio University Press books are printed on acid-free paper ∞ ™

Pioneers Crossing the Ohio River was a mural painted in 1941 by Michael Loew for the Amherst, Ohio, post office. About four feet tall and fourteen feet long, it was photographed by Connie Girard in 1988. The mural depicts the tremendous importance of the Ohio River for early European Americans moving into the Ohio Country. Courtesy of the Ohio History Connection, Image ALO4712.

Hardcover ISBN: 978-0-8214-2635-7
Paperback ISBN: 978-0-8214-2636-4
Electronic ISBN: 978-0-8214-2637-1

Library of Congress Cataloging-in-Publication Data available upon request.

For my wife, Victoria.

Thank you for coming on the journey with me.

Contents

Series Editors' Preface

New Approaches to Midwestern Studies seeks to provide books that are accessible, rich in content, analytically innovative, and timely in the questions they address. Professor Mansel G. Blackford's *Land Hunger: Ohio and the Western Frontiers* is all these things. Blackford moves across time and space and cultures in ways that only a distinguished scholar and experienced author can. He provides a succinct but multilayered synthesis, capturing the dynamic ways that diverse peoples interacted with the environment and one another.

Both ideas and lived experiences shaped land usage, but the environment itself often played a decisive role in shaping outcomes. Without romanticizing Indigenous land usage, Blackford shows how communal views of land management, including brush fire removal, hunting, and limited but nourishing crop pairings, helped Indigenous communities support their vibrant societies through generally sustainable practices. European commercial agriculture brought not only surveyors and privatization but also tilling and deforestation. Draft animals and plant diversification taxed the land, especially when accompanied by hundreds of nonnative weeds. In some places, the draining of swamps lowered the water table, creating conditions for future water shortages. Overhunting by both Native and European American peoples decimated many species of animals until the twentieth century, when different practices and demographic shifts to cities allowed some species of plant and animal life to rebound.

The federal government became an instrument of expansion through force, through expeditions like those led by Lewis and Clark and John Fremont, and through the sponsorship of internal improvement projects. Of particular importance was federal land policy aimed at turning the soil into a commodity that could both fund its existence and ensure western commercial development. Illegal squatters became likely owners, especially after the 1841 preemption law gave them the right to purchase the land. No uniform government policy, though, could fit across the several frontiers: the small homesteads that worked in Oregon provided insufficient lands for success in the arid environment of Kansas.

Land Hunger interlays environmental history with agricultural studies, policy history, and labor practices to show the complex ways that inhabitants shaped, or attempted to shape, the land. It also appreciates the psychological and cultural elements of westward expansion as both romanticism and pragmatism informed the emotions felt by nineteenth-century emigrants and indigenes as they left, arrived at, or defended soil they saw as theirs. The legacy of those feelings appears in interspersed reflections of later twentieth-century authors like European American writers Conrad Richter, A. B. Guthrie Jr., and Hamlin Garland and Kiowa writer N. Scott Momaday.

Part of what makes this book unique and particularly appropriate for our series is its geographic reach. This story starts in Ohio but travels across the broader geographic Midwest, just as large numbers of White and some Black Ohioans traversed the continent, settling in Oregon and in Civil War Kansas. Some of the skills and understandings of the land they acquired in Ohio proved helpful, but others were ill-suited either for effectively using the land or for engaging the Native American peoples they encountered. Misplaced approaches help explain both the continual violence and the environmental and humanitarian disasters like the Dust Bowl.

A seasoned understanding of vast scholarly literatures mingles with snapshots into the real lives of people like Christopher Gist, Joseph and Anna Howells, and Luther Standing Bear to ensure that *Land Hunger* steers clear of many of the simplistic tropes that sometimes define scholarship. The frontier was not an inevitably democratizing force nor one in which the embrace or rejection of abstract capitalist ideas predetermined outcomes. Triumph and tragedy intertwine revealing a story of westward expansion in which men and women,

Black, White, and Indigenous, used what knowledge they had to try, sometimes successfully and sometimes not, to reshape the environment in ways that served them.

Even before Frederick Jackson Turner's famous 1890s "frontier thesis," Americans saw westward expansion as a force that shaped American history and society. Blackford's work draws from an impressive array of scholarship, from the new western history to environmental history to Native American history, to capture the complexity of that interaction. He shows that along multiple frontiers, different environments interacted with diverse human actions to shape the land, settlers' engagement with it, and the interactions that took place on it. By looking back, Blackford's study shows us that we are not the first to grapple with dramatically changing environmental conditions, reminding us that change is possible but usually crisis driven, with success achieved by working with nature rather than fighting it. We are pleased to add this valuable book, the first since Jon joined as a series editor, to our list.

Jon Lauck
Brian Schoen

Acknowledgments

Numerous people have helped me in preparing this book, and I am delighted to be able to thank them for their encouragement, suggestions, and corrections. I would especially like to thank the many staff members of the Ohio History Connection (formerly the Ohio Historical Society), the Columbus Metropolitan Library, and the Ohio State University Library for their kind aid. To some extent, this project has been a family effort. Victoria Blackford, my wife and a librarian, and Kimberly Neath, my daughter and a former bookstore owner, read earlier versions of this work and offered valuable suggestions on how to improve them. Keith Louise Fulton, a professor emerita of English at the University of Winnipeg and my sister-in-law, also read the manuscript history and provided useful comments.

In addition, William R. Childs, Bartow J. Elmore, R. Douglas Hurt, Barbara Mann, and Thomas Weeks read this work in manuscript form and prepared thoughtful critiques. So did two anonymous readers for the Ohio University Press. Many of my colleagues at the Ohio State University provided a congenial atmosphere where I could work in my retirement; but I am especially indebted to Philip Brown, Joseph Duchi, and Philip Smith for their astute comments made over lunch and coffee get-togethers. Likewise, my thanks extend to Barry Keenan of Denison University.

Those at the Ohio University Press helped turn my manuscript history into a book, and for that accomplishment I owe them a lot, especially Beth Pratt, the director of the press, Ricky Huard, the press's editor in chief, and Jon Lauck and Brian Schoen, the editors of the book series New Approaches to Midwestern Studies, in which my work appears. A special tip of the hat is due Lauck for his long advocacy of this project and for his excellent suggestions about how to improve the resulting manuscript for publication. My thanks extend to Dana Johnson and Tyler Balli for their production and editing skills. Their expertise was essential in bringing this work to completion. Finally, in chapters 1 and 2, I have used some material that first appeared in an article I published in *Ohio History* ("Pioneers and Land on the Ohio Frontier," *Ohio History* 125, no. 2 [Fall 2018]: 7–27); and I want to thank Donna DeBlasio, the editor of the journal, for her support of my work. Thanks also to Mary D. Young, the managing editor of Kent State University Press, which publishes *Ohio History,* for permission to use that information in this volume.

I am, of course, solely responsible for any errors of fact or interpretation that may remain in this history.

Introduction

New People in Western Lands

Writing in his journal in early 1751, Christopher Gist gushed about the Great Miami River valley in western Ohio. A locator for the Ohio Company, which claimed rights to land in this region, Gist described the valley as composed of "fine, rich, level Land, well timbered with large Walnut, Ash, Sugar Trees [sugar maples], Cherry Trees &c." Moreover, the land was "well-watered with a great Number of little Streams or Rivulets" and was "full of beautiful natural Meadows, covered with wild Rye, blue Grass and Clover," which abounded in "turkeys, Deer, Elks, and most sorts of Game, particularly Buffaloes."[1]

Gist's words suggest the land hunger harbored by most early European Americans entering the Ohio Country, and more generally North America. They had at times an almost carnal desire to possess land, as they sought present-day survival and future good lives for their families. (What European Americans considered the Ohio Country usually was the land that became the state of Ohio but often also included part of the future state of Indiana and sometimes sections of territories farther to the west.) Native Americans recognized and rejected this lust for land, sometimes stuffing dirt in the mouth of European Americans they had killed.[2]

* * *

Historians of Ohio and the trans–Appalachian West have long identified land hunger as the major motivation for European Americans' invasion of Indian Country. In an essay written for the first comprehensive history of Ohio, published in 1848, John Kilbourne, a surveyor for and founder of the Scioto Company, which purchased and sold lands in central Ohio, observed that the public domain comprised a "bountiful fund, upon which the national government can draw for centuries, to supply, at low price, all its citizens with a freehold estate."[3] In another early history of the Ohio Country, William Dean Howells wrote in 1897 that European Americans "knew that to the westward there was a region, vast and rich beyond anything words could say, and they longed to possess it, with a hunger that was sometimes a pitiless greed and always a resistless desire."[4] In analyzing the history of the trans–Appalachian West, in 1978, historian Malcolm J. Rohrbough also stressed the significance of land, observing, "The acquisition, cultivation, exploitation, and eternal search for more fertile and cheaper lands provide a common theme." Simply put, "land was the lure."[5] Specifically examining Ohio, scholar R. Douglas Hurt made much the same point in 1998, noting that an "Ohio fever," a desire for land, infected large numbers of Americans in the 1780s and later.[6]

More generally, scholars have stressed that land hunger pulled American settlers west. In a seminal essay on the history of United States frontiers published in 1894, Frederick Jackson Turner asserted, "The existence of an area of free land, its continuous recession, and the advance of American settlement westward, explain American development."[7] In 1931, historian Walter Prescott Webb emphasized the land's physical characteristics, especially its arid or semiarid nature, in explaining the settlement of the Great Plains. Land hunger led Americans and others onto the Great Plains, where they had to modify their ways of living, developed in the much more humid East, Webb argued, to cope with the nearly rainless western plains.[8] Through the 1950s, most scholars viewed that settlement as a crowning triumph of the advance of American civilization. More recently, while they have continued to underline the significance of land hunger, historians have seen it in a negative light, as it led to the conquest and destruction of Native Americans and to widespread environmental degradation. Patricia Nelson Limerick, a leading practitioner of the new western history, wrote in 1987, "The history of the West is a study of a place undergoing conquest and never fully escaping its consequences."[9] Over the past three decades or so, frontier history has moved in a multitude of new directions, but many of the recent studies deal with issues involving land and natural resources.[10]

* * *

Land Hunger shows that notions and realities of land use were central to the experiences of European Americans living in Ohio over several centuries. Moreover, this work examines how those Ohioans (and others) sought to transfer knowledge gained in the Midwest to two other regions, the Oregon Country and the Great Plains, but had only partial success. In doing so, this work significantly extends earlier analyses of those experiences. Throughout, the emphasis is on men and women coming to understand and deal more skillfully with environments new to them. This study, thus, addresses questions of importance to students of the environment and the frontier. How did original inhabitants, Native Americans, interact with newcomers over land matters to help shape frontier lives? How much did governments, especially the federal government, contribute to frontier developments? Above all, how did Euro-American conceptions about the environment, especially water and land, shape actions? And what have been the consequences of those actions through today? Questions like these are relevant to our lives as we grapple with the many environmental challenges resulting from climate changes.

The bulk of *Land Hunger* comprises four chapters. The first two chapters examine European American settlement of the Ohio Country in the late 1700s and early 1800s. As an "Ohio fever" gripped them, Americans crossed the Appalachian Mountains by the tens of thousands to take up farming in country new to them. Land was the primary lure, and how European Americans viewed and used that land helped shape Ohio through the twenty-first century. A mix of pragmatic, romantic, and capitalistic ideas guided their actions. It was here that many European Americans formed ideas about land and the environment, and it was in Ohio, specifically, that the new federal government devised ways to survey and sell lands it claimed. Later, some Ohioans took ideas and practices to other regions with different environments, with only limited success. In entering Ohio and other regions, European Americans pushed aside or killed Native Americans who occupied the land and were already changing it through their hunting and farming practices, fire use, and other ways.

European Americans tried to justify their actions in taking Native land in the Ohio Country and elsewhere. They claimed land by right of conquest, arguing that during the American Revolution they had defeated the British and their Native allies and thus had rights to their lands in the Ohio River valley. Sometimes, European Americans claimed Native lands as part of treaty rights, overlooking that Native Americans had not been defeated in battle during the revolution and ignoring that most treaties were secured at least in part by chicanery; many Native leaders whose tribes or nations occupied the lands in question had never signed the treaties. Most basically, European Americans thought they had rights to lands because they would put those lands to better and fuller use than did Native Americans. European Americans viewed their own farming as a higher stage of civilization than hunting and gathering, with which they associated Native Americans. Thus, in his 1751 description of western Ohio, Gist observed that the land "wants Nothing but cultivation to make it a most delightfull Country."[11] Moreover, many European Americans believed the Bible implored them to take the land and cultivate it to the glory of their God. Most, including Gist, adopted the fiction that western lands were vacant and uninhabited. They ignored extensive Native farming and dwelling in many regions, including the Ohio Country.

Chapters 3 and 4 examine how European Americans in Ohio tried to take ideas about the environment and ways of doing things developed in the Midwest to other parts of the United States. Chapter 3 shifts the story from the trans–Appalachian West to the trans–Mississippi West by looking at how European Americans entered and changed the Oregon Country in the 1840s and later. The chapter investigates the development of farming in western Oregon and western Washington. Very humid and rainy, these areas demanded new farming methods and ways of living different from those formed in the Ohio Country. Chapter 4 examines how Ohioans and others moved onto the Great Plains, particularly in Kansas, after the Civil War. Dry weather in a region devoid of trees presented challenges quite different from those encountered in the Oregon Country. How European Americans coped, or failed to cope, with life in the regions new to them is, in part, an Ohio story—a continuation in some senses of Ohio frontiers.

Their invasion of both the Great Plains and the Oregon Country demonstrates the continuing land hunger most European Americans held. The entrance of European Americans into those regions shows as well the need to modify initial ideas about lands when new environmental conditions are encountered. The superhumid Oregon Country and the very dry western Great Plains did not yield well to agricultural methods developed and practiced in the Ohio Country. *Land Hunger* is, then, in its broadest sense, an examination of how people sought to deal with environments new to them. The study focuses on European Americans, for they inundated the Ohio Country in the late 1700s and early 1800s. Nonetheless, the work also regards Native Americans and African Americans throughout, for those groups, too, played important roles in the early development of Ohio. As geographer Timothy G. Anderson reminded others in 2023, "Ohio was from the outset not only a meeting place of diverse groups of people, but also a place where diverse idea(l)s and discourses were contested."[12]

Throughout, the four chapters examine how frontier resources have been pictured in fiction, as one way to uncover what those resources have meant to Americans.[13] For the most part, however, the work relies on a close examination of diaries, letters, and reminiscences, particularly those readily available to anyone who might desire to delve still more deeply into land-development issues. This work is also based on a reading of a broad range of studies published by other scholars, again, especially those generally accessible to the public. The emphasis is on "frontiers," which scholars have defined in many ways.[14] *Land Hunger* treats frontiers as zones or places of interaction between different groups of people, most notably Native Americans, African Americans, and European Americans. As historian Elliott West wisely writes, "A frontier never separated things. It brought them together."[15]

Historian Richard White and other scholars have been showing for about a generation that frontiers were complex places, usually with no single group dominant.[16] While the emphasis of *Land Hunger* is on how European Americans and African Americans dealt with lands new to them, it is important to remember that Native Americans already lived on those lands and had often done so for millennia. Yet Native Americans were anything but static in their histories and in their use of lands and other natural resources. In fact, many Native groups developed new ways of dealing with their environments over time. The Shawnee, to cite just one example, ranged widely across North America east of the Mississippi River before settling mainly in the Ohio Country during the 1600s and 1700s. As they inhabited lands from the Deep South to the Old Northwest, they used different hunting and agricultural techniques.[17]

As European Americans moved west, invading Indian Country, they took prevailing European and eastern American ideas about land with them and then developed new concepts as well. In their descriptions of western lands and resources they often combined pragmatic or utilitarian concepts with romantic ones. As they faced west into the Ohio Country, they viewed lush, green landscapes populated by massive trees as "beautiful," "awesome," and even "sublime." But they also saw land as a commodity that should be individually bought and sold and used for farming. Many European American explorers and settlers were, in fact, interested in capitalistic real estate development as much as in farming. The French social thinker and writer Alexis de Tocqueville, who traveled widely in the new United States, caught this attitude well, observing in 1832, "It seldom happens that an American farmer settles for good upon the land which he occupies; especially in districts of the Far West [then, the Midwest], he brings land into tillage in order to sell it again, and not to farm it." Indeed, the farmer "builds a farmhouse on the speculation, that as the state of the country will soon be changed by the increase in population, a good price may be obtained for it."[18]

* * *

The organization of *Land Hunger* should not be taken to mean that the study endorses American exceptionalism or the spread of American (or more generally Euro-American) civilization across what is now the United States as being in any way a triumphant development or sign of progress. I chose to deal with three regions—the Ohio Country, the Oregon Country, and the Great Plains—because they demonstrate well both commonalities and particularities in European Americans' attitudes toward land and development and because I have some personal knowledge of the areas.[19] My interest in interactions between frontier developments, economic changes, and environmental issues reaches back to my first book, published in 1977, which looked at the intertwining of those matters in

California.[20] More recently, I have examined how those interactions have played out in both urban and rural settings and what their consequences have been over time.[21] How have Americans reached decisions on developmental issues? How have those decisions shaped regions?

My specific interest in the areas covered in this study stems in part from having lived in them and viewed many changes occurring in them. Born in Seattle in 1944, I came of age in a rapidly developing pre-Starbucks Pacific Northwest. No doubt, my father's participation in early king crabbing as captain of a pioneering fishing and processing vessel helped spur my interest in the history of frontier fisheries.[22] My wife grew up in Billings, Montana, on the northern Great Plains, and she and I have spent many enjoyable times exploring the Big Sky State. We have lived in Columbus, Ohio, since 1972, where I taught history at the Ohio State University until my retirement in 2012. Exploring the state on foot, by canoe, and on horseback has helped give me on-the-ground insights into some of the many developments occurring in Ohio. Business historians—and I am one of them—have not usually paid much attention to environmental matters, although that situation is changing. I hope this study spurs more research connecting economic alterations to environmental ones.[23]

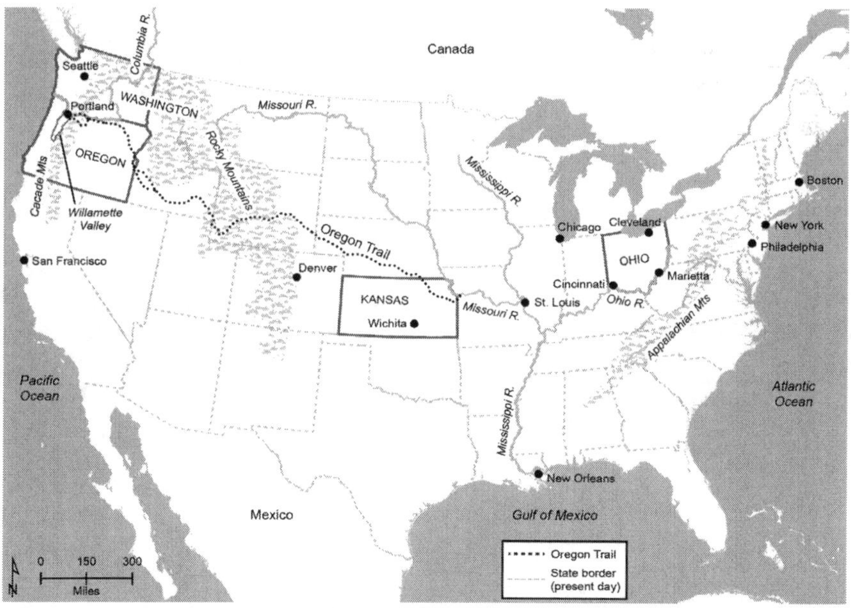

Ohioans were important in the development of frontiers across the United States, including Oregon and Kansas. Map made by Brian Edward Balsley, GISP.

1

Viewing Land in the Ohio Country

The journal of Margaret Dwight, who traveled to Warren, Ohio, from Milford, Connecticut, in 1810, is studded with comments about poor taverns and bad roads. Dwight lamented that she would never see her sister in Milford again because the highways were in very poor repair, leading her to complain, "I cannot think of traversing this road again." Nonetheless, Dwight also observed that people were streaming into Ohio. "I think Ohio," she wrote, "will be filled up before winter, wagons without number."[1] She proved correct, as land hunger drew tens of thousands of European Americans into the Ohio Country. The population of Ohio, which became a state in 1803, increased from 45,000 in 1800 to 231,000 ten years later and soared to 581,000 by 1820. Some 981,000 people lived in Ohio in 1830, nearly all on farms and in small towns. That same year, Cincinnati, Cleveland, and Columbus had a combined population of fewer than 30,000 people.

Lying behind the rush to the Ohio Country lay a lust for land originating in colonial times and even earlier in a shortage of good farmland in Europe, especially Great Britain. Europe's population rebounded, with ups and downs, after the Black Death, or the bubonic plague, abated in the 1400s. The population of Great Britain swelled from 2.1 million in 1430 to 3.8 million in 1603 to 6.9 million in 1700 to 7.8 million by 1760. This population increase put constraints on land ownership and usage. Despite people's movement to cities like London, there simply was not enough land to go around, especially since aristocrats and well-to-do gentry owned most of it. In search of land, Britons migrated to North America, with even those who did so as indentured servants hoping to own land one day. There were additional motivations for migration; some also sought a place where they could practice the religion of their choice, for example.[2] Great Britain was the source of most early non-Black migration to the Eastern Seaboard of what would become the United States, but migrants also came from Spain, France, the Netherlands, and other nations.

Something of the same story was repeated during the mid-eighteenth century in parts of North America's Eastern Seaboard, its population exploding as immigration from Great Britain and other European nations swelled. By 1776, the thirteen colonies had a population of about 2.5 million, including 500,000 African Americans, mainly enslaved, and 100,000 Native Americans. For some, migration westward was again the solution to perceived shortages of good farmland. By the 1760s and 1770s, European Americans were crossing the Appalachian Mountains into Kentucky and western Pennsylvania to seek new land to replace nitrogen-depleted soils exhausted by their farming methods and to acquire land for their sons and their families to develop and farm. Kentucky, which was first a county of Virginia, became a state in 1792. By then, European American explorers, traders, and settlers had been visiting Ohio for some decades. Marietta, the first permanent American settlement in what became the state of Ohio, was founded in 1788.[3]

This chapter focuses on how European Americans viewed lands new to them in the Ohio Country; it begins, however, by looking at Native American groups in the region and how they perceived and used lands for hunting and farming. Both Native Americans and European Americans altered their natural environments, the latter much more so. The changes European Americans made were important in setting the stage for modern-day Ohio.

NATIVE AMERICANS AND OHIO LANDS

Changes to lands in what became known as the Ohio Country began well before the coming of the first European Americans in the 1600s and certainly long before the founding of their first permanent settlements in the late 1700s, as Native Americans began reshaping the land much earlier. In his pathbreaking *Changes in the Land: Indians, Colonists, and the Ecology of New England,* first published in 1983, historian William Cronon emphasizes that early European Americans did not encounter "a Virgin Land, the Forest Primeval, a wilderness which had existed for eons uninfluenced by human hands." To the contrary, "Indians had lived on the continent for thousands of years and had to a significant extent modified the environment to their purposes."[4] As they did throughout New England and most of North America, Native Americans in Ohio altered their natural environments as they hunted, used fire, and cultivated crops.[5] Native Americans were, as anthropologist Joseph A. Gingerich wrote in 2023, "the true pioneers" in Ohio and elsewhere. Native Americans "first saw and explored the North and South American continents."[6]

Paleo Indians entered the Americas via a land bridge across the Bering Strait, called Beringia, linking Asia to North America. Scholars are currently reevaluating exactly when and how the first people came to the Americas. In a comprehensive account, anthropologist and geneticist Jennifer Raff wrote in early 2022, "The history of how people first got to the Americas remains a mystery, a complex puzzle to be solved." She further observed, "Many archaeologists and geneticists now believe that people were present in the Americas far earlier than was previously thought: perhaps by 17,000–16,000 years ago, or even as early as 30,000–25,000 years ago." She has called "the peopling of the Americas" a story of "resilience, compassion, intrepidness, adventure, and loss."[7] When Paleo Indians first came to Ohio is disputed, but they were certainly present by about 13,000–11,000 years ago.[8] Nomadic hunters, they generally trod lightly on the ground.

The period of the Archaic Indians in Ohio dates 9,000–8,000 years ago in Ohio until about 2,000–1,500 years ago. Their lives were defined by hunting animals with spears and spear throwers (atlatls) and gathering food. Also, several plants were domesticated in the southern Midwest and northern Southeast during this time. Agriculture began with small garden plots of gourds, squashes, goosefoot, marsh elder, maygrass, erect knotweed, and barley.[9] Populations increased, villagers became more sedentary, and pottery came into use 5,000–2,500 years ago. Long-distant trade in copper, marine shells, and flint may have begun. (Scholars debate whether true trade, an exchange of goods, began this early. Many prefer the term "interaction sphere" to explain the presence of nonindigenous goods in various scattered places.) Mounds and other earthworks were constructed for social, ceremonial, and astronomical uses. Woodland Indian societies or cultures appeared about 3,000 years ago and lasted nearly into contact times in the 1600s. In Ohio, these included the Adena, Hopewell, and Fort Ancient cultures or societies.[10]

The people of the Adena culture, who lived roughly 2,500–2,000 years ago, were named after the Adena estate of Thomas Worthington near Chillicothe. It was there that one of their mounds was first excavated in 1901. They constructed large burial mounds—for instance, the Conus mound in Marietta—and lived in small villages built on nearby river bottomlands. They hunted, gathered food, and engaged in some agriculture—eating rabbits, deer, nuts, berries, maygrass, goosefoot, barley, sumpweed, and sunflowers, but very little maize (corn). The people of the Hopewell culture, named after a farm in Ross County, where one of their mounds was first excavated, had villages stretching across Ohio, Indiana, and Illinois and flourished about 2,000–1,500 years ago. They built some of the best-known mounds and earthworks in Ohio, such as those in Newark, and lived by a combination of hunting and agriculture, growing maygrass, knotweed, goosefoot, and sunflowers, but not much maize.[11] Their trade reached to the Rocky Mountains and the Atlantic and Gulf Coasts.

After the demise of the people of the Hopewell culture, who may have suffered from disease or simply merged into other groups, major changes came. Around 1,400 years ago, bows and arrows came into common use, replacing or supplementing spears. About 1,000 years ago, maize became a dietary staple, most likely introduced from the Southwest. Beans and squashes accompanied maize, and the three vegetables became known as "the three sisters." Hunting rabbits, deer, and bison was also important. The people built impressive earthworks. Even more than in the past, villages were located on rich bottomlands of rivers, and these villages grew. Some of those who developed this way of life were later called the Fort Ancient people, and their way of living continued among some Indian groups into contact times, as hunting mixed with farming based on maize.[12]

Like their predecessors, postcontact Indians encountered what historian John Mack Faragher has called the "great American forest," forested land sweeping from North America's East Coast westward across the Appalachian Mountains to the Mississippi River. Having "more species of edible and nutritious nuts than any of the world's woodlands," this forest was composed mainly of deciduous hardwoods: beeches, oaks, maples, hickories, and others. These trees produced nuts that could be used as food by men and animals alike. Native people ate *pawcohicora,* an "oily food" made from "the steeped and pounded kernels of the nut." Pecans were "the most prized" of the hickories. Game animals ranging from squirrels to deer, including bears, elk, and bison, also consumed them. "A wide variety of fruit" could also be found in the forest: raspberries, mulberries, strawberries, may apples, cherries, grapes, and the favorite, pawpaws. Like Native Americans, incoming European Americans made use of these forest foods, as did their pigs and cattle. (The nuts and fruit that fell to the forest floor were called "mast" by European American settlers.) Rivers and lakes in the woods contained many types of edible fish: catfish, carp, crappie, bass, sturgeon, and others. In all, there were over one hundred species of fish. Birds passing through on flyways—ducks, geese, and passenger pigeons—were another source of protein. Nonmigratory birds such as turkeys were also important food sources.[13]

Native people relied upon agriculture as well as hunting for their subsistence. In fact, agriculture provided well over half of the food calories they consumed. Like those before them, the Shawnee, Miami, Lenape (Delaware), Wyandot, and other nations or tribes who intermingled and came to dominate Ohio in the 1700s grew maize, beans, and squash. On foot and horseback, they hunted deer, buffalo, and small animals, and they took fish from lakes and streams. In search of good lands and furs, many groups of Native Americans entered and spread throughout Ohio in the 1600s and 1700s.

The Shawnee, inveterate travelers, came from places in the East and South to dominate central Ohio. In 1755, a British superintendent of Indian Affairs called the Shawnee "Stout, Bold, Cunning, and the greatest Travellers in America."[14] Pushed by repeated Iroquois attacks, harmed by diseases introduced by European Americans and for which they lacked immunities, and decimated by slavers seeking Native American victims, the Shawnee left the Ohio Country in the mid- and late 1600s for other regions: the Savannah River area, the region around Kaskaskia, and the northern reaches of Chesapeake Bay. Still other Shawnee groups moved south into what is now Alabama to live in villages, intermingling with the Creek. However, under pressure from farmers wanting more land in the regions to which they had fled, especially Pennsylvania, many Shawnee returned to the Ohio Country in the 1720s and later. In 1727, Shawnee people, along with members of other tribes, founded Logstown eighteen miles downstream from where the confluence of the Allegheny and Monongahela Rivers form the Ohio River, and a few years later, Lower Shawnee Town, where the Scioto River enters the Ohio River. Throughout their many migrations, the Shawnee kept alive their tribal identity through a shared language, ceremonies, and rituals. The Lenape and Wyandot (an offshoot of the Huron—"Huron" being a French slur, according to Native American scholar Barbara Mann) were pushed west by other tribes and European Americans and came to reside mainly in eastern and northern Ohio. The Miami moved into western Ohio from what is now Indiana, partly in search of British trade goods.

For Native people in the Ohio Country, land and its resources were not commodities to be bought and sold. Rather, they were means to gain a living. They believed that no individual or tribe had the right to sell land to European Americans. Indeed, there was no Native tradition that authorized private land ownership; land and its resources were held in common. Well before the charismatic Shawnee leader Tecumseh forcefully put forward that thought, other Native leaders had long embraced it. A leading Ohio Lenape warrior explained to the Moravian missionary David McClure in 1768: "When you white men buy a farm, you buy only the land. You don't buy the horses and cows and sheep. The elks are our horses, the Buffaloes are our cows, the deer are sheep, and the whites shan't have them."[15] Tecumseh spoke for many Native people when he declared bluntly in the early 1800s, "They [European Americans] have taken upon themselves to say this tract belongs to the Miamis, this to the Delawares, and so on. But the Great Spirit intended it to be the common property of all the tribes, nor can it be sold without the consent of all."[16]

In most regions of the Midwest, Native nations, tribes, clans within tribes, and families had *rights to use* the resources of specific areas, including lands for picking berries, gathering wild rice, making sugar, hunting, and farming. Specific spots good for fishing were similarly used by particular Native groups on a regular basis. However, Native people were *not seen as owning* the resources and could not sell them. Instead, they moved from place to place on a seasonal cycle to make use of the various resources. They might make maple sugar at sugar camps in late winter, farm plots of land in the spring and summer (with men clearing the land and women cultivating the crops), pick berries in the late summer, and go hunting for deer in the fall and winter. The home village was near the agricultural fields. That village might well be vacant for much of the year, especially in the fall and winter, as men and women were away hunting and preserving food.

European Americans moving into regions new to them often mistakenly viewed those villages and the farmland as abandoned and seized them as their own, leading to conflicts upon the Native American villagers' return. For instance, in the winter of 1831, Black Hawk, a Sauk and Fox leader, as he later explained, "received information that three families of whites had arrived at our village, and destroyed some of our lodges, and were making fences and dividing our corn-fields for their own use." But his people had only temporarily left the village to go to winter hunting camps.[17] Many Native groups moved on regular twenty- to thirty-year circuits to allow land to lie fallow, thus restoring nutrients to the soil. To European Americans, the seemingly vacant land looked ripe for the taking.

Eventually, Ohio Indians lost to intruding European Americans, who, with their numbers, diseases, and military forces, overwhelmed the Native people. Consequently, land was not to be held in common; it was to be treated as private property to be bought and sold. Weakened by diseases new to them and to which they had no natural immunity—smallpox, measles, mumps, and others—and divided in their ideas and loyalties despite Tecumseh's leadership, Native Americans fell to European American invaders. Native Americans had defeated US armies in major battles in 1790 and 1791, in the later year inflicting the greatest loss ever imposed by Native people on the US military, as measured by the approximately 650 officers and soldiers killed. (For contrast, about 225 soldiers lost their lives at the Battle of the Little Bighorn, or the Battle of Greasy Grass, under Colonel George Armstrong Custer's leadership in 1876.) But the Native Americans lost in 1794. At the Battle of Fallen Timbers, fought in northwestern Ohio in the fall of that year, a well-disciplined army led by General "Mad" Anthony Wayne decisively beat Shawnee, Miami, Lenape, Iroquois, and other Native peoples. In the peace treaty that followed, the Treaty of Greenville of 1795, many Native Americans, under duress, ceded about two-thirds of what is now the state of Ohio to the federal government. But not all did so. Tecumseh, for one, refused to participate in the treaty negotiations or sign the treaty. He never recognized the land cessions. Armed resistance took place again during the War of 1812, when Tecumseh led Shawnee and other Native groups against the European Americans, only to be defeated and killed at the Battle of the Thames in Ontario in late 1813.[18]

Native people left lasting marks on the land of the Ohio Country. They used controlled burning to keep prairies open and to remove underbrush from forests in the interest of improving the habitats of animals they hunted. McClure, the Moravian missionary, found the forest "clear from underbrush" and wrote in his journal about how Native Americans periodically burned the underbrush "that they may have advantage of seeing game at a distance among the trees."[19] Native agriculture created large fields of maize and nurtured some plants over others, with some introduced plants replacing or crowding out indigenous ones. In his 1897 history of Ohio, William Dean Howells commented upon extensive "fields bordering the village" planted in "corn and beans, and the maple groves where they make their sugar."[20] Even Native maple-sugar making altered the landscape. "A productive sugar grove," historian Faragher observes, "requires human care and attention." He notes further: "Indians removed brush that impeded movement from tree to tree, girdled and burned out old trees, and tended replacement saplings."[21]

Maize lay at the center of Native agriculture in the Ohio Country. Each spring the women planted maize in fields, often along riverbanks where annual floods fertilized the soil. Men and women had previously prepared the fields, deadening trees by girdling them with stone-bladed hatchets or with iron-bladed ones acquired in trade. As in New England, Native Americans in the Ohio Country planted the seeds of corn in small hills shaped by hand and hoe. Beans and squash were usually planted with the maize in a symbiotic relationship: beans benefited by being able to climb up toward the sun on cornstalks, and maize benefited from nitrogen returned to the soil by beans, a legume. Maize extracted a lot of nitrogen, needed for most plant growth, from the soil. Without the beans' return of the nitrogen to the soil, the soil would have been quickly exhausted and the fields would have been soon abandoned. Meanwhile, squash benefited from growing in the shade of the maize. Maize, beans, and squash became known as the three sisters. Native Americans did not use plowing in their production. The women cultivated the maize in the spring and summer, weeding the fields and scaring away marauding birds, and harvested it in the late summer and early fall.[22]

This agricultural system proved to be highly effective. Native Americans probably achieved higher crop yields in maize than did contemporary Europeans and European Americans. Historian Susan Sleeper-Smith argues, "Seventeenth- and eighteenth-century Indian women developed a stable, continuous cropping system that maintained the organic matter in their soils by not plowing." She notes, "We now refer to those practices as no-till, or conservation tillage." Maize was especially suitable for no-till cultivation, for the large maize seeds did not require the preparation of a finely granulated bed of soil, which could be made only by plowing. By way of contrast, European

American farmers usually plowed their cornfields, disrupting the soil in the process, thus "oxidizing the soil's organic matter" and, according to Sleeper-Smith, "reducing crop yields." She concludes, "Paucity followed the plow."[23]

The fields of maize cultivated by Native Americans could be quite large; they were not simply garden plots. The Lenape were reported to have farmed three thousand acres, about five square miles, of corn at the forks of the Muskingum River (at the site of Coshocton) in eastern Ohio in 1761. This situation was not unusual. Invading European American armies made a point of destroying Native cornfields as a way of weakening Native American resistance. General George Washington employed this strategy against Iroquois siding with the British during the American Revolution. And General Wayne's soldiers destroyed cornfields for four or five miles along both sides of the Maumee River in northwestern Ohio in 1794. One field was estimated to have consisted of one thousand acres.[24]

Native women were in the forefront of the agricultural changes. Historian David Andrew Nichols observes, "Women produced and provided most of the food Indians consumed: wild rice, maple sugar, strawberries and other wild fruits, and crops like maize and pumpkins." They "also collectively owned local resource sites that sustained their kinfolk: rice lakes, maple groves, berry patches, and fields."[25] Similarly, Sleeper-Smith forcefully argues that women's agriculture (and involvement in the fur trade) created for many decades a prosperous, stable village life for Native Americans in the Old Northwest, especially for those in the Wabash River valley. It was "a kind of paradise," she writes, where women cultivated "extensive fields" of corn, beans, and squash, nurtured apple orchards, harvested "nutritious plants" from wetlands, and gathered fruits, nuts, and sugar from forests. Relatively unaffected by introduced alcohol or diseases, Native Americans thrived in this ecosystem, which was eroded only by American raids, especially by Kentucky militiamen, and then the spread of Euro-American farming. "The Ohio River valley was one of the most fertile landscapes in North America," Sleeper-Smith notes. However, European Americans using "plow agriculture, filling in wetlands, damming rivers, and overhunting animals destroyed this ecosystem."[26]

For all their differences in outlooks and actions, Native Americans and European Americans shared some common ways of living in the Ohio Country, especially by the mid-1700s. Both groups depended in part on wild game for food. Settler diaries are full of accounts of successful hunts for deer, elk, and bison. Farming methods illustrate well both differences and similarities. Of note were the gender differences. Native American women did most of the farming for their people, working in the fields to raise the three sisters of maize, beans, and squash. Men prepared the fields but usually played only a small role in planting, tending, and harvesting crops. By contrast, men in European American communities usually did most of the fieldwork, with women responsible for the home and nearby garden only. Exactly how farming was done also varied. Native American women eschewed the use of plows, planting seeds for maize in holes dug in the earth about a step apart. Once the maize had sprouted, beans and squash were planted. European American men often followed Native planting methods at first, using hatchets to make holes for corn seeds in the ground, taking this type of hatchet planting to the Great Plains in the later 1800s. As soon as possible, however, usually within a year or so, European American settlers turned to plows pulled by horses, mules, or oxen. Farming involved more than field crops. European American men also raised livestock: horses, cattle, and pigs. The pigs were usually turned loose in forests to subsist on mast. By the 1700s, a growing number of Native American men also were raising livestock, including pigs, in the Ohio Country, and after the War of 1812, many more were. Horticulture was another part of farming. Most European American farmers had a few fruit trees, usually apple or peach. Some Native Americans similarly tended trees by the late 1700s, and more did in the 1800s.

Native Americans tended to live in villages, some of which could be large and composed of many homes, whereas European American settlers were more likely to inhabit isolated homesteads. Contributing to this difference were American land laws, which often required settlers to live on their farmland to gain title to it. In housing, however, similarities were marked. By the late 1700s, log houses were common for both Native Americans and European Americans throughout the Ohio Country. European American visitors reported Native log houses to be "well-built," with "stone chimneys, chambers and sellers [cellars]," and "well shingled with nails." After about 1730, European American traders took jewelry, toys, ceramics, and hardware into Indian Country, and Native log cabins came to boast crockery including "creamware" and "tin-glazed earthware." Clothing changed, as buckskin gave way to cloth for many Native Americans in Ohio by the 1760s, including "silk handkerchiefs." New foods beyond the three sisters found their way into Native diets: cabbage, turnips, and cucumbers. Milk and butter became fairly common, a testament to Native animal husbandry. Chocolate and tea were also embraced. Historian Michael N. McConnell concludes, "Taken together, then, native and colonial worlds were at least in some respects becoming more alike."[27]

EUROPEAN AMERICANS VIEW LAND IN THE OHIO COUNTRY

How did incoming European Americans view land in the Ohio Country? A look at the ideas and actions of seven European American explorers, travelers, and settlers representative of the great number of newcomers passing through or moving to Ohio begins to provide answers.[28] The remainder of this chapter describes and analyzes the conceptions of Christopher Gist, who traversed much of Ohio in the early 1750s; Nicholas Cresswell, a young man seeking farmland in the mid-1770s; Colonel John May, a Bostonian who traveled to Marietta in 1788–89 as a member of the Ohio Company of Associates; Claude-François de Lezay-Marnésia, a French nobleman who in the early 1790s sought to establish an agricultural colony near where the Scioto River enters the Ohio River; Francis Baily, a Briton who descended the Ohio River on a North American tour during the mid-1790s; John Melish, a British resident who traveled extensively through Ohio for commercial purposes in 1806–7; and Morris Birkbeck, a wealthy British farmer who journeyed through Ohio on his way to Illinois to found an agricultural settlement in 1818.

How typical were these seven men of the European Americans first encountering land in the Ohio Country? Together with the six settlers, men and women, examined in the next chapter, they represent a cross section of explorers, developers, and farmers. Most saw Ohio lands through pragmatic and romantic eyes and, imbued with a capitalistic outlook, considered land as a commodity to be bought and sold, as well as farmed. (By "capitalistic outlook," I mean they believed in the importance of markets—markets for the buying and selling of goods but also for the employment of labor and the allocation of natural resources.) They had no doubts Ohio lands should be theirs and brushed aside Native land claims. As discussed in the introduction to this study, European Americans firmly believed the lands were theirs by right of conquest and treaty cessions. Above all, they thought their farming represented a higher stage of civilization than Native hunting, gathering, and farming, thus entitling them to the lands.

The European Americans examined in this study, however, differed in several respects from many early European American migrants to Ohio. They were, as a group, a bit older and wealthier than most settlers, and they were more literate. They left diaries, memoirs, and collections of letters that contain discussions of the lands they encountered across the Appalachian Mountains at a time when many Ohioans were illiterate. It was only in 1825 that Ohio's state legislature passed a law requiring counties to levy taxes to support public education, and that law proved inadequate. As late as 1838, some three thousand of Ohio's eight thousand school districts had no public schools. Some Ohioans received private schooling, but, even so, many of the state's citizens could not read or write. Only in the 1850s did one-room schools really begin dotting the state.[29]

Christopher Gist was the son of a surveyor of Maryland's western shore, one of the commissioners who laid out the town of Baltimore. A resident of North Carolina when employed by the Ohio Company, Gist was married and the father of three sons. He fought in 1755 with General Edward Braddock as a scout against the French and their Native allies at the outset of the French and Indian War. After Braddock's defeat, Gist continued to serve in the British military and as an Indian agent, until dying of smallpox during the summer of 1759 in South Carolina or Georgia.[30]

Gist's journals of his Ohio travels in 1751–52 contain numerous references to fertile land that could be put to the plow. As we saw in the introduction to this volume, Gist liked what he encountered in the Great Miami River valley in what would become the southwestern corner of the state. He also praised the valley of the Scioto River in central Ohio for its "fine rich level Land with its large Meadows, fine Clover Bottoms & spacious Plains covered with wild Rye." Like many other newcomers, Gist equated the presence of large trees and forests with good soil waiting to be tilled once it was cleared. He favored the Scioto River valley in part because of its "large Walnuts and Hickories . . . mixed with Poplars Cherry Trees and Sugar Trees." An abundance of game also seemed to indicate a rich land, and Gist lived largely on the deer, turkeys, buffalo, and bears that he shot. But not all land won his approval. Gist found unglaciated western Pennsylvania and eastern Ohio to be hilly with soil that was "mean stony and broken" and, overall, "not very rich." The presence of diseases often detracted from a region's attractiveness, but no descriptions of fevers or malaria mar Gist's account. The reason is simple: settlers brought diseases with them, and there were not yet European American settlers in Ohio in the early 1750s.[31]

Gist saw more than land, for he traversed a region populated by Native Americans. He accepted them and the help some gave him. Nonetheless, Gist clearly believed that Native land could and should be taken and sold by the Ohio Company. Gist was moving through the Ohio Country just before the mid-1752 French and Odawa (Ottawa) attack on Pickawillany, a trading post manned mainly by British traders and the Miami friendly to them, now sometimes considered the opening battle of the French and Indian War.[32] Gist traveled for a while with George Croghan, a British trader and negotiator with Native Americans, sat in on some of the conferences with them, and clearly understood differences among tribes and their tribal leaders. With little comment, he recorded the killing of a White woman held captive by Native Americans.[33]

Like Gist, Croghan saw Ohio as a land of tremendous promise.[34] Descending the Ohio River in 1765, Croghan wrote in his journal on May 16, after a two days' float south of Fort Pitt (later Pittsburgh), of "fine fertile country." On May 17, he observed "fine open country," and on May 31, he described "fine timbered clear wood[s]." Croghan also claimed, "A good hunter without much fatigue to himself could supply daily one hundred men with meat." In part, the good hunting resulted from Native use of fire to clear away underbrush in forests. This game was needed for the subsistence of Native families, and its loss to invading European Americans contributed to the weakening of Native resistance. In 1771, Croghan wrote of "Americans whose predominant passion is to realize an estate."[35]

Besides land and Native Americans, curiosities caught explorers' attention as well. Always observant, Gist wondered about eleven-foot rib bones and four-pound teeth, likely from a mammoth, found in northern Kentucky, probably at Big Bone Lick. He took one of the teeth back to officials of the Ohio Company.[36] Some twenty-four years later, Nicholas Cresswell, a young Englishman searching for farmland in the Ohio Country, detoured to the same spot, which he called "Elephant Bone Lick," where he found "several bones of a prodigious size," along with a six-foot tusk, which he took to be the remains of an elephant. He admitted, however, "What sort of animals these were is not clearly known."[37] Americans and Europeans were fascinated by the fossilized bones of seemingly extinct animals in the West. French explorers had discovered the bones at Big Bone Lick in 1739, and George Croghan rediscovered them in 1765. Thomas Jefferson, always curious, took an interest in the discoveries, calling the unknown animal that was the source of the bones an "incognitum." The discovery of the bones challenged the generally accepted idea that extinctions could not occur because they would contradict the infallibility of God. As president, Jefferson instructed the Lewis and Clark expedition to search for live species of animals "deemed to be rare or extinct" in the Far West.[38]

Like Gist, Cresswell was intrigued with the curiosities of the West. He commented on Indian mounds near the eastern reaches of the Ohio River, which he was descending, by writing, "All of these Hills appear to have been made by human art, but by whom, in what age, or for what use I leave for more able antiquarians to determine." Even earlier, Cresswell went out of his way to visit the battlefield of Braddock's defeat near Pittsburgh, where he "found great numbers of bones, both men and horses" and noted that "the trees are injured." Nearby, he also spied "land very good, but thinly inhabited."[39]

Born in 1750, Cresswell was the son of a well-to-do farmer in Derbyshire, England. He traveled in American colonies for four years, 1774 through 1777, looking for economic opportunities, especially fertile farmland, and satisfying his curiosity about territories new to him. He floated down the Ohio River to a point beyond its confluence with the Great Miami River. On the first page of his journal, Cresswell observed, "I am sensible a person with a small fortune may live much better and make greater improvements in America than can possibly do in England" and stated that farming was "the business I have been brought up to." Land in the colonies was, he wrote, "good and the price is very low," but he never purchased land in the colonies. Caught up in the Revolutionary War, Cresswell, a staunch loyalist, was detained upon suspicion of being a British spy. Released, he sailed back to England in the late summer of 1777. Four years after returning to his family's estate, Cresswell married and began fathering a family. He died at fifty-three years of age in 1804.[40]

To Cresswell, Ohio's lands and other natural resources appeared abundant. Like Gist, he singled out land near the juncture of the Ohio and Great Miami Rivers as particularly desirable. That land was, he thought, "rich beyond conception." Indeed, Cresswell recorded, "Wild clover, what they call wild Oats and Wild Rye [are] in such plenty it might be mown and would return a good crop." Water was always seen as important. Several days' travel upstream on the Ohio River from the mouth of the Great Miami River, Cresswell located additional good land, "the richest and finest . . . ever seen" but dismissed it as "badly watered." Large trees impressed Cresswell as indicators of good soil. Near the confluence of the Little Kanawha and Ohio Rivers he measured a sycamore more than fifty-one feet in circumference and concluded, "Here is excellent land." Cresswell wrote approvingly of deposits of coal and alum and noted numerous outcroppings of limestone. Game abounded, and Cresswell hunted buffalo, deer, bears, and turkeys to supplement supplies of flour purchased at Fort Pitt. Near Elephant Bone Lick Cresswell located "an immense number" of buffalo, which he described as "a sort of wild cattle" with a "large hump on top of their shoulders." Like Gist, Cresswell found little evidence of disease among European Americans—there were then no permanent Euro-American settlements in Ohio—but did note that "flux begins to rage" near Fort Pitt.[41]

The Miami River valley particularly impressed early visitors and settlers to the Ohio Country with its rich lands suitable for agriculture.

Soldiers going through the region in 1793 with General Wayne often remarked on the land's beauty and noted its many hardwood trees in their diaries.[42] Passing through the region in 1804, Gerard T. Hopkins, a Quaker taking Euro-American farming methods to the Miami and Potawatomi peoples, recorded in his journal: "The tract of Country between the two Miamis and thro' which we have passed to day is the most beautiful and desirable country we have yet seen." Continuing, he observed, "The Country lies in Waves of great regularity & is covered with heavy towering timber and the soil [is] inexhaustible Rich."[43] Seven years later, Charity Rotch, who traveled through Ohio with her husband to select farmland, observed that the region near Lebanon, just north of Cincinnati, was "beautiful country considerably improved." Something of a romantic, she paused to pick wildflowers along the Scioto River to the northeast, where she found "a commodious flat."[44] Similarly, Nathaniel Dike wrote in a letter to his brother in late 1817 that "I have seen more good land than I ever saw before" in passing through central and southwestern Ohio. Dike thought that "the country is level and remarkably fertile."[45]

Cresswell was positive in his views of Native Americans. To be sure, he expressed fear of being attacked while descending the Ohio River, but the only "attack" came from a group of friendly Lenape paddling hard to catch up to Cresswell's party near the Kanawha River to engage in trade. Cresswell shared salt and tobacco with them.[46] Sometime later, he visited a Moravian Delaware settlement on the upper reaches of the Muskingum River, which he described as "a pretty town containing about sixty houses . . . built of logs and covered with Clapboards." The town was "regularly laid out in three spacious streets which meet in the centre, where there is a large meeting house . . . covered with Shingles, Glass in the windows, and a Bell." It was all "very clean." Cresswell cohabited for several months with a "young and sprightly" Lenape woman who could "speak a little English." She cooked, took care of horses, and set up camp for Cresswell. Like other Native women, she accepted trade goods as gifts, not as payments for services. Cresswell left his Native companion when he returned to Fort Pitt.[47]

Upon leaving the Ohio Country, Cresswell concluded, "If we take an impartial view of an Indian's general conduct with all the disadvantages they labor under, at the same time divest ourselves of prejudice, I believe every honest man's sentiments would be in favour of them." He further noted, "These beings are endowed with reason and common sense and I make not the least doubt but they are as valuable in the eyes of their Maker as we are, and in general above our level in many virtues." He decried the introduction of "spirituous liquors" and smallpox among Native Americans, writing that "they have depopulated fast." Cresswell's positive judgments clashed with those of the many settlers who viewed Native Americans as savages, nonhumans to be killed at will.[48]

Francis Baily descended the Ohio River from near Pittsburgh through the Ohio Country by flatboat during the winter of 1796–97. Twenty-two years old, he had been born the son of a British banker in 1774. His journey occurred right after he finished serving a seven-year apprenticeship to a merchant in the city of London. Baily was looking for adventure. "I cannot but say," he confided in the journal he kept, "that this opportunity of exploring an unknown country, and of being one amongst the first to found a new colony in an uninhabited place, and to be witness to the first essays of a rising people, gave me a secret pleasure and satisfaction." He conveniently overlooked that Native Americans already lived throughout the Ohio Country and were fully engaged in hunting and farming across the land. Ohio was anything but uninhabited. Still, adventures Baily surely had. About a week after setting out, he and his compatriots found the Ohio River completely frozen just below Wheeling, and about two weeks later, he lost his boat in the breakup of the ice. In a newly constructed vessel, Baily continued his descent for two months. He returned to Great Britain in early 1798, made a good living as a stockbroker in London, and took up astronomy. After retiring from business, he devoted himself completely to his passion, becoming a fellow of the Royal Astronomical Society in 1821 and its president some years later. He died in 1844.[49]

Like Gist and Cresswell before him, Baily was favorably impressed by the potential for agriculture in the Ohio Country. He pragmatically described the soil in the Great Miami River valley as "excellent" and, in fact, "too rich for wheat." Uplands in the region were "rich and level," and very importantly, "abounding with plenty of water." Moreover, Baily observed, "The woods all over this western country produce a variety of spontaneous kinds of grass, some of which grows three or four feet high and affords nourishment for the cattle." In short, Baily found the region to be "a highly fertile and romantic country."[50]

By Baily's time, many European American speculators and squatters had designs on Ohio lands. Large East Coast landowners hoped to replicate positions they held as lords of the manor renting land long-term to tenant farmers. George Washington was one such landowner who was deeply involved in land speculations in the Ohio Country. Thomas Worthington was another. At the same time, individual frontier settlers simply squatted on any lands they could grab, especially unsurveyed lands, building cabins on and farming them without legal ownership. Most hoped to buy the land upon which they squatted once it was surveyed and put up for sale.[51]

Baily combined pragmatic and romantic views of land and nature in his writings about what he saw of Ohio.[52] Romanticism was at the time spreading from Europe to America, with its love of the beautiful, awesome, unusual, and sublime in nature. Baily described Long Reach, a fifteen-mile straight stretch of the Ohio River, as "the most beautiful place I saw in my life." The sun setting on the river there provided "one of the most sublime views I was ever witness to," he wrote, and "the river looked like a little sea of fire." Like many before him, Baily referred to the Ohio River as "the beautiful river Ohio." (*Ohio* is a Seneca word meaning "beautiful river." *O* is "river," and *hiyo* is "beautiful.") In words worthy of the romantic poets George Gordon Byron and Percy Bysshe Shelley, Baily asserted that despite all the hardships he had suffered on the Ohio River, his descent of the stream was wonderful: "Whether it were the novelty of the thing which attracted us, or the scenery of the country, and the sublimity of its views, so very different from what we had been used to in the *old* country, I know not; but certain it is, there is something so very attractive in a life spent in this manner, that were I disposed to become a hermit, and seclude myself from the world, the woods of America would become my retreat: there should I, with my dog and my gun, and the hollow of a rock for my habitation, enjoy undisturbed all the fancied bliss attendant on a state of nature." Yet rationalism tempered Baily's romanticism. Just before his description of Long Reach, Baily explained in detail how he and those with him tapped sugar maple trees, boiled the sap, and made twenty pounds of sugar. He devoted four pages of his journal to that account alone.[53]

Baily was far from alone in conveying an intermixture of ideas. Colonel John May, a resident of Boston and a member of the Ohio Company of Associates who journeyed to Marietta in 1788–89, recorded similar sentiments in his journal.[54] Exploring north of Marietta he "found the land very good" and "started three deer, and two flocks of turkeys." May described the fields around the town as "covered with wheat and corn" and gardens as "large and full of good things." He reported that fifteen thousand fruit trees had been set out and asserted that "madder, rhubarb, cotton, and rice grow luxuriantly." May viewed Marietta's growth rationally, but he also thought romantically. Even as he strained to row a boat upstream on the Ohio River just east of Marietta, he paused to record the passing scene in purple prose: "Could not help remarking again the beauties of the river. On each side mountains, with valleys between, rising progressively to view and filling the mind with admiration and wonder."[55]

Manasseh Cutler, a founder of the Ohio Company and Marietta, and thus a land speculator, not surprisingly joined May in his praise of the first permanent American settlement north of the Ohio River. The lands around Marietta, he wrote in 1787, abounded in wild fruits, "herds of deer, elk, buffalo, and bear." There were, as well, "flocks of turkeys, geese, ducks, swans, teal, pheasants, partridges" and schools of fish, "especially catfish," in the rivers. Rich soil everywhere could be expected to grow bountiful crops of "wheat, rye, Indian corn, buckwheat, oats, barley, flax, hemp, tobacco" and even "indigo, silk, wine, and cotton."[56]

For May, Native Americans were an annoyance, but nothing more. He wrote in 1788 in Marietta, "The Indians have been a little troublesome on the river, but have not hurt us any, nor do I intend they shall." The "troublesome" Indians were probably Shawnee and Cherokee charged by other Ohio Native Americans with keeping European Americans out of the region. May badly misjudged the nature of these interactions; some Native Americans fiercely resisted what they saw as a Euro-American invasion at Marietta. Several years later, in early 1791, a Native American raid killed a dozen settlers from Marietta at Big Bottom on the Muskingum River.[57]

The women who accompanied men to Marietta generally viewed the Ohio Country in a positive light. One wrote to a friend in Massachusetts in September 1788 that she found "the country much more delightful than we have any idea of." Another told a family friend two months later that the area around Marietta "meets every expectation." Still, their lives were demanding, a series of never-ending tasks: cooking, cleaning their log cabin, making clothing, gardening, treating the ill, and raising children. Parties, quilting bees, cornhusking gatherings, and communal events such as weddings enlivened their lives. Those lives were short. In 1775, life expectancy at birth was thirty-four years for White men and thirty-six years for White women in the American colonies. By 1850, the life expectancy for White men and women in the United States had increased only four years.[58]

Related to romanticism, but going beyond that set of ideas in time and space, were notions of pastoralism to which many Americans adhered in the nineteenth century, and some still did in the twentieth century. As historian Leo Marx wrote in 1964, "The pastoral ideal has been used to define the meaning of America ever since the age of discovery, and it has not lost its hold upon the native imagination." Pastoral ideas were important in influencing how people viewed American frontiers, including ones in Ohio. Whether in popular thought or high literature, pastoralism posited the bucolic life as superior to the urban, a rejection of advanced society in favor of an imagined primitive one, a favoring of nature over the machine, a dislike (or distrust) of industrialization, and a search for "peace, leisure, and economic sufficiency." The Roman poet Virgil's herdsman, adapted to American experiences, was pastoralism's token. In the United States, the herdsman became the independent yeoman farmer.[59]

While favoring nature, pastoral ideas stressed the importance of improving on nature. Nature should be used, as in farming—not as in Native farming, however, in which women did most of the fieldwork without horses and plows, but as in Euro-American farming in which men usually guided draft animals pulling plows. This idea quickly became a major rationale for the dispossession of Native lands. European Americans would put these lands, they asserted, to fuller beneficial use than were Native people, thus advancing civilization.

English-language professor William Barillas shows the marked impact of pastoralism on writing about the Midwest. Many writers, especially poets and novelists, picture it as a land of bucolic farms and small towns, even in the twentieth century, ignoring the region's large cities and industrialism.[60] Likewise, historian Peter G. Boag demonstrates the importance of pastoral ideas in how Americans viewed the Oregon Country in the nineteenth century.[61] Pastoral ideas glamorizing yeoman farmers, along with romanticism and utilitarianism, certainly influenced views of Ohio.

For Baily, even more than for Gist or Cresswell, large trees were indicators of good soil. Several day's journey south of Wheeling, not far from where he lost his first boat to ice, Baily observed, "Trees abound, so that it is almost a sure index of a desirable situation for a plantation." He continued, "It is a well-known fact that the Americans judge of the quality of the land when they are in the woods from the kinds of trees which grow on it," with "maple hickory, buck-eye, etc. indicat[ing] the richest soil."[62] Indeed, agricultural historian Robert Leslie Jones observes that for settlers in Ohio, and more generally in the trans–Appalachian West, as soil types, "bottomlands ranked the highest and uplands, which supported the growth of certain hardwoods next." By way of contrast, prairies "were considered little if at all superior to the swamps."[63] This concept is not surprising. Even earlier in the 1600s, British settlers in New England had used the differing natures of tree species as guides to underlying soil types, and New Englanders and others took those notions with them when they migrated to the Ohio Country.[64]

Still, in Baily's eyes, there was more to trees. They formed "a sea of woods, whose tops, just tinged by the setting sun, displayed one of the most beautiful sylvan scenes I ever remember seeing."[65] Baily expressed no fear of the forests. And trees there certainly were. As writer and environmentalist Deborah Fleming observes, Ohio's trees "formed a canopy under which pioneers walked for days without seeing the sky." European American settlers and explorers often remarked that squirrels could cross Ohio without ever stepping on the ground by simply leaping from treetop to treetop.[66]

Like others before him, Baily also commented on the Indian mounds in southeastern Ohio. The "circular and square entrenchments," were, he thought, "curious remains of antiquity." Baily wondered about their origins, concluding that they were "very old" and that "they were built by a race of people more enlightened than the present Indians and at some time very far distant," a common conception then.[67] Thomas Ashe, another British traveler down the Ohio River, reached similar conclusions a decade later. Upon viewing the mounds at Marietta, Ashe observed, "It will be seen that the fallen race, who now inhabit America, are successors of men who have been capable of architectural and other work, that would do honour to any people of any age."[68] Howells concluded in his 1897 history that the "skillfully planned" earthworks required a "knowledge which no savage race has shown" and suggested that ancient Mexicans or Peruvians might have built them.[69] Anyone except ancestors of contemporary Native Americans! If others had built the mounds, European Americans reasoned—falsely—then Native Americans could have no claims on them or surrounding lands.

Not surprisingly, Baily encountered no living Native Americans on his Ohio trip. Ohio's Indian wars of the early and mid-1790s, and the resulting Treaty of Greenville of 1795, had cleared many of the areas along the Ohio River of Native Americans. Beaten at the Battle of Fallen Timbers in 1794, most Indians, as discussed previously, ceded many of their Ohio lands to incoming Americans by the treaty.[70] After the War of 1812, Native Americans lost nearly all their remaining lands in the state of Ohio. At one point, Baily commented, "The most violent prejudices exist on both sides, between the Indians and those white people who live on the frontier."[71]

While Baily met no Native Americans in Ohio, he did encounter many settlers in the new towns springing up along the Ohio River from Marietta to Cincinnati. Baily's journal contains descriptions of the layouts of the towns, their buildings, and their residents. Baily rarely mentioned disease. He was favorably impressed, observing that Americans were "a race of people rough in their manners, impatient of restraint, and of an independent spirit, who are taught to look upon all men as their equals."[72]

Not all visitors and settlers to the Ohio Country were of British or American descent; Claude-François de Lezay-Marnésia was a French nobleman. Born in 1735 in Metz, Lezay-Marnésia was raised on a family estate in the countryside before joining the French army as an officer at the age of twelve. Knighted in the Order of Saint Louis in 1769, he left the military in the same year to devote himself to study, writing, and family affairs. Married in 1766, he and his wife soon had three children. In 1790, Lezay-Marnésia purchased—or at least thought he purchased—22,100 acres from the Scioto Company, which had offices in Paris. (Formed in 1789, the Scioto Company was a land company that had been granted rights by the US federal government to buy three million acres of the public domain in central Ohio.) Deeply influenced by romantics such as Voltaire (François-Marie Arouet) and Jean-Jacques Rousseau, Lezay-Marnésia hoped to establish a French colony, a utopia really, on his Ohio lands. To examine his lands and to escape the turmoil of the French Revolution, Lezay-Marnésia traveled to the United States between 1790 and 1792, getting as far west as the newly formed Marietta, where he spent a long, cold winter.[73]

In several letters to Frenchmen while he was in Pennsylvania and Ohio, Lezay-Marnésia put forth a romantic view of the Ohio Country, untethered from realities. He was, of course, writing a sales pitch for lands he hoped to sell at a profit and was acting a bit as a huckster. Most revealing was a letter penned in late 1791, while he was in Fort Pitt, to another nobleman Lezay-Marnésia was trying to entice to invest in his American lands. The country, Lezay-Marnésia argued, was "almost virgin . . . neither excessively hot nor cold, watered by two superb rivers bordered by rich prairies" and consisting of "prodigious fertility and charming valleys." There were "superb ancient forests . . . sown with trees for the most part unknown in France, far fresher and taller, with more nuanced greenery and more imposing majesty than the trees, so unvaried, of the forests of Europe." The abundance of game, "which still gazes without fear in the forests," impressed him, as it did many Europeans and European Americans. Moreover, he thought, "the vegetable kingdom, so rich in this region, will also be a magnificent source of foods." In particular, "pure wheat flour" would provide bread better than that available in France. Native Americans were not to be feared, as the "good Indians will feel that friends have arrived, and since they really call the French their fathers, they will cover them with a multitude of unaffected and sincere marks of their affection."[74]

At any rate, the wilderness would soon be vanquished. Looking into the near future, Lezay-Marnésia predicted: "The land is no longer a wilderness. Within the space of four or five months, the forests have been replaced by cheerful sites, with fields and prairies adorned by attractive lodges." He further exclaimed, "What a powerful and delightful sensation man feels when, for the first time, he places his hand on a piece of land still virgin, and imprints on it the seal of his power!"[75] Indeed, French observers often commented favorably on American forests. André Michaux, one of France's leading botanists, was sent by King Louis XVI to America to study trees and plants and to ship some back to France to replace those destroyed in repeated crop failures. After hiking in New York's woods and forests with his son, Michaux wrote of "majestic" and "magnificent" trees found there and sent hundreds of specimens home to the Jardin du Roi in Paris.[76]

Lezay-Marnésia's utopian colony was not to be. Unable to ever patent his land, or even see it—for the Scioto Company, it transpired, was fraudulent and never actually owned the land it sold—Lezay-Marnésia failed as a community builder. Then, too, Indian hostilities—the early 1790s witnessing the bloodiest conflicts between Native Americans and European Americans in the Ohio Country—would have impeded any efforts at settlement. Returning to France in 1792, Lezay-Marnésia died there eight years later, bankrupt. It was a common predicament, as swindling was the order of the day. Other French immigrants were also duped by the machinations of the Scioto Company, never able to acquire the land they thought they had purchased. Congress finally gave them 25,200 acres of public domain on the Ohio River to partially compensate them for the swindle. The resulting town, Gallipolis, "City of Gauls," may be seen as their monument.[77]

A brief look at two travelers' accounts penned at the close of Ohio's frontier period rounds out this examination of how visitors to the state viewed its land. John Melish journeyed from Great Britain to the

United States for commercial reasons, descending the Ohio River on one occasion and crossing central and eastern parts of Ohio by land on another between 1806 and 1811. Morris Birkbeck, a wealthy British farmer, passed through Ohio on his way to found an agricultural settlement in Illinois in 1817. Like earlier explorers, they viewed the lands and resources of Ohio very favorably. Birkbeck wrote for both, when he transcribed in his journal, "On entering Ohio from Wheeling, we find a country beautiful and fertile, and affording to a plain, industrious and thriving population, all that nature has decreed for the comfort of man." Ohio, he thought, "contains rich land, good water, wholesome air;—lime, coal, mills, navigation."[78]

Like Baily before them, Birkbeck and Melish looked upon Ohio with utilitarian and romantic eyes, tinged as well with pastoral notions. They recorded the locations of good soil for farming and noted how the quality of soils could be determined by the types of trees. Melish, for example, praised the "fine land" along "very rich bottoms on the Muskingum."[79] Uplands were much less desirable. The trade in land, he noted, was "exactly similar to that of buying any other commodity." Limestone, coal, iron ore, and "freestone" (sandstone) caught their attention. So did water, their journals containing numerous descriptions of rivers, streams, and springs. Yet land and the countryside were more than simply commodities to be bought and sold, as romanticism and pastoralism influenced their views. Near Limestone (later Maysville), Kentucky, on the Ohio River, Melish remarked, "The scenery here was bold and rich." He rejoiced in riding through a nearby "beautiful romantic valley." In fact, he avowed, "The face of nature was smiling around us; the lofty trees spread their branches over our heads; the pure water issued from the fountain, and gurgled by our side; and the feathered choristers [birds] delighted our ears with their song and our eyes with their beautiful plumage." Melish concluded, "I was charmed with this *new* country."[80]

Birkbeck was less enchanted than Melish with forests, which he saw as stifling and confining. Near Mount Vernon, Ohio, he wrote, "To travel day after day, among trees of a hundred feet high, without a glimpse of the surrounding country, is oppressive to a degree which those cannot conceive who have not experienced it."[81] Unlike most settlers, he ended up purchasing several thousand acres of prairieland in Illinois for his settlement. He was not interested in big trees that had to be girdled (Virginia style) or laboriously cut down (New England style). Girdling involved cutting a ring around a tree through its bark and the next layer of wood. Moisture could no longer ascend to the trunk and branches, and the tree died. It could sometime later be burned or cut down at the farmer's leisure. Howells has left a vivid account of girdling trees. Farmers, Howells wrote in 1897, "deadened the trees around them by girdling them with the ax and planted the space between the leafless trunks with corn and beans and pumpkins."[82] In doing so, European Americans followed their previous practices on earlier frontiers and the agricultural methods of Native Americans, who girdled trees and planted maize, beans, and squash, the three sisters, among them. Like forests, prairies could occasionally induce romantic thoughts, but only occasionally. Accordingly, Birkbeck wrote, "In their irregular outline of woodland and their undulating surface, these tracts of natural meadow exhibit every beauty, fresh from the hand of nature, which art often labours in vain to produce."[83]

Writing in 1940, novelist Conrad Richter describes a "sea of solid treetops" and an "ocean of leaves," which he thought made frontier Ohio an oppressive, dark country for settlers.[84] The gloomy, oppressive forest in Ohio, and more generally the Northeast, has been a trope in American literature. Indeed, since at least the writing of Nathaniel Hawthorne in *The Scarlet Letter,* set in New England and published in 1851, the dark forest has been depicted as the locus of evil and the devil. In his 1897 history, Howells wrote of the "gloom of forests" across Ohio and of their "fathomless" depth.[85] Likewise, in 2016, novelist Annie Proulx described the "dark, vast forest, inimical wilderness" of New France in the 1600s.[86] This notion contradicted that of the forest being a source of pastoral retreat.

While Melish and Birkbeck made few comments in their journals about Native Americans—like Baily, they met only a handful in their travels—they were intrigued by the Indian mounds they encountered. Melish was most outspoken after visiting the mounds at Marietta. "They did not come up to my expectations," he proclaimed. "I could hardly view them even as curiosities; and I saw no reason to refer their existence to a different race, or a different state of civilization, than what is to be found among the Indian tribes at present in North America."[87] This conclusion was at odds with that of Baily and many nineteenth-century Americans. Even more than found in Baily's journal, the accounts of Melish and Birkbeck contain numerous descriptions of burgeoning towns and cities along the Ohio River and in the interior of the state of Ohio. They recorded street layouts, the construction of buildings, and the nature of Americans.

Like Baily, they viewed Americans as uncouth but also as independent and friendly. Birkbeck observed, "Intellectual culture has not yet made much progress among the generality of either sex where I have travelled," and he thought that "indolence is the epidemic evil of Americans." Still, when compared to "British peasantry," Americans stood out for their "manners and morals and especially in their knowledge and proud independence of mind." Birkbeck asked rhetorically, "Who would not rejoice to transplant into these boundless regions of freedom, the millions whom he has left behind him, groveling in ignorance and want?" A strain of pastoralism, which saw America as a new beginning, ran through his writings.[88]

As they moved through Ohio, newcomers sought to make sense of what they encountered. In 1806, Melish postulated three stages in Ohio's settlement. First, there arrived "land clearers," or "squatters"; a bit later came those "who have got a little money" to "buy up the improvements of the first settlers, and add to them"; and, finally, there entered a third and last class of those interested in "permanent settlement," who bought "both land and improvements."[89] Melish was not alone in his analysis. In fact, his observations were commonplace. In the same year, Benjamin Rush, a well-known Philadelphia doctor and scholar, described a very similar three stages of settlement.[90] Much later, in 1983, agricultural historian Jones used precisely the same taxonomy and wording as Melish in describing classes of settlers in early Ohio.[91]

The Ohio Country was not the once-healthy region it had been. Disease entered Ohio with European American newcomers. Birkbeck wrote that he heard "much of the agues and bilious fever." Ague was a reference to malaria, which became widespread, and bilious fever meant any of several high fevers. Like many Americans then, Birkbeck subscribed to the miasmic origins of disease, in which it was believed that vapors from rotting organic materials caused illnesses. Birkbeck wrote that "neighborhoods of rivers and creeks, subject to overflow, are the most unhealthy." Millponds were, he thought, "frequently noxious to settlers in their vicinity." "Dry soils" and "elevated situations" were, Birkbeck concluded, healthiest.[92] Melish, too, peppered his journal with accounts of diseases, primarily bilious fevers and ague. In fact, he made a point of claiming that the Virginia Military Tract in southern and central Ohio was "all perfectly healthy, no instance having occurred of bilious fever, or fever and ague."[93] (He may have been exaggerating; after all, lands in that tract were available for sale. Why ruin their chances with a negative report?) Like Birkbeck, Melish associated disease with stagnant waters and rotting organic matter. At Cleveland, Melish encountered "pale, sickly" residents suffering, he thought, from "fever and ague" brought on by vapors from the Cuyahoga River: "I observed the seeds of disease in its slow, sluggish, winding course, choked up with a vast quantity of vegetable matter undergoing decomposition."[94]

The miasmic theory of disease proved false, replaced in the late nineteenth century by germ theory, or the idea that specific bacteria caused many diseases, but illnesses and accidents did shorten lives on the Ohio frontier. In the early 1800s, about 25 percent of children in Ohio, then mainly a frontier area, died before their first birthday, and another 25 percent of children and young adults died by the age of twenty.[95] The United States as a whole possessed what historian Daniel Walker Howe calls a "young society." The median age of Americans in 1815 was just sixteen. Only one-eighth of Americans were as old as forty-three. According to Howe, "One-third of white children and over half of black children died before reaching adulthood."[96]

LAND HUNGER IN OHIO

Land hunger pulled European Americans into frontier Ohio. They went there as largely rational, pragmatic individuals. Land was the lure, as it was on many other American frontiers. Few went so far as Cresswell, who devoted several pages of his journal to a precise, detailed cost-benefit analysis of relocating to Ohio, but nearly all newcomers were drawn to the availability of rich farmland.[97] Still, theirs was a nuanced recognition. Some lands were seen as better than other lands, types of trees seemed to provide a necessary guide, and some resources were viewed as more readily exploitable than others. As early as 1755, frontiersman James Smith, held captive by Indians, observed of central Ohio, "From the south end of the prairie to Ollentangy [*sic*] there is a large quantity of beech land, intermixed with first rate land. . . . The timber is walnut, sugar-tree, ash, buckeye, locust, wild cherry, and spicewood, intermixed with some oak and beech."[98]

In the minds of many European Americans, both pragmatic ideas and romantic notions about land coexisted, especially as the 1800s progressed. Land could be bought, sold, and exploited; it could also be admired for its sublime beauty. Impressions of the country went beyond the rational approaches. Even Lake Erie attracted romantic attention. In 1839, for example, Samuel Hildreth, a doctor from Cincinnati, wrote that the lake "has a sublime and imposing appearance" and that "the white foam of the curling water, glancing on the sunbeams, were seen as far as the eye could reach."[99]

With its many rivers, streams, and springs, Ohio was lauded as well watered; yet those same streams could be, settlers feared, sources of diseases. By the 1800s, settlers' journals included remarks about "the ague" and bilious fevers. Howells complained about "the ague" as a "scourge" throughout Ohio in frontier times.[100] Similar contrasts in views developed about Native Americans; competing ideas existed side by side, often in the mind of the same person. Indians were barbaric "savages" perhaps, but they were also people to be admired in some ways, especially as romanticism and pastoralism shaded thoughts. Indeed, people across Europe and the United States tended to view Native Americans in terms of two competing stereotypes in the nineteenth century, that of the uncivilized "savage" bent on rape and pillage and that of the noble "savage" pure in thought and in tune with nature.[101] And curiosities such as Indian mounds complicated these ideas. European Americans moving into Ohio wondered, Could present-day Indians have conceived of and built them? Probably not, they thought. But if not, who did?

Clearly, understanding frontier Ohio was a complicated process, fraught with both hopes and anxieties. The reports of early European

American explorers and travelers helped prepare the way. They encouraged others to move to Ohio, despite the many challenges in doing so. Many journals were published within a few years of their being written, and all spoke of rich land available for the taking. Native Americans were largely ignored or marginalized. Like the later reports of European American explorers, fur trappers, and missionaries about the trans–Mississippi West, these earlier reports about the Ohio Country contributed to European Americans' westward movement.

In a letter written to his brother from Zanesville in early 1818, Dike tried to balance the pros and cons of moving to Ohio from the Northeast. "What then are the inducements to the people of the Eastern States to emigrate to this country?—I can see but two—the cheapness of land; and a climate somewhat more favourable to vegetation." Against these positive factors, Dike thought, needed to be measured negative ones: the "immense distance" to markets, a climate "not so favourable to the human constitution," harmful diseases, and a lack of good roads, churches, schools, and doctors. Still, people came, as, what Dike labeled "the spirit of emigration," seized Americans.[102]

European Americans moving into the Ohio Country were, above all, struck by the abundance of nature. Just like Britons entering New England at an earlier date, they were amazed by the many fish in streams and lakes, game such as deer, elk, and buffalo in the forests and on the prairies, and especially the many large hardwood trees, such as white oaks, chestnuts, maples, and hickories.[103] Brought up on the reality of wood scarcity in Great Britain, they stood in awe of Ohio's seemingly endless forests. Moreover, European Americans associated the forests with the existence of rich land of fertile soils ready for farming, once those trees were cut down. That abundance did not last long after European Americans invaded the Ohio Country. Within just a few generations, the abundant wild game and seemingly limitless hardwood forests were almost gone, replaced by farms, villages, and domesticated animals.

As European American settlers moved into Ohio, they changed the flora and fauna of the land. "Newly settled areas of North America," historian Mark Barrow notes, "soon began experiencing dramatic transformations." Continuing, he observes, "Once diverse habitats gave way to a more limited range of introduced crops, pesky weeds that seemed to sprout up everywhere, and vexing insect pests." Concluding, Barrow writes, "Newly introduced domesticated animals roamed across the countryside in feral herds that consumed prodigious quantities of native vegetation, fostered shifts in plant species composition, and compacted the soil." He further notes, "Timber became scarce," and, describing the environmental consequences of its absence, concludes, "deforestation, in turn, led to increased rain runoff, wider temperature swings, and soil drying."[104] All these changes, and more, occurred in Ohio. But alterations to the people, flora and fauna, and landscape in the state were only part of similar changes transpiring throughout the Northeast. As observed by Native American scholar Ned Blackhawk in 2023, "Puritan colonization sought to transform American landscapes. Land enclosures, imported domestic livestock, and invasive crops remade the Northeast's ecology."[105]

2

European Americans in the Ohio Country

John Allen Trimble, a storekeeper in Hillsboro, Ohio, wrote of his early nineteenth-century experiences with poor transportation facilities, which made travel difficult: "Turnpikes, rail roads & steam boats were not then in existence; and roads over the mountains were the most indifferent wagon ways conceivable; without grading, ruts & gutters, mudholes and other obsticles [*sic*], never mended, and being hilly & broken, uncommon mountainous country made it toilsome in the extreme."[1] Getting around was challenging in pioneer days, for farmers as well as merchants. Nonetheless, European Americans eagerly tilled farmlands in Ohio. An examination of the lives of six families who moved to different geologic and geographic regions in the Ohio Country during the early 1800s to take up farming reveals some of the motives of the many thousands entering Ohio shortly after it became a state in 1803. It also lays bare the difficulties and rewards they experienced on Ohio frontiers.

Because of its nearness to Pennsylvania and the availability of land surveyed and ready for sale, eastern Ohio was one of the first regions of the state to be settled besides the Muskingum, Scioto, and Miami River valleys, which could be reached by traveling upstream from the Ohio River. This chapter looks at the agricultural efforts of Joseph Howells, who was always on the move searching for better opportunities, farming at several locations near the Ohio River in the Steubenville region beginning in the 1820s, and Joseph and Anna Briggs Bentley, who worked land in eastern Ohio not far from the Howells, again from the 1820s. The chapter also follows the farmwork of Jonathan Hale to their north and west. Hale developed a farm in the Cuyahoga River valley, just south of Cleveland, beginning in 1810. The chapter examines as well the farming of Thomas Worthington, a large landowner in the Scioto River valley in central Ohio, and that of Thomas Rogers, a smallholder living just to the south of Worthington on Paint Creek, a tributary of the Scioto River, as representative of different approaches to farming land in central Ohio in the early 1800s. The labors of members of the Good family and other farmers beginning in the 1830s on one of Ohio's last frontiers, the Black Swamp in northwest Ohio, are discussed near the close of this chapter to show additional ways incoming European Americans tried to develop land. Finally, the chapter examines the life and work of L. D. McMillen, who farmed in Hardin County in western Ohio near the town of Ada during the late nineteenth and early twentieth centuries, to explore how farming had changed in Ohio in the passing of about a century.[2]

CHANGING LAND LAWS AND ECONOMIC CIRCUMSTANCES

American settlers benefited from changed circumstances governing the acquisition of land. In 1820, congressional legislation made it easier for Americans to purchase land from the public domain (land owned by the federal government). The previous Land Act of 1804 had required the purchase of at least 160 acres at a minimum price of $2.00 per acre. The 1820 law lowered the minimum purchase to 80 acres and reduced the minimum price to $1.25 per acre.[3] The nation's land laws had somewhat contradictory goals: to bring in sorely needed revenue for the national treasury in the days long before income taxes but also to quickly transfer land into the hands of frontier settlers. By making land available in smaller parcels at a lower price, the 1820 law favored settlers over the treasury. By late 1821, the federal government had sold about 7.3 million acres of the public domain to individuals in Ohio alone, roughly two-thirds of the land surveyed and available for sale; within four years, another 1.4 million more acres had been sold.[4] Additional legislation further liberalized sales of the public domain. Congressional legislation passed in 1821–24 gave considerable relief to those who had earlier bought land on credit but could not pay for it. For the first time, 1830 legislation allowed preemption sales of the public domain in some areas. That is, squatters living on unpurchased lands were allowed to buy those lands, once surveyed, under certain circumstances. Congress then passed a national preemption law in 1841. Land liberalization culminated in the Homestead Act of 1862, by which settlers could acquire land for nearly free.

Squatters long remained a delicate issue for colonial governments and, later, state and federal governments. Moving westward ahead of other European American settlers, squatters occupied and farmed land they did not own, land which often had not yet been surveyed or even acquired by governments from Native Americans. While sometimes welcoming the actions of squatters as helping to secure frontiers, political leaders and large landholders often disliked the resulting chaos and conflict with Native Americans seeking to defend their lands. Colonial and early national American leaders sometimes used military force to remove squatters from their lands. For instance, in 1761, Colonel Henry Bouquet of Virginia ordered all European American settlers living on unsurveyed lands west of the crest of the Allegheny Mountains to move east. He then sent troops from Fort Pitt to burn the cabins of any squatters remaining along the Monongahela and Youghiogheny Rivers. Such actions, however, were rare and ineffective. Most squatters simply returned to their lands shortly after the troops departed and rebuilt their lean-tos and log cabins.[5]

In the late 1700s, several newly formed eastern states, including Connecticut, New York, and Virginia, gave up extensive claims to lands west of the Appalachian Mountains to the federal government in return for its assumption of their state debts. Those lands became part of the new public domain surveyed and opened to sale to settlers moving west. But not all the western lands were available. Millions of acres were sold to land companies and land speculators—often the same entities—which, in turn, sold them to settlers. Moreover, for some years, eastern states reserved rights to tracts of land in Ohio. For example, the Virginia Military Tract in southern and central Ohio was long kept for gift or sale to former Revolutionary War veterans from Virginia or to those to whom the veterans sold their land rights, their "warrants" to the land.

Dividing and surveying the public domain was done under terms in the Land Ordinance the Continental Congress passed in 1785. The basic land unit was a section of 640 acres, one square mile, a square tract of land one mile per side. Next largest was a township, comprising thirty-six sections, six miles on each side. In the late 1780s and early 1790s, federal government surveyors laid out the first seven ranges of land, east to west, of townships and sections in southeastern Ohio. A range was one township wide, east to west, and any number of townships deep, north to south.[6] Once surveyed, land was placed on the market and sold from a growing number of federal government land offices throughout Ohio. Writing in 1960, novelist and environmentalist Wallace Stegner observed, "Order is the nature of man." True to this observation, ranges, townships, and sections soon marched across the United States, as new parts of the public domain were surveyed and brought to market as neat squares.[7] There were exceptions to this orderly way of surveying land. For instance, land in the Virginia Military Tract was surveyed by a system known as "metes and bounds," which used landmarks such as tall trees or big rocks to delimit boundaries, resulting in irregularly shaped plots of land, not tidy sections and townships.

It should be emphasized, again, that the federal government had no legal rights to the Ohio Country and western lands. The United States had not defeated Native Americans during the American Revolution and so had no rights to the lands by right of conquest. In fact, many Indian leaders were outraged when they learned that Great Britain had ceded their lands to the new United States by the Treaty of Paris in 1783. No Indians took part in the treaty negotiations ending the American Revolution. Nor did the United States legally acquire Indian lands by later treaties or congressional legislation. Those existing treaties (and legislation such as the Land Ordinance of 1785) were, in the eyes of most Native Americans, corrupt bargains never agreed to by the Native tribes and nations occupying and using the lands.

GETTING TO OHIO

Getting to Ohio was a challenge for settlers from the East Coast.[8] Depending on starting points and destinations, journeys were about five hundred to seven hundred miles in length and required, depending on weather and road conditions, one to two months, or sometimes more, to complete. Regardless of the route, European American settlers had to climb the Appalachian Mountains, which reached three thousand feet even through passes. More than geographic journeys, the trips involved psychological breaks with the past, especially for those who thought they would never return to their eastern homes. For women especially, leaving family and friends was a wrenching experience, a situation later repeated by women traveling on the Oregon Trail.

There were several routes west. Especially in the early days of the 1800s, people descended the Ohio River from the Pittsburgh area in "Kentucky boats," large flatboats that floated downstream steered and propelled by large oars called "sweeps." Steamboats came into common use on the Ohio River only in the 1820s and 1830s. Migrants went on horseback or, with more difficulty, by wagon to the Pittsburgh area, where they bought or built the boats. They then piloted the boats downstream to the mouths of the rivers draining Ohio: the Muskingum, Scioto, and Great Miami Rivers. Finally, they ascended those streams to their destinations.

To reach Pittsburgh, they typically followed Braddock's Road, which had been constructed from Virginia and Maryland through the mountains for General Edward Braddock's military force in the mid-1750s. Alternately, they walked or rode along Forbes Road, built slightly later through Pennsylvania to Pittsburgh. Both routes were challenging, featuring ascents and descents over the multiple ranges of the Appalachians. In the early 1800s, European Americans developed several all-land routes directly across New York and Pennsylvania into Ohio. Importantly, Zane's Trace, at first little more than a path, was soon widened and improved into a wagon road crossing Ohio from Wheeling,

Virginia, on the Ohio River through Zanesville, Ohio, and terminating at Maysville, Kentucky. By 1831, at the close of Ohio's frontier period, the National Road provided an east–west route across the Appalachian Mountains, beginning in Cumberland, Maryland, and going through Columbus in central Ohio. Wagons of all sorts were used on these roads, but a short version of the long, canvas-roofed Conestoga wagon later employed on the Oregon Trail was common. Settlers also combined land routes across New York with sailing on Lake Erie to reach regions in northern Ohio.

During their travels, European Americans faced numerous problems. In the early days, there was the danger of Indian attack, especially for those descending the Ohio River, as Native people resisted others invading their lands. Manning swift canoes, Shawnee darted out from the northern shores of the Ohio River to attack those going south and west on cumbersome flatboats. Running battles on the river ensued. For travelers using what passed for roads, bottomless mudholes, rain, and snow during much of the year, steep ascents and descents over hills, and a lack of adequate provisions were common problems. Horses and wagons broke down, and new mounts and supplies were hard to procure. Mosquitoes and flies seemed insatiable. Historian Reginald Horsman observes, "In the first years of settlement reaching Ohio from the East Coast always meant enduring hardships."[9]

The challenges faced by travelers to the Ohio Country were similar in some ways, but different in others, to those encountered a few decades later by those going west on the Oregon Trail. The same physical problems of bad roads occurred on the Oregon Trail, but the journey was much longer, one of several thousand miles taking five or more months, exacerbating problems of securing horses, mules, oxen, and supplies. Few supplies were available beyond Fort Laramie in what is now Wyoming, but by the early 1800s, public houses and inns existed on many of the routes into Ohio, and farmers often let rooms in their homes to travelers, providing them with food and shelter. As much as Ohio travelers complained about poor lodging, including the prevalence of lice and bedbugs, those accommodations were palatial compared to the almost total lack of accommodations along the Oregon Trail.

Finally, moving to Ohio or Oregon meant managing the psychological break of leaving loved ones behind in the East. Yet the trip to Oregon was the more difficult one, involving greater distances across rivers, plains, and mountains. Those moving to Oregon harbored few hopes of ever seeing family or friends remaining in the East. By contrast, those settling in Ohio could realistically expect to visit easterners at some point in the future, and many did so, despite Margaret Dwight's lament that she would never see her sister again.[10] For instance, Anna Bentley, the wife of a farmer in eastern Ohio in the early 1800s, traveled to visit her family in Maryland and received visiting family members at her new Ohio home on several occasions.

EURO-AMERICAN FARMING IN OHIO

European American farmers moving into Ohio entered a country well suited, for the most part, to agriculture. R. Douglas Hurt, a dean of agricultural historians, observes, "The climate and soils of the Midwest were well suited for the production of grain crops, particularly corn and oats for livestock and wheat as a cash crop."[11] Native Americans had successfully grown the three sisters of maize, beans, and squash for centuries, and European Americans were aware of their efforts. Ohio was a humid country. The land composing the state of Ohio—Ohio achieved statehood in 1803—was well watered, with twenty-five thousand miles of streams and rivers, and many lakes, serving the countryside. Rainfall was abundant, more than enough to support growing corn and wheat in most regions. Columbus, in the center of the state, received about thirty-nine inches of rain annually. Wheat required an annual rainfall of about twenty inches to reach maturity, corn somewhat more.[12] As we have seen, trees grew luxuriantly in Ohio's humid climate. Forests covered most of the country, in all about 95 percent of the land area at statehood. As agricultural historian Robert Leslie Jones notes, "Ashes, beeches, maples, and oaks" were "found from Lake Erie to the Ohio River, and others, such as black walnuts, chestnuts, and sycamores" were "characteristic especially of the southern counties."[13]

Several major distinct geologic and geographic regions made up Ohio. The till plains, composing most of the western part of the state, was (and is) by far the largest region. Highly glaciated—that is, having soil ground down by glaciers, which finally retreated from Ohio around 14,000 years ago—the till plains were named after the glacial till—the boulders, rocks, and soil left behind when the Wisconsin glacier returned north. That till could be deep; it was, for example, 110 feet through till to bedrock at the juncture of Broad and High Streets in downtown Columbus. Deep, rich soil covered much of the region. Farther north, the lake plains stretched across Ohio south of Lake Erie. Another glaciated area with generally good soil for agriculture, the lake plains lay north of Ohio's continental divide, an east–west ridge separating waters flowing south into streams feeding the Ohio River and ultimately the Gulf of Mexico from those going north into Lake Erie and eventually the Atlantic Ocean. The Appalachian Plateau to the east was a third region. It had never been covered by glaciers and consequently had never been ground down by ice. Very rugged and hilly, the plateau had poor, thin soil for farming except along some river bottoms. Finally, a finger of Kentucky's bluegrass region, called Lexington Plains, jutted north into south central Ohio.[14]

Ohio soils supported diversified agriculture because of the state's varied topography and microclimates. Native Americans grew maize, beans, squash, and many other vegetables. Similarly, most European American farmers cultivated several vegetable crops, especially corn, and grains, especially wheat, along with beans and squash. They also raised livestock and cultivated fruit trees, as did some Native Americans once they encountered European Americans. In northwest Ohio, incoming European Americans also engaged in dairying, reaching local and regional markets with milk and cheese. Monocultural farming, with an emphasis on just one or two major crops, such as corn or soybeans, came much later. In fact, according to geographer Christopher R. Laingen, the Midwest began shifting from "a mixed crop-and-livestock farming system to one that is highly specialized and focused on cash-grain farming," with farms of only corn and soybeans developing in the 1920s and increasing more significantly after World War II.[15] To spread their risks, European American farmers engaged in diversified agricultural. If one crop failed, another might succeed, ensuring they and their families had a variety of foods and produce needed for subsistence. Especially in the early years, before canals and railroads connected them to large markets, Ohio's farmers grew some of their produce and raised some of their livestock for home consumption. They did so on farms of all types and sizes.[16]

Even on frontiers, farmers used tools and some machinery. Most important were plows. "Farming first meant fieldwork, which meant plowing," historian Hurt observes. Moreover, he writes that the 1800s "was a period of trial and error for plow design as tinkerers, inventors, and blacksmiths, as well as manufacturers, experimented with moldboard curvatures to determine which best slice through the soil." During the early 1800s, Ohio and other midwestern farmers commonly employed wooden moldboard Carey plows built by local blacksmiths and plowwrights. As described by Hurt, "Iron straps rivetted to the moldboard in some fashion helped peel the soil away." Light and maneuverable, the Carey plow could cut through about one acre of soil per day, pulled by a single horse and guided by one person. Like the Carey plow, most farm tools were made mainly of wood—shovels, pitchforks, and the like—as iron and steel were scarce and expensive in frontier times. Ohio forests provided the hardwood needed to make tools, fences, and cabins. Mechanized reapers to harvest grain, self-binders to tie the cut grain in sheaves, and horse-powered threshers to separate grain from chaff came after the frontier stage of development had passed in Ohio, not until the 1830s and later.[17]

There were large individual European American landowners in Ohio. Some sought to acquire estates like those held by large landholders of the Hudson River valley in New York or in parts of Virginia; land brought prestige and social and political power. Others sought land to sell, thus increasing their wealth. In buying and selling, they acted as land speculators, purchasing land in big chunks at low prices from the federal government and then reselling it in much smaller parcels at higher prices to would-be farmers. Land companies such as the Ohio Company also acted in this manner. By 1810, Lucas Sullivant, a surveyor for the Scioto Land Company and the founder of Franklinton in central Ohio in 1797, owned the most land of any individual in the state, possessing 41,459 acres in eighty-six parcels. He had acquired it by taking land in payment for his surveying services in the Virginia Military Tract, a typical practice. Together, the top 10 percent of Ohio property holders in 1810 owned about 33 percent of all properties, and the top 1 percent owned 23 percent of the state's acreage.[18] Most large landowners—individuals or companies—were eager to sell their lands to incoming settlers, hoping to earn large profits. For them, land was a commodity. For instance, Sullivant disposed of parcels along the Scioto River and Alum Creek in central Ohio as early as 1800.[19] But not all sold their lands.

Thomas Worthington sought to create an agricultural empire in the Scioto valley near Chillicothe in south central Ohio's glaciated region, part of the till plains. Hailing originally from Virginia, he was emulating that state's large plantation owners. Rich soil and plentiful rainfall smiled upon his efforts. He eventually created a very large diversified farm, a plantation really. And Thomas played a very active role in Ohio politics, earning the title of "the father of Ohio's statehood."

Thomas had a privileged upbringing living with his brother Ephraim and then with his brother William and his wife. (Thomas's father had died in 1779, when Thomas was six years old.) When William moved to Kentucky, Thomas went to live with Colonel William Darke of Shepherdstown, Virginia. Darke became the father figure Worthington craved, as Worthington later wrote: "This gentleman was to me a father, and his good lady a mother. . . . I lived happily and progressed in my studies." After a stint as a merchant sailor, Worthington set himself up on land inherited from his father in Virginia's Shenandoah Valley and Pennsylvania at the age of twenty. A wealthy landowner, his father had possessed land in both regions. When large amounts of Ohio land became available for purchase following the signing of the Treaty of Greenville in 1795, Worthington, always venturesome, was ready to move.[20]

Two scouting expeditions to examine and buy land led Worthington to Ohio. The first trip took him down the Ohio River from Wheeling to the mouth of the Scioto River, where he paddled upstream by canoe in the summer of 1796. Passing newly established Chillicothe (then called Massie's Town after its founders Nathaniel and Henry Massie), Worthington continued north to Paint Creek. He liked the land he saw there, especially the land along stream and river bottoms, where there were several species of big trees, and bought 600 acres on Brush Creek. Back home in Virginia, he married Eleanor Swearingen and started planning to move west. A second scouting trip intervened. In the summer of 1797, Worthington, accompanied by Edward Tiffin, a doctor and his brother-in-law, returned to Ohio to look at more land. Worthington bought another 7,600 acres in the Virginia Military Tract near Chillicothe. (Duncan McArthur, who located and surveyed the land, received 20 percent of the acreage for his services.) Worthington also purchased three town lots in Chillicothe, and with Tiffin's help, he immediately built a log cabin on one of those lots to fend off squatters. Worthington continued to buy land in later years, amassing a whopping 18,272 acres by 1800.[21]

After disposing of his Virginia land and house and freeing the enslaved people, Worthington moved to Ohio with his family in the spring of 1798. He was one member of a substantial group, including—in addition to Thomas and Eleanor's own growing family, the first of ten children being born in late 1797—his brother Robert Worthington, Robert's wife and three children, Eleanor's two brothers, Tiffin and his extended family (his parents, two brothers, and two sisters), along with a Mr. Woods and his family, several adolescent boys who were millwrights, and a group of African American servants (formerly enslaved). Traveling by wagon, they journeyed across the Appalachian Mountains to Pittsburgh, descended the Ohio River by flatboat to the mouth of the Scioto River, and rode horseback north on a path paralleling that stream to Chillicothe. The trip took just over a month.

Two motives prompted the move. Worthington wanted to live in a region without slavery, and slavery had been illegal in the Ohio Country since the passage by Congress of the Northwest Ordinance in 1787. Even more important was his land hunger. According to Worthington's biographer, "the economic motive of bettering his condition by moving into a country where land was rich and cheap" was paramount in Thomas's thinking.[22]

Near Chillicothe, Worthington engaged in large-scale, diversified farming on his estate. His land produced corn, wheat, flax, hemp, and other crops. Fruit trees soon bore peaches, apples, and cherries. Livestock raising included horses, cattle, pigs, and sheep. To process his and his neighbors' grain, Worthington built gristmills at the falls of the Hockhocking River and on Kinnikinnic Creek. As Worthington recorded in his diary in 1802, the latter mill, just north of Chillicothe, "grinds for 3/4 of the people in Fairfield and Ross Counties." Soon, Worthington also had sawmills and gristmills on Paint Creek and the Mad River. In 1810, Worthington built a ropewalk to process his hemp in Chillicothe as well as a cloth mill to weave his flax and wool (he also imported cotton from the South for the mill). Worthington continued to speculate in land and became one of the organizers of the Bank of Chillicothe.[23]

In 1802, Worthington built a log house atop a hill on his land two miles outside of Chillicothe, beyond the reach of the "bilious and intermittent fevers" that plagued the lowlands. Just a few years later, Worthington supplemented it with a multistory stone house, Adena Mansion, designed by noted architect Benjamin Latrobe, which still stood in the early 2000s. Adena means "places remarkable for delightfulness of their situation," and Ohio's state seal shows the view of hills from Adena Mansion. From this comfortable headquarters, Worthington went into politics, serving at various times as one of Ohio's senators to Congress and as the governor of Ohio.[24]

Few landowners operated on Worthington's regal scale. Mary Howitt's fictional account, *Our Cousins in Ohio,* first published in 1849, offers a vivid and remarkably astute portrayal of family farming just after the close of Ohio's frontier period. Located near the Hocking River close to Athens, one river valley to the east of Worthington's estate, the diversified farm pictured in Howitt's novel produces corn, oats, and potatoes for commercial sale. Orchards grow peaches, cherries, and apples. A substantial vegetable garden provides the farm's dinner table with asparagus, rhubarb, beets, carrots, beans, peas, turnips, squashes, melons, sweet potatoes, and tomatoes. The size of the farm is never given in Howitt's writing, but its lands are worked by family members with seasonal help from a handful of hired hands.[25] George Dell's *The Earth Abideth* provides another fictional depiction of farm life in early Ohio, with its action set on a small family farm near Lancaster, just south of Columbus. The protagonist loves his farmland studded with big trees: "It was the land that caught Thomas's eye—the long, low swell of the fields, undulant to the brow of woods at the back line. There was walnut and oak in the woods." Thomas plants corn and hay, nurtures apple trees, and keeps horses, cows, and pigs. The farm is the source of his income, but the farm means more than money to Thomas: "This was his life—the land. Here not only his few acres belonged to him, but the seasons and eternal hills as well."[26]

These fictional depictions are accurate. In 1810, the median holding of an Ohio farmer was 150 acres—more than enough for prosperous agriculture—at a time when 40 acres was about the most a person could keep cultivated.[27] Despite inequalities in land ownership, Ohio contained relatively large family farms. Even tenant farmers and farm laborers—only 45 percent of men over the age of nineteen owned real estate in Ohio in 1810 or 1850—could realistically aspire to land ownership in Ohio's burgeoning economy at some point in their lives. Throughout the late colonial period and into early national years, American farms were typically about 75 to 100 acres, with roughly 15 to 35 acres of those planted in crops. As late as 1920, the United States possessed many more farms smaller than 250 acres than farms larger than that size.[28] Farms in Ohio, then, were considerably larger than the national norm. Land was available for purchase at reasonable prices from land companies and from the federal government, especially after the passage of the Land Law of 1820.

Thomas Rogers was a typical smallholding farmer living in Paint Valley near Worthington's major landholdings. Born in 1782 in Virginia, Rogers traveled with his family to Kentucky before moving with them to Ohio. A dislike of slavery and a search for fertile farmland prompted his family's moves, just as they did Worthington's.[29] After several exploratory trips north of the Ohio River, the Rogers family moved to the Paint Creek region, just off the Scioto River, about four miles west of Chillicothe. Here Thomas's father found "beautiful, rich rye grass, bottoms, and beautiful streams of water." He bought 200 acres in 1796 and immediately put in a crop of corn. Wild game, especially turkeys and deer, tided the family over until harvest time. Within a few years, the family was taking thirty-four wagonloads of corn to market each fall. Local markets in nearby farm towns were increasingly connected to larger regional and even national markets by roads and canals during the 1810s, 1820s, and 1830s.[30]

At the age of twenty-three, Thomas left his family, married, and started his own farm nearby. "So, I fell to work," he later recalled, "as I had no other shift, and worked almost night and day." He planted five acres in corn and "made a pretty fair crop." He also put in potatoes, fruit trees, and a patch of wheat. Every spring thereafter, Rogers cleared an additional field for his growing farm. Still, wild game long continued to be an important source of food. "When I settled on Paint Creek,"

Rogers remembered, “there was game in abundance, and especially deer and turkeys, and some bears.” In his memoirs, Rogers described at length “the largest deer I ever killed.”[31]

His family lived in a log cabin. In *Stories of Ohio,* writer William Dean Howells describes a one-room pioneer log cabin probably very similar to that in which Thomas and his family resided. The cabin was “framed of the round logs, untouched by the ax except for the notches at the ends where they were fitted into one another.” The chimney, he observes, was made of “small sticks stuck together with mud,” and the floor was formed of “rough boards called puncheons, riven from the block with a heavy knife.” Howells describes the roof as being constructed of “clapboards split from logs and laid loosely on the rafters and held in place with logs fastened athwart them.”[32]

To the east in Ohio, Joseph Howells, a Quaker born in Wales in 1783, had mixed success farming much rockier and hillier unglaciated land than the glacial till owned by Worthington and Rogers. Near the western border of Pennsylvania, Howells's land on the Appalachian Plateau had not been ground up by glaciers and had thin, poor soil. In short, this unglaciated land possessed soil largely unsuitable for most types of agriculture.

Howells immigrated to the United States in 1808 to go into working wool, which he did for several years in New York. Hired by a fellow Quaker, Howells, who had married, moved with his family to eastern Ohio to establish a wool factory in Jefferson County. After a wagon trip over very rough roads, the Howells family arrived in 1813 at Warrenton, Ohio, about fourteen miles south of Steubenville. The region was, as Joseph Howells's son, William Cooper Howells, later recalled, already “well cleared up and settled.” Joseph Howells sought with only limited success to build a wool works and enter the wool trade over the next four years, as the War of 1812 put a damper on business. In 1817, Joseph bought his first farm, forty acres five miles from Steubenville, of which only twenty-five acres could be cultivated, the rest “being stony hillside.” William remembered, “It had always been a doctrine in the family that we ought to move onto a farm and father looked forward to the time he could buy a farm and devote himself to the cultivation of it.” Land hunger ran in the family, a good example of how previous experiences with shortages of land in Great Britain and the eastern United States spurred a lust for land in European Americans in Ohio.[33]

Farming the rocky, "hopelessly poor" land, some of which was exhausted from previous agricultural efforts and all of which was full of rattlesnakes, proved difficult, and within a few years the Howells family moved to another farm not far away. Again, stony, thin soil plagued their efforts, as they tried to grow corn and wheat, nurture an orchard of peach trees, and raise sheep. Joseph found that he had to work in Steubenville to make ends meet, returning to his farm and family only on weekends. Theirs was a hardscrabble existence, endured for three years into 1822. Giving up this farm, Joseph and his family moved to one nearby of twenty-three acres, which Joseph rented. It had "a good spring," a grove of "sugar trees," and soil that was "tolerably good." Still, farming was a challenge. William later wrote, "The great difficulty with the family was that we did not belong to the farming class." They had to learn everything about farming from scratch.[34]

The Howells family moved yet again. Using a legacy from the death of his father in 1824, Joseph and his family decamped to a 160-acre farm, which Joseph purchased in Harrison County, thirty-seven miles from Steubenville. There, the land was "tolerably good" but "very hilly."[35] The family had some success, girdling trees to clear fields. (As mentioned previously, in girdling trees, farmers cut rings through the bark and next layer of growth around the trunks and allowed them to die while standing. Only several years later were the trees burned or cut down and removed from fields. Meanwhile, corn was planted around them.[36]) Like most early European American farmers in Ohio, Howells ran a diversified operation, raising corn, wheat, flax, and, for a time, tobacco.

Logging bees, in which settlers cooperated in clearing woods of trees, cornhusking parties, during which they removed the husks (outside leaves) from ears of corn after fall harvests, religious meetings, and trips to nearby villages provided social contact with other farmers and entertainment. It was not enough. "The farming operations," William recorded in his journal, "were a failure here, because we were not expert farmers." Joseph sold the farm and moved to Wheeling, Virginia, where he bought a house and worked in the wool trade. Meanwhile, the now-adult William went into printing, journalism, and other occupations. In 1834, Joseph, his wife, and younger children moved again, this time to Chillicothe, where Joseph bought yet another farm. Within three years, however, Joseph sold the farm and moved to Hamilton, Ohio, where he purchased a drugstore in which he did "fairly well." Still later, he went into journalism, politics, and gristmilling. He died at the age of eighty-seven in 1870, an unusually advanced age at a time when most Americans were dead by the age of about thirty-five or forty.[37]

Women were important on Ohio's frontiers. Joseph Howells's wife ran their farms whenever her husband was away working in wool. She operated as what many historians have called a "deputy husband." More commonly, however, women worked alongside their husbands in making and then operating farms. Frontier life was often a difficult existence for women. In her reminiscence of farm life in western Ohio during the early 1800s, Liwwat Boke painted a dismal picture: "Life is a long struggle. We must fell trees, but also cope with droughts, deep snow, sudden flooding, cloudbursts, forest fire, swarms of deer-flies, and mosquitoes and midges, snakes, wolves, and twice the wolves were mad." Moreover, she averred, "In time some people go completely mad, change, commit suicide." Historian Stephane Elise Booth indeed concludes that in the isolation of the Ohio frontier, "domestic abuse was an all-too-common occurrence and murder of a spouse was not unknown." Women throughout Ohio had many tasks. In Marietta, they cooked, made clothes, raised children, kept gardens, and took care of the sick. Gender lines sometimes blurred, as women worked in fields. Then, too, women interacted with visiting Native Americans while their husbands were away laboring in fieldwork. They sometimes supplemented their family's income by weaving and running inns, and a few women were landowners in their own right.[38]

More successful at farming in eastern Ohio than the Howells family was Anna Briggs Bentley and her family. Born in 1796 and raised in Maryland by a prominent Quaker family, she married in 1812. With her husband, Joseph, she moved to Columbiana County in eastern Ohio near the Pennsylvania border in 1826, where fellow Quakers awaited them. About eight thousand Quakers lived in eastern Ohio then. This area was the same generally rocky region of unglaciated soil that the

Howells farmed. However, Anna's husband had previous knowledge of farming and, it appears, enjoyed more help from his Quaker neighbors than did the Howells. The Bentley family succeeded in agriculture in the inhospitable land; for Anna, life was not the dismal scene pictured by Boke. Life was considerably varied for women on Ohio's frontier.

Within just a few days of their arrival, Joseph, assisted by other Quakers, was, as Anna wrote friends in Maryland, "grubbing, mauling, and burning" to clear land for a family farm. The hard work paid off. Walking around her family's land in July 1826, Anna observed "beautiful hills" and "majestic Oaks." Five or six acres had been cleared for farming on a "fine piece of land," which Anna viewed as "an inheritance for my children." Three months later, she celebrated an "overflowing abundance" of produce, including "the finest fruit" and "barns full, herds, flocks, swine, and poultry, the garden flourishing." She exclaimed, "Oh, this is a favored spot." A year later, Anna recorded "excellent wheat" and "flourishing corn," along with "watermelons, cantelopes [cantaloupes], cimbuns, pumpkins, beans, and cucumbers." Peach, apple, and cherry trees bore bumper crops, and chickens and cows did well. Over the years, Anna and Joseph's farm and family increased in size as prosperity attended their efforts.[39]

Members of the Bentley family were commercial farmers. Like nearly all Ohio agriculturalists, they raised a variety of produce for sale in regional and even national markets as well as for their own consumption. The Ohio and Erie Canal was built through the Bentley's neighborhood in 1834, spurring market developments. By the mid-1840s, two canal systems running north–south linked communities throughout Ohio. Canals allowed farmers to get their heavy and bulky crops—such as wheat, corn, cheese, and fruit—to distant markets at reasonable prices for the first time. Road transportation had been expensive, limiting Ohio produce to local outlets. Financed by the state of Ohio but constructed by local contractors who often employed area farmers to dig the ditches, canals revolutionized the economy. Anna observed the changes locally. "A great change is occurring in our neighborhood," she noted in late 1834. She wrote further: "Little Hanover is rapidly improving, buildings going up; lots that sold for $80 last summer sold 2 weeks ago for $280." In fact, she exclaimed, "they are rushing on with this canal tearing up trees by the roots." New opportunities appeared. Joseph found employment selling coal "as fast as he could haul it in Hanover."[40]

Log rollings, house raisings, in which settlers cooperated in building houses and barns, Quaker meetings, visits to towns, and even attendance at a traveling circus provided amusements and a chance for sociability for the Bentleys. Life was rarely dull. Not all was enjoyable, however. Beyond the never-ending hard work of making a farm lay the specter of disease. Bilious fevers, typhus, whooping cough, scarlet fever, smallpox, and toothaches afflicted Anna's family and her neighbors at one time or another. Still, the Bentleys lived long lives. Joseph died in 1865 at the age of seventy-six, and Anna died in 1890 at the age of ninety-four. By the times of their deaths, Ohio had passed far beyond its frontier stage of development.[41]

Historian Harry N. Scheiber summarizes well the alterations that canals and, a bit later, railroads brought to Ohio, thinking it a "remarkable transformation." Continuing, he concludes, "In 1820 Ohio had barely gone beyond the frontier stage of development, except in a few settled areas along the Ohio River and its major tributaries; yet by 1861 it had become one of the nation's leading states in population and in industrial and agricultural development." Canals reoriented Ohio's trade. Originally, nearly all the state's commerce had passed down the Ohio and Mississippi Rivers to New Orleans and then had gone by sailing ship to the East Coast and abroad. That trade had linked the North and the South. However, new trade routes developed with canals and railroads, joining Ohio to eastern states, especially New York and Pennsylvania in an East-West nexus. The growing acrimony over slavery contributed to this reorientation as well. The Ohio River, once a bridge between Ohio and the South, became a boundary.[42]

Ohio's European American farmers were certainly market oriented, eager to send their produce wherever they could earn profits. At first, this meant shipping whatever they grew downstream to Cincinnati or New Orleans by flatboat or, from 1817, by steamboat. As early as 1800, a farmer descended the Great Miami River to the Ohio River via a flatboat with five hundred venison hams. He then went down the Mississippi River to New Orleans, where he sold them. River trade was extensive. From November 24, 1810, through January 24, 1811, some 197 flatboats and 14 keel boats carried 18,611 barrels of flour, 520 barrels of pork, 681,000 additional pounds of meat, 2,373 barrels of whiskey, 3,759 barrels of apples, 1,085 barrels of cider, 817 venison hams, and many other items down the Ohio River.[43]

Yet a page from the daybook of Daniel Kaufman, a farmer in Richmond County in central Ohio, illustrates how commercially minded farmers blended business with noncommercial matters, even well beyond frontier times. Covering the last week of 1864, the page shows that Kaufman kept careful track of how he used his time in the interests of business rationality. Daybook entries also reveal that Kaufman bought and sold goods at the nearby market town of Mansfield, hired workers for special tasks such as butchering hogs and beef, paid those workers in cash, and settled his accounts at the end of the calendar year. Yet personal comments, such as those about the weather noting "the soft rain," interspersed his business accounts. Notable, too, is that Kaufman abstained from all work on Sunday, the Sabbath.[44]

In their approaches to agriculture, European American farmers in Ohio resembled their counterparts across the United States. American farmers combined subsistence farming, growing crops for their own use, with, whenever possible, producing crops for market.[45] Farmers viewed growing crops, nurturing fruit trees, and raising livestock for their families' use as virtuous activities, as protecting them into the future. In the opening decades of the nineteenth century, as historian Daniel Howe writes, "the most common and popular utopia of all was simply a family farm." Continuing, Howe observes, "There the average white American could enjoy the dignity of freehold, exchange help with neighbors during stressful seasons, entertain the expectation of a good harvest, and hope to build a competence that would see a couple through old age with something to pass on to their children." None of these activities precluded engagement in markets. "A composite family farm," Howe notes, "could simultaneously live in a local world of barter and engage in international commerce." Moreover, he concludes, "Market success and a measure of self-sufficiency were not even incompatible goals."[46]

About 80 percent of Americans were farmers during late colonial and early national times, and many, probably most, equated farming with republican virtue. That is, farming was viewed as much more than merely a way of making a living. It was a way of life. Farming was seen as giving a person independence through the ownership of productive property, land that a nonfarmer simply did not have. That liberty gave a person, many thought, republican virtue. Artisans, even those who possessed their own tools, did not have that independence and virtue because they were dependent on merchants and market forces. Similarly, American merchants were often dependent on their British counterparts and certainly on markets. Although farmers, too, bought and sold in markets, especially as commercial farming spread, they could always, it was imagined, fall back on subsistence farming if necessary, thus preserving their independence and virtue.[47]

As historian Gregory S. Rose says of developments in the Midwest, "The yeoman farm—carved from the forest or prairie, developed and worked by the family, and the basis of the family's prosperity and inheritance—formed the conceptual ideal."[48] Writing to his son, who was moving to Marietta from New England, Manasseh Cutler, one of Marietta's founders, advised, "I have earnestly wished for you to have a good farm, to establish a good landed interest in preference to trade . . . for there is nothing in this country that will render a man so completely independent and secure against difficulties."[49]

Historian Richard Bushman argues cogently that subsistence farming, which he calls "self-provisioning," and market farming went together in colonial and early national America as farmers sought "to add to family well-being." For farmers, family "well-being," present and future, was the primary goal of their lives. That meant ensuring they had enough land to pass on to their sons when they came of age—a circumstance which, in turn, Bushman stresses, spurred movements to frontiers where lands were available. "The expansive impulse," Bushman writes, was "driven less by raw economic necessity than by a judgment about the good life." Native Americans, Bushman points out, lost their struggle against Euro-American expansion, pushed aside or destroyed in European Americans' quest for land.[50] For families seeking a good life based on gaining more land for sons, moving to Ohio seemed to be an answer. George Washington, who speculated in western lands and always tried to present them to others in the most positive light possible, observed in a 1785 letter to the Marquis de Lafayette that "the fertile plains of the Ohio" were a "land of promise, with milk and honey."[51]

In contrast, Native American farming was more for strictly subsistence needs. On occasion, however, Native Americans sold to European Americans maple sugar they made, maize they cultivated, and wild rice they collected. Also, Native Americans were often active participants in the fur trade, seeking profits and bargains. The Miami even moved eastward into Ohio from Indiana in part to be closer to British traders, who offered higher-quality goods at lower prices than French traders farther west.

African Americans joined European Americans in sentiments about the land and commercial farming. For African Americans, land ownership may have meant even more than it did for European Americans. Like others, African Americans in Ohio embraced the republicanism of land ownership, that it gave them a certain amount of independence and freedom. Even more, land ownership was seen favorably by many African Americans in an almost religious light and as an antidote to slavery.

Entering Ohio, African Americans found a state and people ambivalent in their attitudes toward them. The federal Northwest Ordinance of 1787 and the State of Ohio Constitution of 1803 forbade slavery. Neither, however, gave African Americans the right to vote, and Ohio's constitution permitted indentured servitude. More than that, between 1803 and 1807, the Ohio legislature passed a series of laws known collectively as the "Black Laws" or the "Black Code," designed, in the words of historian Stephen Middleton, "to make life for African Americans in Ohio so intolerable that these men and women would not use the free state as a refuge from the oppression of slavery." The Black Laws required that African Americans have European American sponsors to move into an area and that African Americans place a deposit of $500, a large sum then, with the local government to live in the state. Laws forbade African Americans to vote, serve on juries, testify against White people in trials, or serve in militias. Laws also upheld the federal Fugitive Slave Act of 1793, which permitted slaveholders to pursue enslaved people who had run away to free states. Other states in the Old

Northwest (Indiana, Illinois, Michigan, and Wisconsin) adopted their own versions of Ohio's Black Laws during the early and mid-1800s. Repeal of the Black Laws in Ohio occurred only as public attitudes toward African Americans became more favorable from the 1840s into the 1880s. The last Black Law was repealed in 1887.[52]

African Americans viewed the Black Laws with dismay. John Malvin, an enslaved man in Virginia, was a carpenter by trade who moved to Ohio in the 1820s. In his new state, Malvin wrote, "I thought upon coming to a free state like Ohio, that I would find every door thrown open to receive me, but from the treatment I received by the people generally I found it little better than Virginia. I found every door closed against the colored man in a free state, excepting the jails and penitentiaries."[53] Even so, African Americans entered Ohio in significant numbers, lured by thoughts of land and freedom. Only 337 African Americans lived in Ohio in 1800, but 4,723 did in 1820, and 9,568 resided in the state in 1830. About 25,000 African Americans made Ohio their home in 1850. While some lived in emerging cities, especially Cincinnati, many lived in the countryside, where they farmed.[54]

By the 1850s and early 1860s, there were 338 African American agricultural settlements in the Old Northwest, including 95 in Ohio alone. About 63,000 African Americans lived in the Old Northwest in 1860, some 73 percent on farms.[55] Above all, African Americans sought fertile farmland. An 1843 Michigan convention of African Americans advised, "Agriculture is the bone and sinew of our country." They further resolved, "We recommend it to our people as best calculated to promote their rise and progress."[56] African Americans saw land and citizenship as linked and, despite the Black Laws, succeeded in establishing farms. A Quaker making an 1837 visit to the African American community of Lexington in Columbiana County, Ohio, not far from the Bentley family's farm, found a "settlement of 51 families, numbering 264 individuals." Some 1,860 acres valued at $29,200 were being farmed.[57]

Thoughts about the positive moral value of farm freeholds echoed into the twentieth and twenty-first centuries. Ohio's best-selling writer and gentleman farmer Louis Bromfield embraced such notions during the mid-twentieth century, expostulating that there was "in all the world no finer figure than a sturdy farmer standing, his feet well planted in the earth, looking over his rich field and beautiful shiny cattle." At his farm about fifty miles northeast of Columbus, which he named "Malabar" after a portion of the Indian coast he had once visited, Bromfield experimented with ecologically sustainable agriculture. He also hobnobbed with Hollywood celebrities. Humphrey Bogart and Lauren Bacall were married at Malabar. For Bromfield, the land was everything. His goal in life was "to be on my own land, on an island of security, which could be my refuge, not only for myself and my family but my friends as well."[58]

To the north and west of the Bentley and Howells families, Jonathan Hale and his family developed a farm in the Cuyahoga River valley, just south of Cleveland, on the lake plains. The soil of this land was deep and rich in nutrients. Well watered, the land was suited for diversified agriculture. Moreover, Hale came from a farming family and brought with him knowledge gleaned from working on his family's farm in Connecticut, which grew many of the same crops Hale cultivated in Ohio. Agricultural success seemed likely for Hale.

Born in 1777, Hale had grown up on a family farm near Hartford. Its principal crops were rye, wheat, corn, flax, tobacco, onions, turnips, and apples, and its livestock included chickens, pigs, and cows. Hale and one of his brothers-in-law, Jason Hammond, swapped their lands in Connecticut for Ohio lands held by a proprietor of the Connecticut Land Company. That company owned about three million acres purchased from the state of Connecticut, which had claims to part of northern Ohio. Hale acquired five hundred acres of new land. "When Jonathan Hale whipped his team onto the flat-bottomed ferry which crossed the Connecticut River at Rocky Hill," a biographer notes, "he left behind him the rich bottom lands, the ploughed fields, pastures, and hilly woodland on the farm that had been the home of his family for five generations." Hale was an experienced farmer when he moved to Ohio at the age of thirty-three in 1810, well used to the many demands of diversified agriculture. One of his grandsons later recalled that his grandfather moved west to acquire new and better land, to escape debts, and to avoid being at the "tail of the heap" in his family.[59]

By the time Hale migrated, land in the Cuyahoga valley had been recognized for its agricultural potential for decades. As early as 1758, a European American held captive by Native Americans recorded in his memoirs, "The bottoms are rich and large," and "the timber is walnut, locust, mulberry, red haw, black haw."[60] Passing through the valley twenty-five years later, Moravian missionary John Heckewelder praised the bottom lands, observing "Wild hops of excellent quality" and noting that the region abounded in "Elk, Deer, Turkeys, Raccoons, etc."[61]

Hale went to Ohio by wagon in the early summer of 1810. It was a journey of thirty-two days, a trip which he later estimated to have been 646 miles long. In late July, Jonathan, who had arrived at his land a few weeks earlier, wrote his wife, Mercy, who had been temporarily left behind in Hartford, saying, "The land here is much better than I had expected." Indeed, Hale recorded in late 1810, "The land I live on is as good as any man can wish for." Hale was impressed by the "various kinds of timber," which included white oaks, black walnuts, cherry trees, boxwood, butternuts, and sugar maples, which "grow to great size 5 & 6 feet in diameter." Mercy and their three young children joined Jonathan on the land that fall, after their own demanding journey of forty-two days across the mountains of Pennsylvania. Meanwhile, Jonathan acquired a log cabin and several acres planted in wheat from a squatter on his land in a swap for his worn-out horses and his wagon. The cabin had a stone chimney, a window, a loft where the children slept, and a lean-to on one end. The Hale family lived in that cabin for seven years. Several other family members took up nearby lands.[62]

Over the next two decades, Jonathan and his family built up a prosperous diversified farm, much like the one left behind in Connecticut. The Ohio farm's commercial produce included corn, wheat, oats, flax, potatoes, and turnips. Various vegetables were grown for home consumption. Most important was corn, which historian Geoff Cunfer calls the "quintessential American pioneer crop." Relatively easy to plant and cultivate, corn was low in proteins but high in carbohydrates and thus in energy. Both people and livestock could eat it.[63] And it could be distilled into corn liquor for easy shipment to markets. Honey came from several hives, and sugar was made from sugar maple sap late each winter. Cattle, oxen, horses, pigs, and sheep were the farm's livestock, along with chickens, turkeys, geese, and ducks. Peach and apple trees were soon bearing fruit. Ohio's farmers especially favored peach trees because they bore fruit within just three years of being planted; apple trees took several years longer. The peaches could be eaten, made into peach brandy, or preserved by drying into "peach leather."[64] The work was continuous, as land needed to be cleared and then put into crops. Smoke hung in the air as downed trees were burned.

Hale developed several side businesses that boosted his farm's profits. He burned limestone found on the farm to make lime, from which he produced mortar needed in stone and brick construction, and he made bricks from clay located on the farm. Meanwhile, Mercy and her daughters—the couple had five children who lived to maturity—spent their time on household tasks, which included spinning and weaving flax into homespun clothing. Trained as a seamstress, Mercy also cut garments for other women in the neighborhood, bringing in needed funds. Socializing accompanied making the farm. Jonathan enjoyed singing and playing the violin and often did both at local parties. The Hale family especially celebrated holidays with friends—Thanksgiving, Christmas, New Year's, and the Fourth of July.[65]

The growing prosperity of the Hale family assumed tangible form in the construction of a large, three-story brick house to replace their log cabin. Using local materials mainly from the farm, and with Jonathan and his two adolescent sons providing much of the labor, the house went up in the late 1820s.[66] Called "Old Brick" by family members and known as the Jonathan Hale House, it still stood in the early 2000s.

Mercy did not enjoy the new house for long. Tired and suffering from an unspecified illness, she died in 1829 at the age of fifty. Jonathan had suffered intermittently from malaria (he called the ailment "fever and ague") from his first autumn in Ohio and was too ill to attend his wife's funeral. Still, he soon remarried and lived into 1854, when he died at the age of seventy-seven. Such a sequence was common on the Ohio frontier, where men often outlived their wives. All too frequently, women died in childbirth or indirectly of overwork. Jonathan's second wife passed away in 1855.[67]

Far to the west, Howard Good's grandfather developed a family farm in Ohio's Black Swamp, moving there from Lancaster, Pennsylvania, in 1836. Located in northwestern Ohio on lake till, the Black

Swamp was "the product of three poorly drained rivers: the Maumee, the Auglaize, and the Portage."[68] Some thirty to forty miles wide, the swamp extended about 120 miles southwestward from the western end of Lake Erie. Living in villages spaced around its outer margins, Native Americans had used the swamp as a valuable source of fish, waterfowl, fur-bearing animals, and plants. Euro-American movement into the area had begun with the conclusion of the War of 1812, which led to the removal of Native Americans from the region and the opening of land for purchase.

"No doubt," Howard Good later wrote, "the principal attraction for all was the low cost of the land." The very level land of the Black Swamp had been compressed over millennia by glaciers and was poorly drained. "Great reaches of water . . . dark and motionless" covered "much of the flat terrain." Still, the swamp boasted big trees—hickories, oaks, sycamores, elms, maples, ashes, and box elders—which "stood like straight, giant poles" and were seen as indicative of good soil. That soil consisted of about a foot of rich topsoil, "dark and waxy," underlain by layers of yellow and blue clay, which impeded drainage. The region also harbored extensive wildlife—bears, wolves, deer, and fish.[69]

Clearing the land of trees and draining the land of water were the first major tasks farmers faced. They cut down and removed trees in logging bees, community efforts that Good described as "frontier social affairs."[70] After felling trees, the settlers typically burned them, using the ashes to make potash, which could be employed in manufacturing soap and glass, as Hale had done. Removing obstructions from streams began the work of drainage, soon followed by digging drainage canals to sluice away standing water. Placing clay tiles underground to drain additional water from below the surface, accomplished mainly in the 1880s and later, completed the process. In *At the Edge of the Orchard,* published in 2016, novelist Tracy Chevalier sets her story in part in Ohio's Black Swamp during the 1830s and 1840s. She observes that clearing the swamp of trees and taking out the "goddamn stumps" was seen as progress by incoming European Americans.[71]

Environmental changes accompanied alterations to the land. The introduction of livestock, especially cattle and sheep, led to the trampling and then sedimentation of the banks of streams. Invasive grasses and weeds replaced native vegetation in affected areas. One type of weed, with which most incoming farmers were unfamiliar, could poison cow's milk, leading to sickness and even death among infants and young children. Then, too, the region's water table fell with drainage and deforestation, leading to water shortages whenever rains failed during growing seasons of crops. Those crops were many, for diversified farming dominated agricultural efforts in the Black Swamp as they did elsewhere in frontier Ohio: oats, wheat, rye, corn, potatoes, and grasses for hay. Invasive insects accompanied farming. For instance, chinch bugs spread from Central America to North America, including the Black Swamp, where they attacked fields of corn. Orchards produced cherries, peaches, and apples. Livestock included cows, pigs, and sheep. Sugar came from sugar maples, and honey from bees' nests in trees.[72]

Most early Euro-American farms in Ohio were worked within a division of labor. Men cleared and drained the land and cultivated crops, only occasionally assisted by women in the fields. Women took care of children, did the cooking and laundry, made clothes, tended gardens by the home, milked cows, and raised poultry. Egg and butter money made from the sale of those items to country stores gave women some financial independence. Still, as Good recalled, there was a lot of truth to the adage "Man works from rise to set of sun, but women's work is never done." He noted, too, that "monuments in old cemeteries bear the names of many women who succumbed in what are now regarded as the middle years of life," a situation he attributed to overwork, diseases, and the dangers of childbirth.[73]

Just to the south of the Black Swamp and just north of Dayton lay the Mad River valley, settled as an American farming region in the early 1800s. "The story of Champaign County and its Mad River Valley," historian Timothy H. H. Thoresen writes, is a "story of the Ohio Country and, with reference to agriculture, it is a story of America and its rural heartland." Continuing, he explains, "It is the story of land-hungry migrants." In fact, "land was the reason. Land gave identity. Land also gave purpose." As elsewhere in Ohio, would-be farmers selected their lands by looking at the trees. "The settlers of the Old Northwest," Thoresen notes, "were adept at reading the trees as a way of finding the kinds of soil they were familiar with working." Once cleared, land was used for diversified agriculture, growing and raising corn, wheat, vegetables, livestock, and fruit trees. Farmers wanted to provide food for their families, but they also were eager participants in regional markets made accessible by wagon roads, canals, and railroads.[74]

Wherever they farmed in Ohio and throughout the Midwest, European American agriculturalists laid out their spreads in common ways. When possible, they placed their farmsteads on hills and ridges to avoid floods, to enjoy cool breezes, and to have views that might reveal errant livestock or approaching enemies. The homesteads, and especially houses, were positioned below the crest of hills and on the lee side of prevailing winds. Farmsteads were also located east and south of trees, which could serve as windbreaks (prevailing winds blew from west to east). Doing so, historian and geographer James E. Davis explains, minimized "odors, flies, jarring noises, and the threat of fire spreading from barns to houses." Barnyards and hog lots were generally placed east and south of barns to speed sunrays' early-morning drying of the ground. Similarly, houses, barns, henhouses, and the like were situated to take advantage of local environmental conditions.[75]

WATER AND SETTLEMENT

Water was also seen as essential to the settlement of Ohio. Attitudes and actions toward the Scioto River, which runs north to south in central Ohio and empties into the Ohio River at Portsmouth, were typical. Ohioans followed precedents set by residents of eastern states in their use and legislation of water. Having plenty of water, at least initially, most New Englanders adhered to the doctrine of riparian rights inherited from Great Britain's unwritten common law. Under such doctrines, people could divert water from rivers and streams for their private use, as in turning waterwheels for gristmills or sawmills, if they returned that water in good condition to the waterways and did not impede others' use of water downstream.[76] (This approach to water ownership and usage changed as miners and settlers moved into the much more arid trans–Mississippi West. There, the doctrine of prior appropriation was adopted, giving most water rights to whoever first used or appropriated the source. That is, the person who first turned the water to "beneficial use" in a region could claim and use all that water: "First in time, first in right.")

Ohioans generally adhered to the riparian-rights approach to water, employing water power in all sorts of mills and using rivers and lakes as arteries of commerce. In all cases, water was to be returned to streams for use by others. No one owned the water; it could be taken for temporary use only. In this respect, European Americans in Ohio resembled Native Americans, who viewed water as a bounty for all to use.

Nonetheless, water usage could sometimes lead to conflict. Employed for commercial purposes, the Scioto River in central Ohio became something of an open sewer, the recipient of waste from sewers draining the growing town of Columbus. Matters first came to a head on this issue in 1827. What the *Ohio State Journal*, a Columbus newspaper, called "a goodly number of respectable citizens" tore down a milldam built across the Scioto River by the owners of a gristmill. The citizens wanted to make their river navigable again, but they also wanted to release stagnant waters behind the dam that they blamed for creating miasmic airs and spreading diseases. No one was prosecuted.[77] Similarly, in 1824, owners of keelboats and flatboats threatened vigilante actions against milldams obstructing navigation on the Great Miami River to the west of Columbus.[78]

In their attitudes toward rivers, Ohioans shared ideas with people throughout the Midwest. They liked rivers for their utilitarian value, especially as transportation arteries, and artists sometimes pictured midwestern rivers in romantic ways. However, Ohioans also disparaged them as sources (real and imagined) of diseases and as places frequented by gangs of criminals. Rivers were not seen in a totally positive light. In his 1818 account of his journey from the East Coast through Ohio to Illinois, Morris Birkbeck concluded that most American town builders chose "convenience or profit to salubrity" in building on rivers and therefore "after all are bad calculators."[79] Even more vividly, the editor of the *Scioto Telegraph* of Chillicothe, a town located on the Scioto River, observed in early 1820, "The angel of disease and death, ascending from his oozy bed along the marshy margin of the bottom grounds . . . floats in his aerial chariot and in seasons favorable to his prowess spreads mortal desolation as he flies."[80]

By the 1830s and 1840s, land clearing was being finished in most parts of Ohio, one exception being the northwestern section of the state, home to the Black Swamp. The frontier era was fast ending. The passing of the frontier occurred in slightly different times in different parts of the state, but three major developments signaled its demise. First was the achievement of statehood in 1803, which marked a new stage of political maturity.

Second, the new state government was able over time to help fund transportation improvements, which brought economic growth to Ohio, further hastening the close of the frontier era. Usually commercially minded, Ohio's farmers were better able to get their produce to markets with the construction of canals in the 1830s and 1840s and railroads from the 1850s. Canals and railroads proved more effective in moving heavy, bulky goods such as coal, corn, and wheat. The Ohio and Erie Canal opened in 1834, joining Lake Erie to the Ohio River. We have seen its importance to the Bentley family in eastern Ohio. Canal boats could carry large amounts of heavy freight long distances at reasonable rates. However, canals had serious drawbacks. They were slow, they froze in the winter, and they were unusable in times of low water in the summer and fall. Railroads were faster and far more flexible. In the 1830s and 1840s, railroads in the United States ran at an average speed of about fifteen or twenty miles per hour, and they ran year-round. The first railroad to begin operations in Ohio was the Erie and Kalamazoo, which did so with horse-drawn cars in the fall of 1836.[81] By the 1850s and 1860s, steam-powered railroads had crisscrossed much of the state. In the 1850s, railroad mileage in the Midwest rose from 1,276 to 9,715. By 1860, Ohio ranked first among the states in railroad mileage.[82]

The third marker that the state's frontier era had ended was the removal of Native Americans from Ohio. From the 1600s, Ohio had been a place of interaction between Native Americans and European Americans. Once defeated in battles during the late 1700s and early 1800s, many Native Americans in Ohio voluntarily moved west across the Mississippi River to try to avoid further encroachments. Others, however, tried to stay in the Buckeye State on reservations granted them by the Treaty of Greenville and later agreements. They adopted Euro-American farming methods, with Native men (not women) plowing fields to grow corn, wheat, and other crops. They lived in log cabins and raised livestock and nurtured orchards. Many adopted Christianity. None of these moves allowed them to remain in Ohio, however, once invading European Americans coveted their lands. Under the terms of the federal Indian Removal Act of 1830, nearly all Native Americans still living in Ohio were removed to lands new to them west of the Mississippi River. For more than a century, almost no Native Americans lived in the state of Ohio. Only in the 1960s and later did many Native Americans return.[83]

Throughout the 1800s, Ohio farmers responding to the growing demands of regional and national markets took steps to boost their productivity. To combat soil exhaustion caused especially by the depletion of nitrogen in the soil, many adopted crop rotation schedules, first developed on the East Coast and in Great Britain, to try to preserve the fertility of their fields by growing corn, wheat, oats and barley, then hay and clover in successive years. The hay and clover returned some nitrogen to the soil, and farmers manured all their crops, which further increased the soil's nitrogen content. In the mid- and late nineteenth century, most Ohio farms remained diversified, but some specialization began as farmers sought to boost productivity. Corn and hogs were increasingly raised in southern Ohio; wheat came to dominate much of the northern part of the state; dairying predominated in northeastern Ohio; and fruits and vegetables were grown along Lake Erie.[84] These changes were taking place across the United States, with Ohio in the forefront.

A brief look at the operations of L. D. McMillen's 125-acre farm in Hardin County in the late nineteenth and early twentieth centuries shows some of what had changed but also much of what remained the same from the early 1800s. Like earlier farms, McMillen's spread was diversified in its crops. To improve the nitrogen to the soil, he adhered to a three-crop rotation system, growing wheat or oats, clover, and corn in successive years, and manuring all of them. Fruit trees produced cherries, peaches, apples, pears, and plums, and a garden near the house provided a broad range of vegetables for home consumption.[85]

The gendered division of work so typical of early times continued, with McMillen's wife in charge of the children and activities in the house, while L. D. took care of the cultivation of crops and livestock (horses, cattle, hogs, and sheep). Most farmwork remained unmechanized in this age before tractors. Eggs and butter were his wife's domain and, as in the early 1800s, provided some financial independence for the woman of the house.

Yet there were major changes. The farmhouse, which replaced the log cabin in which the McMillen family had lived for a decade, boasted a coal-fired furnace and kitchen stove. Hot water was available in the house. Communications were greatly improved. The McMillens had rural free delivery of mail and packages, took a daily newspaper from 1898 or 1899, and owned a telephone from 1913. In 1912, L. D. purchased his first automobile, a Ford touring car. These communication improvements tied the McMillens more tightly than earlier farmers into a market economy and contributed to their fuller social life. With the automobile facilitating trips to town, visiting stores, fairs, circuses, and churches became more common, and isolation vanished. Vacations became possible. The McMillens found time to visit the St. Louis World's Fair in 1904.[86]

The achievements of Ohio's frontier farmers were significant and set the stage for later agricultural developments. Into the early twentieth century, most Ohio and other midwestern farmers were, like their frontier ancestors, "diversified with wheat, corn, and oats, with varying degrees of emphasis, with wheat being the cash grain crop."[87] Most kept livestock, usually horses, pigs, and a few "milch" cows, and many nurtured small orchards of at least a few apple and peach trees. A gendered division of work, sometimes blurred on the frontier, remained. Women took care of the home, children, and kitchen garden; men worked the fields, nurtured the orchard, and cared for the livestock. Farms in frontier times and in later years produced for home consumption and for the market. Ohio's farmers were always market oriented, but they were concerned as well about their families' present and future overall well-being. Republicanism ran in their veins as they juggled competing thoughts and actions. For farmers, "the family and the household were the building blocks of society," and "the household was also the workplace."[88]

Further alterations took place in Ohio farming during the twentieth century, paralleling those occurring across the United States. In the Scioto Township in central Ohio, for example, farms became highly mechanized, with tractors replacing horses in the 1920s, 1930s, and 1940s, and, still later, with the use of more expensive equipment, such as giant combines. Farms also became larger, as the use of such equipment encouraged consolidation. Family farms gave way to corporate ones. Then, too, as monocultural farming became the norm after World War II, farmers came to depend very heavily on the use of artificial fertilizers and herbicides. The production of the same crops, such as corn, on the same fields year after year meant that farmers used increasing amounts of artificially produced fertilizers to try to keep up their farms' output as postwar crop specialization became common.[89]

A NEW LANDSCAPE

The consequences of the movement of hundreds of thousands of European American and African American settlers imbued with land hunger to the Ohio Country were many and fundamental. On the positive side, the newcomers to the Midwest, including Ohio, created a society, as historian Jon Lauck describes it, possessing a "common culture . . . grounded in the ideals of the Revolution, free-labor beliefs, Victorian norms, entrepreneurial ideals, love of the republic, and democratic egalitarianism." For all its continuing inequalities, especially discrimination against African Americans and the exclusion of Native Americans, the Midwest of the 1800s was probably, as Lauck concludes, "the most advanced democratic society" in the world.[90] As noted earlier, some 981,000 people lived in Ohio by 1830, nearly all in small towns or on farms. "Ultimately, the most impressive thing about the settlement of Ohio," historian Andrew R. L. Cayton wrote in 1986, "was how quickly the frontier period passed." Moreover, he observes, those settling Ohio strove, successfully, to create an open, democratic society, at least for adult White males. "Whatever the specific issue," Cayton avers, "the settlers of Ohio constantly returned to larger questions of sovereignty and the viability of a liberal, democratic society," concluding that "their foremost concern was with personal independence or liberty."[91]

There were substantial costs, however. Most obviously, Native Americans lost their lands (and sometimes their lives) and were removed from Ohio by the mid-1840s. In 1897, William Dean Howells wrote, "Whenever the English came, the Indians' woods were wasted and the Indians were driven out of the land."[92] Native Americans were still trying to reclaim lost lands in Ohio during the opening decades of the twenty-first century. Following their removal, few Native Americans lived in Ohio again until after World War II. Many of those Native Americans moving into Ohio from the 1960s and onward came from tribes on reservations on the Great Plains and not from tribes or nations once indigenous to the state. As part of a poorly conceived and executed program to move Native Americans from reservations into urban areas where they might find more and better jobs, the federal government designated Cleveland, Ohio, as one of about a dozen national relocation centers. Thousands of Native Americans were relocated to Cleveland, a city soon in economic decline, but many of them drifted to other Ohio cities, including Columbus, during the late twentieth century.[93]

Perhaps less immediately apparent were alterations in Ohio's natural environment. European Americans cut forests, drained swamps, and eventually cultivated even prairies and meadows. When John May described the orchards and fields of crops around Marietta in 1788–89, he was describing a fundamental change then just beginning: the state's shift from being a forested land to a countryside of farms. In the late 1700s, forests covered about 95 percent of Ohio, but by 1900, just 10 percent. Historian Cayton bluntly states, "Heavily forested Ohio was stripped bare." Indeed, he concludes that "immigrants completely revised the landscape of Ohio."[94] As early as 1839, Ohio led the nation in wheat production, and a decade later, was the number one state in growing corn and raising sheep. Cincinnati was well known as "Porkopolis" by 1820 because of its many hog-processing plants, and large woolen mills existed in Steubenville. (In 1820, nearly six hundred books and broadsides were published in Ohio, and fourteen years later, Ohio possessed 48 of the 598 newspapers operating in the United States.[95]) "To us today, with lumber so scarce and expensive," Good wrote in the 1950s about the area that had once been the Black Swamp, "large-scale destruction of fine timber seems a rank, outrageous waste. It did not seem so at the time."[96] By 2000, with the abandonment of some farms and with considerable reforestation, trees covered about 33 percent of the land area of Ohio.

With the adoption of Euro-American agriculture came new plants. In Ohio, some eight hundred alien species of plants were introduced over the years, including the dandelion, valued for salads; wild carrot (Queen Anne's lace); teasel, which was used in carding wool (preparing raw wool for spinning); and garlic mustard. Meanwhile, indigenous plants lost their habitats to agriculture and were crowded out. By the 1900s, fully 18 percent of Ohio's native plants were endangered, including the painted trillium, cliff greens, small yellow lady's slipper, and lakeside daisy; another 4 percent had been extirpated. About 29 percent of the state's plants were invasive species.[97]

New animals, too, replaced older residents. The abundance of wild animals did not last long once European Americans entered the Ohio Country. Buffalo, wolves, bears, cougars, beavers, deer, and turkeys were wiped out from Ohio, giving way to cattle, horses, sheep, and pigs. Buffalo were gone by 1814. Beaver, taken in large numbers for the fur trade, were extinct in Ohio by about 1830. White-tailed deer were eliminated from Ohio by 1890, killed for their food value, their hides, and the damage they did to farmers' crops. Turkeys were erased from Ohio by 1904. Large community-wide, and sometimes countywide, hunts were held to rid the vicinity of wild animals, as they were seen as incompatible with settled agriculture. In the Great Hinckley Hunt of December 24, 1818, as the slaughter of wildlife in several townships came to be called, some six hundred men and boys surrounded and killed 300 deer, 21 bears, 17 wolves, and many other creatures, including turkeys, foxes, and raccoons. Some animals, most notably deer and turkeys, were successfully reintroduced in the twentieth century, and others, such as bears, returned on their own. Beavers, migrating back into Ohio from Pennsylvania and New York and reintroduced by the state of Ohio, flourished. By 1976, about 8,000 beavers could be found in forty of the state's eighty-eight counties. Turkeys were reintroduced in the mid-1950s. By 2016, some 180,000 wild turkeys and 30,000 beavers lived in Ohio and were spotted in all counties.[98]

Of all the introduced animals, pigs were the most destructive of the natural environment. Some escaped from farmers and lived wild. Feral pigs competed with deer, turkeys, and squirrels for food supplies such as acorns. The pigs' grubbing for tubers and other foods tore up forest soil, hastening erosion and opening the way for invasive plant species, such as bush honeysuckle. Their wallowing in streams polluted water supplies. This damage caused by pigs was not short-lived. In 2016, an estimated 6 million feral pigs lived in at least thirty-five states. Some 2,000 thrived in national forests in southeastern Ohio, leading Craig Hicks, Ohio's feral swine coordinator, to denounce them as an "ecological train wreck."[99]

Even insects were affected, although much less is known about them and other arthropods than about mammals, birds, and plants. Writing in 1998, Carolyn Platt, a faculty member at Cuyahoga Community College, observed this about spiders in Ohio: "Knowledge of exactly which spiders live in Ohio today and how their population may have changed since settlement is also quite limited." More is known about several specific insect species. European honey bees, for example, moved west with settlers, staying about twenty miles in advance of them. In a symbiotic relationship, bees fed on nectar and pollen as they pollinated the peach and apple trees of early Ohio, and farmers received their honey, a major sweetener then. Less fortunately, chinch bugs from Central America invaded Ohio and attacked corn, and mosquitoes carrying malaria brought the "shakes and ague" to settlers.

Did Ohio's farmers wage war on their environment? Or did they quickly come to understand it and live in some harmony with it? Historian Peter Boag has raised these important questions about farmers in Oregon's Willamette Valley.[100] The contrast is too stark, for the situation, at least in Ohio, was nuanced. In Ohio, as in Oregon later, European Americans tried to choose the best land available for settlement. That usually meant settling on land they could reasonably get to and easily develop, land generally close to water transportation routes but away from swamps and often-wet prairies. They developed intimate relationships with their landholdings, learning quickly where to plant their various crops. All these matters suggest that they did, to some degree, understand their natural environment. On the other hand, their community hunts, like the one in Hinckley, suggest an invasion of Ohio little short of war. So, too, do the wholesale girdling, cutting, and burning of trees to make way for fields and the draining of the Black Swamp to create additional farmland. In the end, their pragmatic and romantic views of nature and land, together with their embrace of capitalism and its treatment of land as a salable commodity, led European Americans to impose an ecosystem based overwhelmingly on commercial open-field farming, domesticated livestock, and fruit trees on an earlier one predicated on forests and wild animals, along with Native Americans' more limited crop growing and nature management.

3

European Americans in the Oregon Country

In what became Yellowstone National Park a generation later, fur trapper Osborne Russell paused to speculate in 1834: "Near these was an opening in the ground about 8 inches in diameter from which hot steam issues continually with a noise similar to that made by steam issuing from a safety valve of an engine and can be heard 5 or 6 Mls. Distant. I should think the steam issued with sufficient force to work an engine of 30 horsepower." Russell trapped beaver throughout the Far West for several different fur companies in the 1830s and 1840s and, like most European Americans, looked upon the West with pecuniary eyes. A budding capitalist, he yearned to put nature to work. Yet Russell also expressed romantic sentiments. He called the northeastern section of Yellowstone, a region that became known as the Lamar River valley, "a beautiful valley . . . surrounded by dark and lofty mountains," and he praised its "wild, romantic scenery."[1] Thus, both pragmatic concerns, such as the possibility of using steam power from a geyser to move machinery, and romantic notions, as featured in his description of the region, permeated Russell's account, as they did many Euro-American journals about the Oregon Country. (Many Americans considered much of what would become the states of Wyoming and Montana part of the Oregon Country then.)

This chapter looks at the massive European American migration west along the Oregon Trail to the Pacific Northwest, a movement motivated by both pragmatic and romantic concepts of the land and country. As in the case of "Ohio fever," land and its resources (including furs) were the lures stimulating the migration. Ohioans and other midwesterners were numerous among those trekking to Oregon. Even as Ohio's population rose from 1,980,000 residents in 1850 to 2,340,000 a decade later, some 400,000 Ohioans left the state to move farther west. Of those Oregon immigrants who left written accounts of their journeys, about three-quarters came from Indiana, Illinois, Iowa, and Missouri. Most of the rest came from bordering states, such as Ohio. Missourians ranked first in Oregon's European American population in both 1850 and 1860. And many of those Missourians had recently come from the Midwest, including Ohio.[2] Settlers from those regions developed many of Oregon's Euro-American farms. Emigrants from New England, in contrast, tended to live in Oregon's nascent urban centers, giving Portland, for instance, a conservative, almost puritanical, tone.

The Oregon Country, in the words of geographer and historian William A. Bowen, "included the vast territory stretching westward from the Rocky Mountains between the forty-second and forty-ninth parallels." The region consisted of present-day Washington, Oregon, Idaho, and western Montana.[3] Chapter 3 examines how European Americans held land in the Oregon Country, how they put that land to use by farming, and what the environmental results of their actions were. This chapter looks especially at the movement of Americans to the Willamette valley in western Oregon and to the Puget Sound region in western Washington. Having a climate like that of the Ohio Country, one marked by plenteous rainfall and humidity, the Oregon Country seemed familiar in some ways to Americans moving there from the Ohio Country and other parts of the Midwest. Yet, even here, changes in farming methods were needed, as Ohioans and other European

Americans encountered an environment that in other ways was somewhat different from those to which they were accustomed.

Chapter 3 shows how land hunger continued to motivate European Americans—including many Ohioans—throughout the nineteenth century. After discussing the geology and climate of the Oregon Country, the chapter examines first, however, how Native Americans viewed and used the lands and waters of the Oregon Country. It is important to bear in mind that Native Americans successfully lived in these regions (and still do) well before the intrusion of European Americans. Contrasting notions of land ownership and use lay behind many of the conflicts between these two groups.

THE GEOGRAPHY AND CLIMATE OF THE OREGON COUNTRY

The climate and geography of the "Puget Sound-Willamette lowlands," which Carlos Schwantes, a dean of historians of the Pacific Northwest, calls "the heart" of the Pacific Northwest, shared marked similarities with those of the Ohio Country: both had plenty of rain for agriculture, both were covered with large trees that seemed to indicate to would-be farmers the presence of rich soil, and both had numerous bodies of water that could be used for transportation. Examining the movement of Americans to the Oregon Country, and then their early farming there, highlights how settlers similarly viewed the Ohio and Oregon regions. Not surprisingly, European Americans passed over the dry, alien Great Plains to the much more familiarly humid Oregon Country. As late as 1990, about two-thirds of Oregon's residents lived in the Willamette valley, extending about one hundred miles south from Portland to Eugene. Seattle, located on Puget Sound, dominated the state of Washington.[4]

The Oregon Country, especially its western reaches in the late 1700s and early 1800s, was a land defined by wind, mountains, and rain. Trade winds blowing from west to east swept humid air over the land from the Pacific Ocean. Some of that humidity took the form of rain that fell on low coastal ranges of hills and mountains that ran north–south just inland through what would become the states of Washington and Oregon. On the Olympic Peninsula in western Washington, rainfall measured at 120 to 140 inches annually. Farther east, the higher Cascade Mountains, extending north–south like the coastal ranges, blocked the movement of humid air eastward. Some 30 to 50 inches of rain fell on the Puget Sound-Willamette lowlands each year, about the same amount that fell on most of the Ohio Country.

The rain fell throughout most of the year, not just mainly in the spring and late fall as was typical in Ohio. In 2020, it rained about 150 days of the year in Portland and Seattle, making those cities the two cloudiest, large urban centers in the United States.[5] Columbus, Ohio, was a distant number eight. This excessive cloudiness meant that some crops that were easily cultivated in the Ohio Country, which boasted long, sunny summer days, did not grow well in the Oregon Country, most notably corn. East across the Cascade Mountains rainfall was much less. Lying in the rain shadow of mountains, the land received enough rain only for dryland farming of crops like wheat. Diversified family farming was not possible over much of the vast regions of eastern Oregon and eastern Washington without irrigation.

Historian Gray Whaley describes the climate of the western parts of the Oregon Country as having "relatively mild winters between late September and late June," and he notes that "autumn, winter, and spring blur into each other as an often chilly 'rainy season' broken periodically by brief periods of welcome sun and warmth."[6] Nationally known journalist Timothy Egan aptly titled his 1991 collection of thirteen essays about the Pacific Northwest *The Good Rain*.[7] The mildness of the climate, which compared favorably in the minds of many settlers to the heat of Ohio's summers and the coldness of that region's winters, came from ocean currents that brought relatively warm waters to Pacific shores. Rich soil, suitable for most types of agriculture, welcomed farmers. Much of the soil in the Oregon Country was twice-blessed. It was glaciated like much of that in the Ohio Country, ground up by advancing and retreating glaciers over tens of thousands of years; and the soil was alluvial, washed down from hills and mountains by ever-present rain. The water, which overlay much of the western Oregon Country in the forms of rivers, lakes, and ocean inlets, was beneficial in another manner: it provided a way for European American farmers (and lumbermen) to transport their produce to markets. Almost from the first, they grew food and cut timber not for their own consumption alone but also for sale to residents in urban markets, including those in booming San Francisco.

Schwantes argues convincingly that "geographic isolation fundamentally shaped the course of Pacific Northwest history" and consequently "contributed to a pronounced time lag in its historical development."[8] Indeed, although inhabited by Native Americans for millennia, the Pacific Northwest became widely known to European Americans only in the nineteenth century. But once it became known to sea captains, army explorers, fur trappers, missionaries, and farmers, the Oregon Country was depicted as a veritable Garden of Eden by most of those reporting on it. One enthusiast wrote with considerable exaggeration and some humor that the region was a "pioneer's paradise" where "pigs are running around under the great oak trees, round and fat, and already cooked, with knives and forks sticking in them so that you can cut off a slice whenever you are hungry." It was said that a person could plant a nail in the rich, black Oregon soil and grow a spike! Given such boosterism, European American settlers rushed to Oregon lands. Ohioans and others moving there soon found they had to adapt some of their farming and living methods to a new environment.

NATIVE AMERICANS IN THE OREGON COUNTRY

European Americans found many Native tribes and groups inhabiting the Oregon Country and speaking different languages and dialects. Still, the Native groups had much in common, especially those in the western regions. Like Native Americans in the Ohio Country, they drew upon multiple sources for their subsistence. Hunting in prairies and wooded hills provided deer, elk, and small game, such as rabbits. But above all, the Pacific Ocean and the rivers flowing into it yielded the bounty of the sea. Along the shore could be found oysters, clams, and seaweed; and many types of fish could be taken from shallow waters. By far, the most important fish, however, was the oceangoing salmon. Five types of salmon swarmed up the rivers of the Oregon Country to spawn (breed) each year and then die. Taken by the millions by the various Indian groups—one method being to use dip nets at narrow choke points on the rivers, such as at Celilo Falls on the Columbia River and Willamette Falls on the Willamette River—salmon could be preserved by drying and smoking and were the staff of life for many tribes. Native people living along ocean shores also took to sea in large canoes to hunt marine animals, including seals and sea lions, fur-bearing sea otters, and even whales. They still do so today. The Makah living on the northwestern tip of Washington hunt a limited number of whales each year using ceremonies preserved orally for generations, much to the displeasure of some environmentalists who would like to end all whaling. Writer Linda Hogan captures well the tensions and controversies about Makah whaling in her novel *People of the Whale,* published in 2008.[9]

One major difference in subsistence methods between Native Americans living in the Ohio Country and those in the Oregon Country was that the latter practiced no agriculture; they did not grow maize, beans, and squash. They did not need to, for camas roots, a tuber, grew in natural prairies kept open by burning off bushes each year. Other vegetables, fruits, and nuts could be found and gathered in profusion.[10] Then, too, the cloudy climate was not conducive to the cultivation of corn. As they did in the Ohio Country, Native Americans altered their physical environments in the Oregon Country. On occasion, they drained swampy land to make more room for camas and other root crops. More commonly, they used low-intensity fires to prevent forests from encroaching on prairies, especially to maintain areas growing camas roots. In doing so, Native Americans created a "parklike" land, what historian Robert Bunting calls "a garden" that "appealed to Euroamerican aesthetic tastes and a cleared, fertile landscape that met settlers' practical farming needs."[11]

In the western sections of the Oregon Country, most Native Americans lived in a "diffuse, kin-based network of villages." No single chief controlled any large area or group of villages. One European American trader called those villages "little sovereignties." From those villages, which were typically located on river or ocean shores, the people moved to food-gathering, hunting, and fishing sites seasonally, much like their counterparts in the Ohio Country. Moreover, they engaged in commerce with other Native groups through well-established trade networks and routes, some of which reached eastward to, and even beyond, the Rocky Mountains. In the early 1800s, enterprising European

American fur traders tapped into those networks and routes to facilitate their commerce.

For Native Americans in the western Oregon Country, their identities as groups usually lay with their home villages. Most commonly, "whole communities composed of multiple families" had rights to *use*—but *not to own*—"limited resource sites, particularly for fishing." Individual ownership of natural resources was almost unknown.[12] Nathaniel Wyeth, a fur-trapping entrepreneur, observed that the Native Americans of the Pacific Northwest "have no actual ownership of the soil, but rove over it to hunt."[13]

EUROPEAN AMERICAN EXPLORERS AND FUR TRAPPERS VIEW THE OREGON COUNTRY

Reports about a vaguely defined Oregon Country came to European Americans from various sources, all of which stimulated excitement about rich lands far to the west. British and American sea captains coasting Pacific shores and United States army explorers, fur trappers, and missionaries to Indians all wrote accounts that raised Americans' awareness of Oregon. By the 1840s, an "Oregon fever," like the earlier "Ohio fever," had infected Americans. And like early Ohio, the land of Oregon was pictured through rational and romantic eyes, with explorers and travelers stressing both the fruitfulness and the beauty of the country through which they journeyed.

In the mid- and late 1700s, American and European seafarers mapped the geography of the Pacific Coast. However, those oceangoing explorers hardly penetrated inland. Nor had explorers moved much farther west than the eastern Great Plains by land. A large swath of country, roughly the region west of the Mississippi River between latitudes 40° and 50° north, lay mainly unknown to European Americans. (The border between the United States and Canada lies at latitude 49° north for much of its length.) The United States had acquired much of the land west of the Mississippi and Missouri Rivers from France in 1803 with the Louisiana Purchase, and Americans, especially President Thomas Jefferson, wanted to know about the region's lands and resources. As historian Gordon S. Wood argues, Jefferson always "faced west."[14] Perhaps Jefferson dreamed the area contained the fabled Northwest Passage, eagerly sought after as a trade route to China. Perhaps the region had plants and animals unknown to European Americans, maybe even ones thought to be extinct, such as mammoths and mastodons. Surely the West boasted Native American tribes new to European Americans. A scientific exploration as well as a search for trade routes, the Lewis and Clark expedition was charged with many tasks. Jefferson sent the westbound expedition, formally titled the Corps of Discovery, to uncover the secrets of a region largely mysterious to European Americans.

Named after its two leaders, Captains Meriwether Lewis and William Clark, the military expedition was under orders to ascend the Missouri River to its source in the Rocky Mountains, called at that time the Stony or Shining Mountains, and cross over the "highlands" in what was expected to be an easy portage of about twenty miles to the headwaters of the Columbia River. The corps would then descend the river in easy stages to the Pacific Ocean. (Clark was actually a lieutenant, but Lewis always treated him as a captain.) It was hoped that a practical Northwest Passage using the Missouri and Columbia river systems could be pioneered, opening an easy trade route to Asia. The expedition was also to bring back samples of flora and fauna found in the West, along with detailed written descriptions, and to develop amiable relations with Native Americans encountered along the way.

Ably led, the Lewis and Clark expedition of thirty-one people achieved its goals and more.[15] Leaving St. Louis in early 1804, the corps reached the Pacific near the mouth of the Columbia River in late 1805 and returned to St. Louis, already becoming known as the gateway to the West, in the summer of 1806. Detailed reports on the West's resources were brought east, some tentative friendships with Indians were made (the Blackfeet being a notable exception), and the possibility of the existence of a workable Northwest Passage was laid to rest. Some two hundred very difficult miles—not twenty easy ones—separated the headwaters of the Missouri and Columbia river systems. Indeed, the members of the corps suffered great physical hardships and near famine in crossing the mountains. The fabled Northwest Passage, Lewis and Clark showed, simply did not exist.

More significantly, the Lewis and Clark expedition helped establish American claims to the Oregon Country in competition with British ones and gave Americans a sense that the West was theirs. The rapid "publication of the official and unofficial records" of the corps, historian Schwantes observes, "stimulated the curiosity and commercial ambitions of those who followed."[16] As pioneering western historian and writer Bernard DeVoto noted in 1953, the expedition "gave not only Oregon but the entire West to the American people as something with which the mind could deal." The reports of the corps made the trans–Mississippi West seem real.[17]

But what exactly did those reports contain? And how did they picture the land of the Far West? In the reports were recorded pragmatic details of the country and its flora and fauna. On the Missouri River, just north of the Platte River, the explorers wrote, "This bluff contains alum, copperas, cobalt, pyrites; and alum rock, soft and sand stone." On the Missouri River near the Yellowstone River, they observed "mineral appearances of salts, coal, and sulphur." The Great Plains were seen as beautiful and possibly fertile but as lacking in trees, which disturbed the explorers. Anticipating many later explorers and settlers, Lewis described the plains in Montana as having "the appearance of an ocean" with "not a tree or shrub to be seen." While portaging the Great Falls of the Missouri River, the explorers noted, "It is worthy of remark that the winds are sometimes so strong in these plains that men informed me that they hoisted a sail in the canoe and had driven her along on the truck wheels. This is really sailing on dry land." In Oregon, they remarked on the availability of farmland in the Willamette River valley: "The highlands of this valley are rolling, though by no means too steep for cultivation. They are generally fertile, of a dark rich loam and tolerably free of stone."[18]

Romanticism also suffused the journals. The Great Falls were, they thought, "a sublimely grand" spectacle. In northern Montana near Marias River, Lewis wrote, "The hills and river cliffs which we passed today exhibit a most romantic appearance." He thought, "The water in the course of time in descending those hills and plains, on either side of the river, has so trickled down the soft sand cliffs and worn it into a thousand grotesque figures, which, with a little imagination, and an oblique view, at a distance are made to represent elegant ranges of lofty free stone [sandstone] buildings, having their parapets well stocked with statuary."[19]

Orderly nature, as in a pastoral garden, was especially admired. On the Missouri River near the Teton River, Lewis and Clark recorded: "The shortness and verdure of the grass gave the plain the appearance, throughout its whole extent, of a beautiful bowling green in fine order. . . . The scenery, already rich, pleasing and beautiful, was still further heightened by immense herds of buffalo, deer, elk and antelopes, which we saw in every direction."[20] One can almost imagine a member of the romantic Hudson River school of painting of the 1800s penning those lines in a sketch book. It was about this time that British gentlemen, as part of their Grand Tour of Europe, went hiking in the Alps. They wanted to view nature, but not untamed nature. They often walked along mountain trails looking downward into a box that held an array of mirrors through which they could see the mountain peaks. They thus viewed nature neatly framed and tamed in a sort of camera device.[21]

In their depictions of Native Americans, Lewis and Clark were largely realistic and did not resort to the use of stereotypes.[22] Only once did they remark upon Native Americans as being of "brute creation."[23] Lewis and Clark differentiated among the tribes they met as best they could and, almost like anthropologists, recorded physical descriptions, lifestyles, numbers of individuals, and numbers of tribes. Still, some groups fared better in their records than others, with those that more nearly approximated Euro-American standards of beauty doing best. The Sioux were "a stout, bold-looking people; the young men handsome and well-made." The Arikara, another Plains tribe, were "dirty, kind, poor, and extravagant, possessing national pride, not beggarly, receive what is given with great pleasure, live in warm houses, large and built in the octagon form." In contrast, Indians of the Pacific Coast—"Clatsops and Chinooks, Tillamooks"—were seen as "generally low in stature, proportionally small, rather lighter complexioned, and much more illy formed than the Indians of the Missouri and those of our frontiers."[24]

Lewis and Clark distributed medals, flags, clothing, and other presents to try to win Native Americans over to the United States and wean them away from Great Britain, and most of the relations between members of the corps and Native Americans were congenial. Clark's enslaved servant York traveled with the corps, and the actions of this reportedly large, agile African American man helped establish friendly relations with Native Americans. In a 2003 assessment, scholar Darrell M. Millner concluded, "York made critical contributions to the expedition's success, and perhaps none was more important than the unplanned and unexpected role he played in the diplomatic relations with the native people the expedition encountered."[25] Some of the men cohabited with Mandan women during the winter of 1804–5 and later suffered from venereal disease contracted during their encounters. Then, too, Native Americans rescued the corps as it faced famine in crossing the Rocky Mountains in the fall of 1805, providing the explorers with supplies and horses. Here, the expedition may have been helped by the presence of Sacagawea, a Shoshone; her husband Charbonneau, a trader; and their baby Pompey. On the other hand, conflict between Lewis's men and the Blackfeet on the return trip to St. Louis resulted in the death of one tribal member in 1806.

Most important in the short run, the journals of the Lewis and Clark expedition were studded with findings of beaver out west. Near the juncture of the Missouri and Platte Rivers, they noted, "Five beaver caught near camp, the flesh of which we made use." On the Missouri River approaching the Yellowstone River, they recorded, "Our party caught three beaver last evening. . . . There was much appearance of beaver." And again on the Missouri River near the Yellowstone River, they observed, "Beaver are very abundant."[26] Fur trappers, mountain men, soon began heading out of St. Louis to go upstream on the Missouri River and its many tributaries to trap beaver, whose thick, glossy fur was made into top hats for gentlemen. In fact, Lewis and Clark met two trappers far up the Missouri River even as the corps was descending the stream on its return to St. Louis. They advised the men on geography and beavers.[27] In the 1820s and 1830s, trappers penetrated all the Far West, including the Rocky Mountains and the country beyond them.

A study of the lives of 446 of the 900–1,000 mountain men who plied the fur trade between 1805 and 1845 shows that most of the trappers entered the beaver trade to advance socially and economically. Only a few stayed in the mountains for more than four or five years. Most remained just long enough to make a grubstake to go into business or farming elsewhere. Like later gold seekers in California, they were looking for mobile wealth. They certainly saw beauty in western nature, but they also viewed the West as a treasure trove of pelts to be gathered, land to be farmed, timber to be cut, and minerals to be mined.[28] A capitalistic ethos suffused their thoughts, in sometimes uneasy coexistence with romanticism.

Fiction writers—most notably novelist A. B. Guthrie Jr., in *The Big Sky*, published in 1947—tried, with some success, to capture the lives of mountain men. Born in Indiana, Guthrie grew up in Choteau, Montana. After graduating from high school there, he moved to Kentucky to engage in newspaper work, then two decades later, he returned to live in the Big Sky State. *The Big Sky* revolves around Boone Caudill, who at the age of seventeen runs away from his farm home in Ohio after almost killing his father in a fight. Caudill flees to St. Louis, where he joins beaver trappers heading up the Missouri River. Guthrie follows Caudill's exploits as he becomes a mountain man trapping on the upper reaches of the Missouri River and in the Rocky Mountains from 1830 to 1843. Caudill works with two other trappers—Dick Summers, an older man, and Jim Deakins—most of the time. Hot-tempered and possessing a dark streak, Caudill eventually kills Deakins in an argument about Caudill's wife, a Blackfoot. The novel describes well the mechanics and difficulties of beaver trapping: the challenges of hauling keelboats loaded with supplies upstream, mosquitoes that "made a cloud about every man," water "so cold it knotted the flesh," venereal disease, Blackfoot attacks, and ambushes by other trappers.[29]

Overall, however, Guthrie presents an overly romanticized image of mountain men. He stresses their imagined love of unspoiled nature. Upon coming upon the Great Plains for the first time, for instance, Boone is struck by its immensity: "It was open country now, bald and open, without an end. It spread away, flat now and then rolling going on clear to the sky. . . . It made the heart come up. It made a man little and still big, like a king looking out." Largely unconcerned about earning money, Caudill stays out west as a trapper for twice as long as most men did. Summers, who returns to Missouri to become a farmer with $343, about the average grubstake earned by trappers, is dismissed as not being a true mountain man. At the close of the novel, Caudill, visiting Summers on his Missouri farm, reminisces in words unlikely to have been uttered by any mountain man: "It's all sp'iled, I reckon, Dick. The whole caboodle."[30]

Summers and Caudill return to the Far West in two later novels penned by Guthrie—*The Way West,* which appeared in 1949, and *Fair Land, Fair Land,* published thirty-three years later in 1982. In the *Way West,* which won the Pulitzer Prize for Literature, Guthrie describes the journey of farmers to the Oregon Country via the Oregon Trail, with Summers acting as a guide for a wagon train. The farmers were different, Summers thought, from fur trappers: "These couldn't enjoy life as it rolled by; they wanted to make something out of it, as if they could take it and shape it to their way if only they worked and figured hard enough."[31] In *Fair Land, Fair Land,* the third novel of his western trilogy, Guthrie explores Summers's searching for the last idyllic spots of wilderness in the Far West and losing propositions as the region was built up.[32]

Guthrie's trilogy about the settlement of the trans–Mississippi West invites comparison with Conrad Richter's three accounts of the settling of the Ohio frontier—*The Trees, The Fields,* and *The Town*—published around the same time. Both trilogies picture the settlement of American frontiers in a generally positive light, despite their nostalgic look at past, wilder days. Both see the march of American civilization, and the demise of Native Americans, as inevitable, if at times regrettable. Novels in both trilogies won Pulitzer Prizes for their authors. And both were products of their time. Writing when the United States was under attack during World War II and then seemingly under siege during the Cold War, Richter and Guthrie praise American life, even as they offer some criticisms of it. Romanticism, and even pastoralism, run through parts of their works.

The writings of trappers, however, tell a somewhat different story than those that Guthrie wrote—a more realistic one, although romanticism entered trappers' accounts as well. Osborne Russell, who took beaver during the 1830s and early 1840s, certainly viewed the West with flexible eyes. While trapping in northern Utah, he wrote, "This place which now looks so lonely, visited only by the rambling Trapper or lonely Savage will doubtless at no distant day be a resort for thousands of the gay and fashionable world, as well as invalids and spectators." In

Montana, he recorded seeing "large quarries of gypsum almost transparent of the finest quality and also appearances of Lead with large rich beds of Iron and Bituminous coal." In the Rocky Mountains, he found oil seeps spilling into streams of water.[33] Russell's observation, like his speculation that a geyser might be harnessed to produce steam power, suggested that nature should be used.

Nonetheless, Russell also saw the West through rose-colored glasses. Upon viewing the Lamar River valley, he rambled for a page in his journal about its beauty:

> There is something in the wild romantic scenery of this valley which I cannot nor will I attempt to describe but the impressions made upon my mind while gazing from a high eminence one evening as the sun was gently gliding beneath the western mountain and casting its gigantic shadows across the valley were such as time can never efface from my memory but as I am neither Poet Painter or Romance writer I must content myself to be what I am a humble journalist and leave this beautiful Vale in obscurity until visited by more skillful admirer of the beauties of nature who may chance to stroll this way in the future.

More prosaically, Russell's journal recorded many of the hardships of the trapping life: loneliness, danger of drowning in rivers, Blackfoot attacks, thirst and famine, buffalo stampedes, and seemingly ever-present mosquitoes.[34]

Enthusiasm for Oregon came from multiple sources, such as sea captains, army explorers, and fur trappers. They viewed the Far West and the Oregon Country with both pragmatic and romantic eyes—there were profits to be made in a beautiful land—similar to how many newcomers had once looked upon Ohio. Most were budding capitalists. Even Lewis and Clark, while mainly interested in geography and natural science, faithfully recorded in their journals natural resources that might be profitably exploited. A major maritime expedition mounted by the United States Navy touched upon the Pacific Coast in 1841, losing one of its ships, the *Peacock,* to shipwreck at the treacherous sandbar extending across the mouth of the Columbia River. Charles Wilkes, its commander, wrote of Puget Sound, "Nothing can exceed the beauty of these waters." But Wilkes also viewed the Oregon Country with utilitarian eyes. He selected a millsite on the Willamette River with great care.[35]

To these groups must be added missionaries to Indians. Beginning in the 1830s, Protestant and Catholic missionaries proselytized among Native Americans in the Oregon Country. Their letters home to relatives and friends in the East stressed the availability of good farmland out west and were frequently reprinted in widely read religious newspapers of the day. Some missionaries to Oregon, most notably Jason Lee and his nephew Daniel Lee, abandoned missionary life to become farmers and merchants there, and were unabashed boosters for the land.[36]

Jason Lee and fellow Methodists established a mission to Native Americans in the Willamette valley during the mid-1830s. In explaining why he chose to site the mission there, Lee picked his words carefully. The valley, he asserted, had a "beautiful river" and was a "delightful valley" with "beautiful groves of trees." Above all, it had a mild climate and fertile soil ripe for farming.[37] Historian Whaley explains that under Lee's leadership the Willamette mission "built and operated mills, cultivated significant acreage . . . constructed dwellings and schoolhouses, and possessed substantial livestock." Euro-American civilization, as well as religion, was taught to Native Americans, who were instructed in farming. The Methodist mission, Lee stated, had "all the necessaries . . . of a civilized society." Within a few years, however, the mission's governing board, located in the East, closed the mission. The board's members thought the mission had become too worldly and was not doing enough to Christianize Native Americans. Still, the mission had a marked impact on Oregon in attracting European American settlers.[38]

MEN AND WOMEN ON THE OREGON TRAIL

One of those immigrants to the Oregon Country was my maternal great-great-grandmother, Mary Jane Kinney, who was born in Iowa in 1836 or 1837. She traveled across the Oregon Trail as a child in 1847, just as the route was being opened and several years before the California gold rush, in a fully loaded Conestoga wagon as part of a wagon train headed west. In her handwritten reminiscences, Mary left a vivid account of her family's experiences on the trail. On the open plains west of the Missouri River, Mary recalled, Indians "arose from an ambush all around" and had to be "placated by presents." Her family then plodded uneventfully to Fort Laramie on the North Fork of the Platte River, in present-day Wyoming, which Mary remembered as "a pretty place." They continued past Fort Hall in the Rocky Mountains in today's Idaho and finally limped onward to the lush Chehalem valley in Oregon, where Mary's father took up land.[39]

Mary's traveling party had difficulties with Indians. In fact, she later recalled that Indians, who she remembered as being Pawnee, had "raised the war-whoop" and tried to steal children in an ambush. One Indian rode alongside "the girls" for "two or three days" before seizing one "around the waist" and trying "to lift her from her horse to his," but he was thwarted by the girl's uncle, who "suspected the attempt" and successfully interceded. The Pawnee proved especially troublesome to travelers moving west in 1847. There were also more mundane challenges along the trail. Mary later remembered, "At times they used buffalo-chips [dung] for fuel. At one place they had to travel through sand all night and 2 days because of scarcity of water." They made only about "12 miles per day" on the trail and were "about 6 mos. on the trip." Still, they persevered and made it to Oregon.[40]

Mary's father was Robert Crouch Kinney, and it was he who led the family to Oregon. Born in 1813 in Illinois, he had taken up steamboating on the Mississippi River, making Burlington, Iowa, his headquarters. After crossing the Oregon Trail with his family, Robert paid $300 for land in the Chehalem valley. His family lived initially "in one end of a double loghouse" on the property. The house was, as its name suggests, two, one-room log houses joined by a covered breezeway. Other family members who had crossed the Oregon Trail with Robert and his family lived nearby. The Kinney family resided in the Chehalem valley for about a decade, engaging in diversified farming before moving to McMinnville, Oregon, where Robert went into the flour business. He also bought flour mills in Brooklyn, just across the Willamette River from Portland. Robert died in 1875 of injuries sustained in an accident caused by a runaway horse.[41]

The Kinneys were far from alone in their travels. The United States was a nation on the move in the nineteenth century, especially as Americans rushed west hoping to benefit from farming and mining opportunities. In 1845, newspaperman John L. O'Sullivan wrote of "our manifest destiny to overspread the continent allotted by Providence for the free development of our yearly multiplying millions." His phrase "manifest destiny" stuck with Americans and inspired them to move west. Echoing historians, writer Mike Blakely observes in his novel about Americans' expansionism in the mid-1840s, *A Sinister Splendor,* published in 2019, "From the halls of Congress to the meanest taverns, Americans lusted for lands beyond their borders."[42]

Some 350,000 Americans crossed the Oregon Trail between 1843 and 1869, at a time when their nation's population was about thirty million.[43] The first sizable emigrant company, one of over one hundred families, left for Oregon in the spring of 1842, and a still-larger one the next year. About 4,000 migrants entered Oregon in 1847, and another 1,300 in 1848. The gold rush diverted all but 450 migrants to California in 1849, but in 1850 some 6,000 settlers moved to Oregon. About 3,600 settlers took the trail to Oregon in 1851, some 10,000 more in 1852, and an additional 7,500 in 1853. In sum, between 1840 and 1855, about 46,000 settlers moved to Oregon.[44] Emigration by wagon continued until the completion of the nation's first transcontinental railroad in 1869 eliminated the need for wagon travel. Traveling west on the trail, Margaret Frink from Indiana recorded in her diary the scene near Fort Kearny in Nebraska in May 1850, capturing well the crowded trail: "The country was so level we could see long trains of white-topped wagons for many miles. It appeared to me that none of the population had been left behind." Frink concluded, "It seemed to me that I had never seen so many humans before in all my life."[45]

It was always an arduous trip, typically requiring about five or six months to complete. However, very few settlers had the difficulties with Indians that the Kinneys did.[46] Native Americans viewed European Americans on the Oregon Trail as invaders but usually left them alone. By the first Treaty of Fort Laramie of 1851, many Native leaders, though far from all, granted European Americans on the way to the Pacific Coast the right to pass through Native lands on the Great Plains.

Accidents, caused especially by inept usage of firearms, and diseases carried by polluted water—typhus, cholera, and dysentery—were more dangerous, killing thousands of overlanders over the years. Lucia Loraine Williams from Ohio lost her son on the trail in 1854. She lamented in a letter to her mother, "Poor little fellow, we could do nothing for him," and observed, "Oh, how suddenly he was beyond our reach."[47]

The Oregon Country possessed great amounts of land like the country that European American settlers were used to from farming in the Midwest. The western slopes of Washington and Oregon were humid, well watered, and well timbered. Large trees, seen as the mark of good land, were everywhere. It was this land that westering farmers sought. The countryside seemed familiar. Eastern Washington and eastern Oregon, by contrast, were arid and treeless, the plains marked by sagebrush. A guidebook written by a missionary layman living in Oregon in 1842 praised the Willamette valley for farming but described eastern Oregon as "entirely unavailing of any purposes of civilization."[48] Not until the twentieth century did settlers enter most of the eastern stretches of the Oregon Country in any numbers, and then only with the aid of irrigation. As they moved west, European Americans took preconceived notions about land and farming with them. (They later did the same when they moved in numbers out onto the Great Plains after the Civil War.) However, the realities of the environmental conditions forced changes in ideas about farming methods.

The destination of most migrants to the Oregon Country, especially during the 1840s and early 1850s, was the Willamette River valley. Running north–south along the Willamette River in western Oregon, the valley was (and is) about thirty miles wide and one hundred miles long. The valley lies between the Coast Range to the west and the Cascade Mountains to the east. Today, the city of Portland is near the confluence of the Willamette and Columbia Rivers at the northern end of the valley. Would-be farmers were willing to pass over the much more alien Great Plains, which seemed dry and barren, to travel all the way to Oregon to begin new lives in the Far West.[49]

In America's westering society, it was usually men who made the decision to move west, reflecting its patriarchal nature during the antebellum years. Men usually headed the family, with women holding subordinate positions. Men were searching for better economic conditions, especially new land, and adventure. Describing the motives of those who traveled to the Sublimity area in the southeast section of the Willamette valley, rural historian Dean L. May observes, "It was land they sought—more land, and better land. They were people of the soil."[50] For many, there were additional matters of importance. Male migrants often called traveling to Oregon and California "seeing the elephant," by which they meant having new and exciting experiences. Indeed, as historian Bowen observes, many motives impelled male migrants to Oregon. They "attached great value to the ownership of real estate," which "translated into cheap or free land," but they also sought escape from diseases common in the Ohio and Mississippi valleys—tuberculosis, influenza, scarlet fever, typhus, cholera, and malaria.[51]

Women were often more reluctant westerners. They disfavored leaving family and friends more than men did. Only about one-third of the women gladly agreed to go west with their husbands. The other two-thirds did not want to move but had little choice in the matter. A popular song in the Midwest during the 1850s captured gender differences in thoughts about going west. "Dear wife, let us go, and don't let us wait. / I long to be doing, I long to be great," sang men. To which women replied, "Dear husband, remember your land is to clear, / It will cost you the labor of many a year. / Your horses, sheep and cattle will all be to buy, / And before you have got them you are ready to die."[52]

With their farms in the Midwest sold, families typically moved with their supplies in the late fall or winter to a "jumping-off" place for the West: Council Bluffs, Iowa; St. Joseph, Missouri; or Independence, Missouri. There, the emigrants usually bought their last supplies and formed wagon trains. A fairly typical traveling group of Ohioans (and a few Pennsylvanians) in 1850 consisted of forty men, eight women, and their children in eighteen wagons, with about 150 cattle walking alongside.[53] Plodding over the first leg of the journey began in April, when spring grass was available for the oxen, mules, and horses.[54] This leg took emigrants from the Missouri River jumping-off points to the United States Army's Fort Kearny on the Platte River in central Nebraska, a distance of roughly 320 miles. The weather was usually mild, the hills low and rolling, and supplies of wood and water plentiful.

Fort Kearny typically saw the most emigrants arriving in late May. Next was movement toward the foothills of the Rocky Mountains along the Platte River to Fort Laramie, a fur-trapping post taken over by the army in the 1850s. The trail remained mainly flat, but the weather grew warmer. Wood was no longer available, and buffalo chips, gathered by women, had to be used as fuel for cooking fires. Along this 300-mile stretch, emigrants saw high buttes and rock formations, such as Chimney Rock and Scotts Bluff. From Fort Laramie, the last post at which any supplies could be purchased, it was 280 miles to South Pass, an easy route across the Rocky Mountains at an elevation of about eight thousand feet. Along the way, emigrants passed Independence Rock, known as "the register of the desert," where many carved their names in the sandstone. By now, it was mid-July. From South Pass through the Rockies in Wyoming travelers went southwest to California or northwest to Oregon.

Those going to Oregon still had a long, difficult trip ahead of them. They journeyed 110 miles through rough country to Fort Hall, a fur-trading post on the Snake River, usually arriving by mid-August. Then came 175 grueling miles along the south side of the Snake River northward to the Boise River. Only slightly easier were the 100 miles along the bottomlands of the Boise River to Fort Boise, another fur-trading post, followed by 150 miles across desert scrub to reach the base of the Blue Mountains in eastern Oregon. That range was crossed only with great difficulty, with wagons pulled up some very steep grades by ropes attached to winches. From the Blue Mountains, emigrants followed the Columbia River westward to its confluence with the Willamette River, near present-day Portland. They typically arrived at the river valley to take up farmlands in mid-October.

The thousands of travelers moving across North America on the Oregon Trail affected the environment, changing the biota along a broad swath of territory. The Oregon Trail was not a narrow band across the continent. In places, it stretched ten or even more miles wide, as emigrants ranged the land looking for clean water, fresh forage, and game. Cholera bacteria, left in the water by overlanders, spread to the Pawnee, Cheyenne, and Lakota Sioux, causing an epidemic in the late 1840s, part of a worldwide pandemic. Along the trail, plants and animals began changing. In the 1840s and 1850s, some 1.5 million oxen, cattle, horses, and sheep used the Oregon Trail. European Americans cut trees sorely needed by Native Americans for their survival during cold plains winters. The separation of buffalo into northern and southern herds, often attributed to the building of transcontinental railroads, may date back to the use of the Oregon Trail. Then, too, as historian Sarah Keyes describes in a provocative article, the noise generated by emigrants along the trail represented a "sonic conquest of the West." She writes, "The cadences of the emigrant wagon trains—cracking pistols and rifles that rent the air, punctuating the chorus of hallooing men, lowing oxen, braying mules, and rumbling, grinding wagons marked a pivotal moment in transforming the 'wilderness' into American civilization."[55]

The diaries of men and women on the Oregon Trail, like the writings of explorers and fur trappers before them, often contained pragmatic observations about life and work on the trail and discussions of family matters combined with romantic descriptions of the lands through which they passed. In 1852, Abigail Scott described the view from bluffs above the Platte River as a "romantic spectacle." A bit later, as her wagon train closed in on Chimney Rock and other rock formations along the trail, she wrote, "The hills have a truly grand romantic appearance . . . approaching almost to sublimity."[56]

EURO-AMERICAN FARMING IN OREGON

Once in Oregon, European Americans found a ticklish geopolitical situation that made it difficult for them to establish ownership of their lands or set up a local government. By an agreement made between the United States and Great Britain in 1818, which was renewed in 1827, the Oregon Country was open to settlement by citizens of both countries, a policy called "joint occupancy." The vast area had no effective laws or government at first except those provided by the private British firm the Hudson's Bay Company, whose traders and trappers had led developments in the area. As Americans arrived in substantial numbers in the 1840s, they called for changes. In 1843, settlers, mainly Americans, tired of waiting for outside recognition or action, organized a grassroots government of their own. Finally, in 1846, Great Britain and the United States agreed upon an international boundary line at latitude 49° north. The Hudson's Bay Company withdrew north of that line into what is now the Canadian province of British Columbia. Two years later, the United States Congress organized Oregon as a territory. It had a European American population of 9,000.[57]

Oregon became a state in 1859, with Washington following suit in 1889 and Idaho in 1890. Even before Oregon achieved statehood, the Oregon provisional government passed legislation in 1843 (modified in 1844) to permit European American settlers to claim land in blocks of up to 640 acres, though some found ways to claim considerably more acreage. The land could be marked and surveyed in irregular claims by the "metes and measures" system, like that used in the Virginia Military Tract in Ohio. That is, land claims did not have to adhere to the bounds of ranges, sections, and townships specified by the federal Land Ordinance of 1785. Still later, Oregonians acquired land under the terms of the Donation Land Claim Act passed by Congress in 1850, under which male European American citizens eighteen years or older who had become Oregon residents before December 1, 1850, could claim 320 acres of land. If married by December 1, 1851, their wife could claim an additional 320 acres. If a single man of at least twenty-one years of age became an Oregon resident between December 1, 1850, and December 1, 1853, he received 160 acres or, if married, 320 acres. Claimants had to live on their land for four years to win title to it. No African Americans or Native Hawaiians, a sizable number of whom lived in Oregon, and no Native Americans or Chinese Americans, could claim land.[58]

Racism accompanied frontier life in the Oregon Country just as it had in the Ohio Country. Historian Schwantes notes, "Most pioneer settlers were antiblack, but differed over whether slavery should be permitted in their territory." In setting up a provisional government in 1843 and 1844, Oregonians outlawed slavery but also forbade free Black people from living in their territory, giving them two years to leave Oregon. When Oregon became a state in 1859, its constitution repeated those terms: no slavery was allowed in Oregon, but free Black people were forbidden from living in the state. Public attitudes toward African Americans were like those in Ohio, which is unsurprising since many migrants to Oregon came from Ohio and other midwestern states. They took their cultural baggage with them.[59]

Few African Americans settled in early Oregon. Discouraged by the state's anti-Black laws and by the cost of travel to Oregon, they went elsewhere, to the Great Plains, for example. African Americans composed about 3 percent of those crossing the Oregon Trail.[60] Only 207 African Americans lived in Oregon in 1850, and just 128 did so a decade later. The anti-Black clause was removed from Oregon's constitution only in 1926, but just a scant 2,000 African Americans lived in the state in 1930. Unlike in Ohio, most African Americans living in Oregon did so in small communities within large cities like Portland. They eschewed the isolated farm life.[61]

Despite the prevalence of racism, republican ideas ran through the thoughts of many who took up farming in the Oregon Country. As historian Gray Whaley observes, "Republican discourse was readily apparent in the writings and debates of early colonists in the Willamette Valley." Settlers drew on the "rhetoric of classical republicanism" and "touted yeoman citizenry and the common good and bemoaned banking and economic speculations that had caused the financial panics of the day." There was still plenty of room, however, for land speculation by individuals in republican concepts about land. Settlers in the Oregon Country saw no contradictions in their ideas on this matter. Between 1843 and 1851, before the Donation Act went into effect, European Americans claimed large expanses of land, intending to sell some of it at high prices later. "Speculative ventures" covered as many as three square miles. Even after the passage of the Donation Act, which required claimants to live on their plats to patent them, incoming settlers often found ways to speculate in land. During its five-year existence, the Donation Act saw about eight thousand claimants acquire three million acres.[62]

Euro-American farming in the Oregon Country resembled that in the Ohio Country of a generation before in important ways, a situation which might be expected since, again, many settlers came from the Midwest, including Ohio. But there were differences as well. As in Ohio, farmers in Oregon girdled trees or cut down and burned them, clearing land upon which they then planted several crops. Here, a problem developed. Those trees were conifers (evergreens)—Douglas firs, pines, hemlocks, spruce, and so forth—as well as deciduous trees—oaks, beeches, and maples—more common in the East and Midwest. The conifers, especially the Douglas firs, were huge, much larger than even the biggest trees in the Ohio Country. European Americans viewed the trees with dismay, as barriers to settlement. They called the forests that often extended to water's edge, "gloomy, somber, dark, wild, and savage."[63] No romanticism here! Sometimes, they bored large holes into tree trunks, set fires inside those cavities, and tended the blazes until the trees collapsed.[64] More commonly, they tried to avoid trees as much as possible by settling on prairie lands and uplands, not in densely forested river valley lands and lowlands, a different selection strategy than that usually followed in Ohio, where great trees were sought as guides to rich soil. Historian Bowen argues persuasively that in much of the Willamette valley incoming farmers sought burned-over prairies on which to settle from the earliest days to avoid the hard labor of having to cut down massive trees.[65]

Rain, sometimes falling very hard, but more often descending as a mist for hours or days at a time, provided plenty of water west of the Cascade Mountains. Forty to fifty inches of rain fell in the Willamette valley each year. Riparian-rights doctrines generally governed how water rights were handled, at least west of the mountains. There was plenty of water, and anyone could use it, if they returned it to streams for others to also use.

This soggy situation contrasted to the dry one prevailing in the Oregon Country east of the Cascade Mountains. Novelist Wallace Stegner depicted the conditions in this arid land in his fictional account *Angle of Repose,* published in 1971. This novel follows the life of a mining engineer and his family from California moving through the West—the Dakotas, Colorado, Idaho, and Mexico—as he accepts various assignments. In eastern Idaho, he oversees the design and construction of an irrigation project, one that ultimately fails. Arguably one of the finest pieces of writing about the Far West, *Angle of Repose* tells of a family always seeking, but never quite finding, the pot of gold at the end of the rainbow. Indeed, the West disappointed many who sought to exploit the region's riches for quick gains through mining, cattle raising, and farming.[66]

Farming in the Oregon Country was very much a family affair in the early years, with families producing diversified goods for their own consumption while sending staples to emerging markets.[67] Diversified composite farms producing for both the subsistence needs of settlers and the commercial demands of markets were the norm, like the situation among farmers in Ohio. Republican ideals of the yeoman farmer combined with a lack of capital, technology, and markets kept most farms relatively small family affairs despite some land speculation. Only in the mid- and late nineteenth century did large, specialized wheat farms and ranches develop in parts of Oregon and Washington, like the growth of large monocultural farms in Ohio. It was not until 1850 that the California gold rush created a major market for Oregon's wheat, with 208,000 bushels shipped from Oregon to the Golden State that year, allowing some crop specialization to begin. Wheat was usually the main commercial crop of Oregon's farmers. The number of farms in the Willamette valley rose from 4,592 in 1870 to 11,536 in 1890, but the average size of a farm declined from 324 acres to just 212 acres during those years. As more settlers entered the valley, earlier ones sold some of their land to them, and overall farm sizes shrank. Also, only parts of those farms were cultivated.[68]

Farmers produced a mix of corn, wheat, oats, and potatoes, kept several oxen and cows along with horses or mules, raised pigs, and took care of flocks of chickens, geese, and ducks. Many also nurtured fruit trees. Raising chickens, ducks, and geese was the domain of wives and children. Household gardens, also kept by women and children, produced cabbages, peas, turnips, onions, carrots, tomatoes, beans, and parsnips. Farmers soon found that corn, however, did not usually grow well in the cloudy climate, so they turned to other crops. With corn requiring lots of sunny days in the summer to mature, some farmers turned to potatoes as a replacement crop. In the Willamette valley, European American farmers and their families lived in "a variety of simple structures that ranged from teepees, willow huts, and tents to log cabins and adobe buildings." Double log cabins, such as that lived in by Robert Kinney and his family, were common. Dirt floors and windows covered with stretched, translucent deer skins (glass was expensive) predominated.[69]

Lured by news of the Willamette valley's rich farmlands, European American intruders poured in from the East. In 1843, about 160 European Americans lived in the valley. A year later, 2,100 did. By 1848, some 9,000 made the valley their home. In 1850, about 23,000 European Americans resided in the Willamette valley. The population of Native Americans dropped precipitously. Decimated by diseases, hurt by small-scale warfare, and simply pushed aside or murdered by incoming European Americans, Native Americans saw their numbers in the valley fall from about 15,000 in 1830 to roughly 2,000 in the mid-1840s.[70]

As settlers moved into the Willamette valley and the nearby valleys created by its subsidiary rivers, such as the Calapooia River, which feeds into the Willamette from the southeast, they found a land already shaped by Native Americans. Native people had burned prairies to grow camas bulbs, one of their major sources of food, keeping the land clear of shrubs and trees for generations. The actions of European Americans altered the Calapooia valley still more. At first, European Americans farmed on rolling, dry hillsides, removing trees and replacing them with fields. Later, when the best uplands had been taken up, newcomers moved out onto the wet prairies, drained them, and plowed them up for crops, just as Ohioans had drained the Black Swamp. These actions displaced both Native Americans and animals, such as ducks and geese, that had depended on the prairies and nearby hills to supply them food. Historian Peter Boag, who has examined the development of the Calapooia valley in rich detail, argues that settlers moving into the area quickly came to understand its environment very well, planting crops on appropriate lands and building houses out of local materials. Boag may go too far, however, in asserting that European Americans lived in harmony with nature there, that they did not wage war on nature or the environment. Whether they lived in sweet harmony or in sharp tension with their surroundings, or most likely something in between these extremes, the result was the same. The Calapooia valley, like the much larger Willamette valley, became a varied agricultural domain. Forests and prairies gave way to fields. The frontier period decisively closed with the introduction of the railroad into the region in 1870–71.[71]

Named by an early European American settler in 1852, the rural area of Sublimity lay along a river valley in the southwestern portion of the Willamette valley. Its name suggests the romantic beauty some saw there, but it was the ability of the valley's rich soil to produce bountiful crops that led European Americans into the valley, just as it had been in the Calapooia valley. Nearly all who came were farmers from the South and the Midwest, "seeking farm land, enough to sustain themselves for generations to come." They grew wheat, barley, oats, and potatoes, raised horses, sheep, cattle, and hogs, and kept small apple orchards. They desired farmland not just for immediate economic gain but, as historian May shows, also for the benefit of future family members. Land was seen as an investment in the future, at least at first. Settlers actively farmed many fewer acres than they owned, and did so on purpose. "The Sublimity farmers," May argues, "chose to farm only enough of their land to fill their basic needs so they could conserve the rest for their children."[72] Too many children and not enough land for inheritance purposes was a basic problem, as it had been for many farmers east of the Mississippi River, encouraging the westward movement of European Americans. For Oregonians, there was nowhere farther west to go. This partial orientation toward the future broke down, however, in the 1870s and later as farmers in the Sublimity region turned increasingly to the market production of foodstuffs.[73]

Alterations in the land can also be seen in Island County in western Washington as described in a history prepared by Richard White, a leader in western American and environmental history.[74] Just north and west of today's Seattle, the county consisted of two major islands, the larger of which was (is) Whidbey Island. At thirty-eight miles in length, it was second in size only to New York's Long Island among islands in the contiguous United States. Island County covered about 208 square miles of land in Puget Sound. Watered well by twenty to thirty inches of rain per year, it was mainly forested land, with only about 5–10 percent of its area in prairies. In general, American farmers were much slower to settle north of the Columbia River than south of it in the Willamette valley, for there simply was less good farmland to the north. Also, even more than to the south, large trees, especially Douglas firs, grew to the water's edge. Still, there was some farmland north of the Columbia River, and Whidbey Island was appealing.

As in Ohio, changes began with the actions of Native Americans, in this case members of the Salish. Hunter-gatherers and fishers who took salmon and many other types of fish, the Salish also came close to engaging in agriculture. They used fire to promote the growth of plants they used as food sources: nettles, bracken, and camas roots. Those fires kept prairies open and free of other vegetation. Intentional burning in forests to keep underbrush down for improved hunting allowed Douglas firs to dominate those woods. As a result, deer and elk, which adapt best to recent burns and early succession forests, dominated wildlife in the forests of the islands. "Through observation and tradition," White concludes, "Indians altered natural communities to fit their needs."[75]

Many more changes accompanied the entrance of European Americans. The first European American farmer arrived on Whidbey Island in 1850, hailing from Missouri and, before that, living in Illinois and Ohio. By 1860, 294 farmers had taken up lands under either the Donation Act or the Preemption Act of 1841, which allowed settlers to buy 160 acres of land at $1.25 per acre. By 1860, they had claimed 15,381 acres, nearly all of them on or next to prairies. Allowed to run free, farmers' cows and pigs dug up prairies, destroying beds of camas roots and fields of bracken and nettles prized by the Salish. By 1860, 1,158 head of cattle and 3,409 hogs roamed across Whidbey Island. Replacing these food sources with potatoes was easily adopted by the Salish, for nurturing them and then digging them out of the ground resembled taking care of and harvesting camas roots. In fact, Salish people had planted potatoes a decade before the first European American farmers moved to Whidbey Island, having acquired seed potatoes off island. By the Treaty of Point Elliott in 1855, the Salish under duress ceded rights to land in Island County to incoming European Americans.[76]

European American farmers introduced new crops, oats and wheat, in addition to potatoes, which began changing the land. Corn, a staple in the Midwest, was not grown to any great extent, as the climate was too cool, rainy, and cloudy, just as was the case in the Willamette valley. Most of the initial farming in Island County was done on the open prairie lands, not on cleared forest lands, unlike in frontier Ohio.

Plowing the lands and cutting roads opened vectors for the unintentional spread of invasive species of plants as weeds: European foxtails, shepherd's purse, sow thistle, American black nightshade, knotweed, and, most damaging of all, Canada thistle. This plant invasion was part of a national trend. In the early 2000s, botanists estimated that 258 of the 500 weed species in the United States were plants from the Old World. Plowing also changed the environment by reducing the capability of some soils to hold moisture, thus limiting the types of vegetation those soils could support.[77] Still later, American farmers and lumbermen turned their attention to the trees on Whidbey Island, cutting most of them down, an act that resonated with the destruction of forests in Ohio.

THE CLOSING OF FRONTIERS IN THE OREGON COUNTRY

The most obvious impact of Euro-American imperialism and land hunger lay in the displacement and deaths of Native Americans in the Oregon Country, just as had occurred in the Ohio Country several decades earlier. In his careful examination of relationships between Native peoples and newcomers throughout western Oregon and western Washington, historian Whaley shows that Native Americans were able to at least partially maintain their concepts of lands and people—Whaley uses the Chinook term *Illahee*—in the face of Euro-American challenges for four or five decades. Illahee was a concept based on use, not ownership rights to land, webs of personal and familial relationships, and spiritual beliefs based on the sacredness of specific places. By the 1850s, however, Native people were overwhelmed by new ideas of private property, a centralized state, and Christianity brought by European Americans.[78]

The proximate cause of Native defeats in the Oregon Country was diseases unintentionally imported from other regions, smallpox as early as the late 1700s, but especially malaria, smallpox (again), mumps, measles, diphtheria, and influenza in the 1820s and 1830s. Malaria "virtually depopulated" the Willamette valley of Indians. The number of local Chinook and Kulupuyan plummeted by almost 90 percent. By 1840, introduced diseases had reduced the number of Indians living in the Puget Sound region by about one-half.[79] From the 1840s into the 1860s, Native Americans in the Oregon Country and northern California were further weakened in wars: the Cayuse War, the Mariposa War, the Rogue River War, the Klamath War, the Yakima War, and the Modoc War. Historian Anne Hyde writes, "Individual sets of grievances coalesced into desperate war as Native people realized they were losing their homelands."[80] The United States Senate refused to ratify nineteen treaties drawn up with Oregon tribes in the early 1850s because the tribes were seen as retaining too much power and land. However, new treaties drafted later in the same decade, by which the tribes ceded much of their land to the federal government, won quick approval (the treaties did not give up Native fishing rights). At this point and later, many Native people were forced to leave their lands for reservations sometimes created on land far from their ancestral homes.[81] For instance, as late as the 1850s, some ninety longhouses, home to an estimated ten thousand Native Americans, dotted the Duwamish River watershed just south of the newly founded town of Seattle; within little more than a generation, none remained. Diseases, wars, and land losses all took tolls on the Native population there.[82] Historian Bunting concludes, "Within a century of sustained Euroamerican contact, the Northwestern native population had been reduced by more than 80 percent."[83]

Nonetheless, Native Americans did not disappear from the Oregon Country. Living on and off reservations, many found seasonal work as agricultural laborers and in salmon canneries in the late nineteenth and early twentieth centuries. After World War II, a wider variety of occupations became available. Even in the largely industrialized Duwamish River watershed, Native Americans remained and, indeed, played leading roles in the revitalization of that polluted stream.[84]

Oregon became an American territory in 1848 and achieved statehood in 1859, and these political changes contributed to the closing of the frontier in Oregon, just as similar ones had in Ohio. Like members of the Ohio legislature, those of the Oregon state legislature did what they could to further the growth of commercial agriculture. They especially favored transportation improvements, and the state backed the construction of roads and railroads. The state also encouraged steamboating on the Columbia River through the removal of snags and the blasting of reefs (rocks) in rapids. With transportation improvements, diversified family farming in western Oregon was increasingly supplemented by large, expansive wheat farms and cattle ranches in eastern Oregon. A new stage in the Oregon Country's history had been reached, one going well beyond frontier developments.

As in Ohio, the land cover was altered in Oregon. Largely surveyed in square sections of one mile on each side and townships of six miles per side from 1850—a form of surveying reaching back to the Land Ordinance of 1785 and the first ranges laid out in eastern Ohio and one that soon replaced surveying by metes and bounds in Oregon—the state's countryside increasingly became a commodity up for sale and resale, despite romantic notions that some people held about it. Even more than Native Americans, European Americans drained wetlands and used fires to clear land for farming. Those fires often got out of hand and burned thousands of woodland acres in high-intensity conflagrations.

As in Ohio, cultivated farmland replaced forests and meadows, and wild animals—wolves, bears, cougars, deer, and elk—yielded to domesticated ones—cows, horses, goats, and pigs. Often running free while foraging for food in whatever woods remained, pigs especially rooted up the ground, sometimes destroying native plants and preparing the way for invasive species, just as occurred in Ohio. Inadvertently introduced weeds—Scotch broom, tansy ragwort, and thistles—pushed aside native plants. This certainly occurred in the Willamette River valley and on Whidbey Island, but similar changes took place throughout the Pacific Northwest.[85] Even before the founding of Seattle in 1851, Luther Collins, who had failed in the California gold rush, cultivated land in the Duwamish River valley just to the south of Seattle, planting fruit trees in "uniform orchard rows," replacing "native cedar, spruce, and a riparian assortment of alder, willow, and cottonwood." By 1855, some one thousand trees in Collins's orchard bore three hundred bushels of salable peaches.[86] The fruits and vegetables grown in the valley got Seattleites through the especially hard times they faced during the winter of 1856.[87]

The actions of federal government officials were important in bringing about changes in the Oregon Country. Exploring expeditions led by army officers, from Lewis and Clark in the early 1800s to John C. Fremont in the 1840s, popularized ways west. And the establishment of Fort Laramie on the Oregon Trail in the foothills of the Rocky Mountains helped commit the federal government to the West and aided emigrants, as did the role of federal negotiators—often backed with the force of arms—in arranging treaties with Native Americans.

4

Moving onto the Great Plains

After the Civil War of the 1860s, railroads advertised lands they had acquired on the Great Plains for sale to European American settlers in extravagant, even fraudulent, terms. One advertisement promised, "Coming to Kansas means a life of ease, perpetual June weather, milk and honey." Another ballyhooed, "The truth is a poor man may live richer, and a rich man easier in this portion of Nebraska than in most parts of the world's domain." That advertisement continued, "A farmer with but little means can come into this section now, and by following the dictates of prudence and economy soon become a very nabob." On the wide, open plains, settlers, the advertisements claimed, no longer had to use trees as evidence of fertile soil. But the reality was vastly different from what the advertisements depicted. Holding pragmatic as well as romantic and capitalistic notions about lands on the Great Plains, would-be settlers rushed to the lands new to them. Yet, even with unremitting toil, farmers had difficult times succeeding on the Great Plains.[1] Struggles with their physical environments were common in the lives of most European American settlers on nearly all North American frontiers, but nowhere were they more pronounced than on the Great Plains.[2]

This chapter turns to the Great Plains, especially Kansas. The settlement of the Great Plains by European Americans, including many from Ohio, provides a marked contrast to that of the Oregon Country or the Ohio Country and is worthy of examination for that reason.[3] On the Great Plains, European Americans encountered environments very different from those they had grown accustomed to elsewhere. The region was not like Ohio or Oregon, as farmers learned to their dismay. Becoming higher and drier moving from the Mississippi River west toward the Rocky Mountains, the Great Plains, especially the western portions, such as western Kansas, were characterized by aridity, a lack of trees, and rolling hills. Lying in the rain shadow of the Rocky Mountains, the Great Plains lacked the humidity and lushness of vegetation found in either the Ohio Country or the Oregon Country. New farming methods were needed to work the land, but even with these methods, settlers struggled to prosper, or even survive. Yet, drawn by land hunger, continued liberalization in their nation's land laws, and deceptive advertising, they tried.[4]

Like men, most women, historian Joanna Stratton notes, "embarked upon their journey to Kansas in quest of greater economic opportunities."[5] Still, leaving their established homes on midwestern farms, from which most of them came, was difficult. As it was for women traveling the Oregon Trail, it was hard to give up networks of family and friends. One woman leaving Ohio for a new life on the Plains wrote, "To leave permanently one's home and friends, parents, brothers, and sisters; to journey a thousand miles . . . requires the greatest courage." Another recalled that she had little choice: "To me it spelled destruction, desperadoes, and cyclones." Continuing, she observed, "I could not agree with my husband that any good could come out of such a country, but the characteristic disposition of the male predominated," and in 1879, she traveled with her family to what she ruefully labeled the "Promised Land." Yet she and many other women went because, as Stratton observes, "land was the great lure of Kansas."[6]

In his pathbreaking study of western Kansas, historian Craig Miner emphasizes the diversity of those moving onto the Great Plains. "Blacks fought dust and wind with whites," he writes, and "women 'manned' the homesteads while their husbands worked in distant towns." Too,

Miner observes, "Catholics built cathedrals and Orthodox Jews broke prairie sod," and "sheepskin coats, embroidered boots, and samovars were as much part of western Kansas as Levi overalls and sunbonnets."[7] Using prairie schooners, stagecoaches, steamboats, and railroads, migrants entered Kansas and other parts of the Great Plains in large numbers after the Civil War. Diversity there was, but about 60 percent of the women going to Kansas came from the states of Illinois, Ohio, Indiana, Iowa, and Wisconsin. Like those traveling on the Oregon Trail, they were predominantly midwesterners.[8]

It is telling that European American migrants moved out onto the western Great Plains only after the Civil War, often several decades after the conflict. They moved onto the Great Plains in appreciable numbers a generation or two after earlier settlers had claimed the richest agricultural lands in western sections of the Oregon Country and about three generations after Euro-American settlement of the Ohio Country. Would-be farmers were willing to endure the long, hard trek across the Great Plains and mountain ranges to the western Oregon Country before they settled on the Plains themselves. Only when nearly all the humid, well-watered, and well-timbered lands had been taken up in the Midwest and along the Pacific Coast did European Americans tackle the arid, treeless country west of the 98th or 100th meridians (longitude 98° or 100° west), imaginary lines running north–south through the Dakotas, Nebraska, Kansas, Oklahoma, and Texas. West of those lines, rainfall was so sparse, less than twenty inches annually, that farming was generally difficult, if not impossible, without irrigation or the development of specialized dry-farming techniques.[9] Only once most other parts of the public domain had been claimed did farmers move into this alien region.[10]

The reluctance of European Americans to move onto the western Great Plains is understandable, for the rainless area had a poor reputation for settlement. As writer Wallace Stegner noted in 1953, "The notion of a Great American Desert east of the Rockies is almost as old as the public domain."[11] Zebulon Pike, the army officer who explored parts of the Southwest, reported in 1810 on finding a desert between the Missouri River and the Rockies. Likewise, the army expedition of Major Stephen Long a decade later during a severe drought solidified the idea of the Great Plains, especially their southern portion, as the Great American Desert. The Long expedition's reports and maps "seared the notion of a Great American Desert on the American mind."[12] An 1822 atlas featured a map of the Arkansas Territory with the words "Great Desert" emblazoned across the lands between the Mississippi River and the Rocky Mountains. Even after the Civil War, William Tecumseh Sherman, who commanded the western military forces of the United States then, wrote, "In general terms the settlements of Kansas, Dacotah and Iowa have nearly or quite nearly reached the Western limit of land fit for cultivation, parallel 99 degrees of West Longitude." He continued, "Then begins the Great Plains 600 miles wide, fit only for Nomadic tribes of Indians, Tartars, or Buffaloes."[13]

Americans were, another army officer thought in the mid-1800s, "upon the shore of a sea, up to which population and agriculture may advance, and no further."[14] The vast sea of grass on the plains was frequently viewed as an "ocean," and settlers' wagons were known as "prairie schooners." Lewis and Clark had likened the Great Plains to an ocean as early as 1806. These were not romantic, friendly, or enticing metaphors and images so common in describing the Ohio Country or the Oregon Country. The Great Plains, especially their western reaches, were initially seen as hostile, forbidding territory. Not surprisingly, when European Americans finally moved onto the Plains, they viewed conquering nature and putting the land to what they saw as productive use through farming as their overriding goal.[15] Miner observed in 1986, "Western Kansas was one of the most arid areas to which it was seriously contemplated that nineteenth-century agricultural civilization might be imported whole." But would that attempt work? The result of trying, Miner concludes, was a "recurring cycle of hope and despair," as European American settlers sought new ways to come to grips with a hostile environment.[16]

NATIVE AMERICANS ON THE GREAT PLAINS

Native Americans already living there saw matters differently. They viewed the Great Plains as anything but hostile. On the contrary, the Great Plains' openness to the sun and their rolling hills were viewed as full of life and bounty, and as almost sacred. In fact, the Black Hills of South Dakota, so named by European Americans because the pine trees made the hills appear black from a distance, were regarded as sacred by the Sioux.[17] The sun dance was one of the most sacred ceremonies of the Sioux and still is. To the south, the Comanche, too, regarded the sun dance as central to their belief system and way of life.[18] Members of both northern and southern Plains tribes viewed their tribal lands as their homes and resisted efforts to be ousted.

Luther Standing Bear, a Sioux who grew up on the northern Great Plains before being sent to a Pennsylvania boarding school in 1879, described well what the physical environment meant to many Plains Indians in his writings: "We do not think of the great open plains, the beautiful rolling hills and winding streams with tangled growth as wild. Only to whitemen was nature a wilderness, and only to him was the land infested with wild animals and savage people. To us it was tame." He concluded, "Earth was bountiful, and we were surrounded with the blessings of the Great Mystery."[19] The twentieth-century Kiowa writer and poet N. Scott Momaday made many of the same points about the Great Plains. "The earth unfolds and the limit of the land recedes," he has written. "The sun follows a longer course in the day, and the sky is immense beyond all comprehension." Momaday goes on, "The great billowing clouds that sail upon it are shadows that move upon the grain like water, dividing light." He further observes, "The sun is at home on the plains. Precisely there does it have the certain character of a god."[20]

Many of the Native Americans living on the Great Plains in the nineteenth century were relative newcomers, having settled on the Plains only after they acquired horses in the 1600s and 1700s. The Sioux reached the upper Missouri River area in the mid-1800s, for example.[21] Once on the Great Plains, however, the Native groups who adopted the horse adjusted well to life there, living most of the year in small, mobile groups to hunt buffalo, which provided nearly all their needs for food, shelter, and clothing. Mounted, buffalo-hunting Indians such as the Sioux, Cheyenne, and Comanche shunned settled agriculture, trading instead with other Native peoples for their maize, beans, and squash. The Sioux and Cheyenne on the northern Plains traded with the Mandan, Hidatsa, and Arikara, who resided in sedentary, agricultural villages along the Missouri River. Pushed aside and marginalized by the Comanche entering the southern Plains from 1706 on, many of the Apache took up agriculture and traded some of their crops with the Comanche for bison meat and robes. In this way, the Comanche received necessary carbohydrates in the form of maize. Pueblo Indians and the Navaho also traded maize with the Comanche. Enterprising European American traders tapped into Indigenous trade routes on both the northern and southern Plains to reach migratory tribes. Both intertribal commerce and trade between European Americans and Native Americans were substantial.

For almost two centuries, the Comanche held sway in what was the southern Great Plains and in what became the American Southwest. In their Comancheria—an area covering much of Arizona, New Mexico, and Texas—they built what historian Pekka Hämäläinen has rightly labeled an "empire." The Comanche Empire warred with other peoples, conducted extensive diplomatic relations with other Native tribes as well as with Spanish, Mexican, and American representatives, maintained extensive trade and raiding routes, and developed its own internal structure and sense of identity.[22]

Moving down from the Rocky Mountains in 1706, the Comanche, who were sponsored by the Ute Indians, fully adopted the horse and, along with that animal, a nomadic lifestyle. Hunting the buffalo on horseback they soon surpassed the Ute, who had only partially adopted the horse, in numbers and power. Expanding their trade and raiding in many directions—the Comanche viewed commerce and raiding as being on the same continuum of activities—they became the predominant power in their regions by the late 1700s. Despite suffering several epidemics, the Comanche boasted thirty thousand to forty thousand members in their empire by the early 1800s. Some were captives taken in raids and adopted into the Comanche nation; others were enslaved members, also acquired in raids. By their raiding and warfare, and often just by the threat of violence, the Comanche subjected others to their will. The Apache and Wichita were among the many tribes that were at various times enemies, allies, trading partners, and peoples subject to the Comanche.

Even Spanish and (later) Mexican New Mexico often acted almost as a province of Comancheria. Similarly, people living in large parts of Texas, both when it was a territory of Spanish America and (later) Mexico and when it was an independent republic, were subject to the power of the Comanche. A common language, a religious system based on the sun dance, and a flexible political system by which the Comanche reached major decisions by consensus gave them a sense of identity. Only in the 1840s and later was the power of the Comanche Empire eroded, and eventually destroyed in the 1870s. Environmental degradation caused by overgrazing of the huge horse herds, decimation of buffalo herds by overhunting for subsistence and trade, and the massive strength of the industrializing United States combined to bring down the Comanche Empire.

Throughout the existence of Comancheria, the Comanche thought of their land as a common possession of all tribal members. Hämäläinen writes, "Although rancherias [major groups] and divisions had distinct geographical identities, Comanches regarded Comancheria as a common domain to all."[23] Other forms of property were recognized as belonging to individuals—horses, for example—but not land. Land was held, grazed, and hunted in common. This way of thinking caused problems when Comanches and Americans sought to agree upon treaties. Those treaties, from the American point of view, gave Comanches rights to hunt on certain lands but did not give them ownership of the lands. However, Comanches saw hunting and grazing rights as tantamount to the ownership of lands and saw themselves as custodians of the specified lands.[24]

In the Central Plains, the dominant Native force was the Cheyenne. Like the Comanche, the Cheyenne (and the nearby Arapaho and Kiowa) gave up an agricultural way of life to move out onto the Great Plains as mounted warriors hunting buffalo. Around 1680, the Cheyenne began moving from the upper Mississippi River westward, forming new villages near the Mandan, Hidatsa, and Chippewa on the Missouri River by the 1770s. Within about a decade more, the Cheyenne, ravaged by smallpox and measles, moved toward the plains proper. They acquired horses, abandoned agriculture, and hunted buffalo. Moving southward to the Central Plains, they lived in the area later to become Kansas, Nebraska, and Colorado. Like the Comanche, the Cheyenne spent much of the late spring, summer, and early fall on the move— hunting, gathering in large groups for ceremonies like the sun dance, and raiding other tribes. In the winter, again like the Comanche, the Cheyenne moved into settlements in timbered areas along river valleys, which the historian Elliott West rightly calls "sanctuaries," to escape the cold wind and driving snow that repeatedly swept the plains. Like other Plains tribes, the Cheyenne built up extensive horse herds, which gave them the mobility they needed to live on the Central Plains, but over time, the horses came to overgraze parts of their homeland, degrading the environment.[25]

The Sioux dominated the northern Great Plains, moving into the region in three steps. They began migrating west from the western Great Lakes in the 1700s, displacing the Omaha, Oto, Cheyenne, Missouri, and Iowa tribes in the process. They did so in search of beaver for the fur trade and because they had acquired horses with which they could more easily hunt buffalo than on foot. Like the Comanche, the Sioux fully adopted a nomadic way of life. They moved into the middle Missouri region farther west in the late 1700s and early 1800s searching for additional beaver-trapping areas, new buffalo-hunting grounds, and more horses. Finally, by the mid-1800s the Sioux came to dominate even the far upper Missouri River region, stretching into the area that would become Montana, as they moved ever farther west in search of buffalo whose hides they traded with incoming European Americans. From the 1820s on, the Sioux sought to wrest control of the western Great Plains from the Arapaho, the Crow (who were an offshoot of the Hidatsa), the Blackfoot, and other tribes—and were largely successful.

Not all Native peoples accepted the horse, buffalo hunt, and nomadic way of life. Some remained agricultural tribes growing maize, beans, and squash for their own subsistence and for trade with the more nomadic tribes, such as the Sioux. The Mandan, Hidatsa, and Arikara living along and above the Great Bend of the Missouri River in what became North Dakota continued their sedentary, agricultural lives into the 1800s. Residing in earthen lodges, they tended their crops and periodically ventured away from the river to hunt buffalo on the nearby plains. Living close together, members of these tribes were particularly susceptible to introduced diseases such as smallpox, measles, and mumps and were severely harmed by a series of epidemics beginning in the late 1780s and lasting into the mid-1800s.[26] (Living in small, mobile groups most of the time, the Sioux were less susceptible to such diseases.) The Arikara, Mandan, and Hidatsa, greatly reduced in numbers and strength by disease, grew increasingly dependent on the Lakota Sioux, who came to treat them almost as their servants, as handy sources of maize to be taken in trade or raids. The beans, maize, and squash raised by the village-dwelling tribes provided the Lakota Sioux with essential carbohydrates, vitamins, and amino acids.[27]

It was with the Mandan that members of the Lewis and Clark expedition wintered during 1804–5. It was a cold winter, with the temperature, according to one of the expedition's thermometers, dropping to 45 degrees below zero on December 17. Clark observed that the Mandan lived in "houses that are round and very large containing several families," and he noted that "the Mandans speak a language peculiar to themselves." The men of the Corps of Discovery maintained friendly relations with the Mandan, coming, in fact, to depend on them for corn. For instance, Clark recorded in his journal how the men of the expedition gladly accepted eleven bushels of corn from the Mandan in early November 1804.[28] In his account of the expedition, historian Stephen Ambrose writes, "It was Mandan corn that got the expedition through the winter," stating that "had the Mandans not been there, or had they had no corn to spare, or had they been hostile, the Lewis and Clark Expedition might not have survived its first winter."[29]

Like other fully mounted Plains tribes, the Sioux developed a lifestyle based on following buffalo. For most of the year, they lived in loosely allied, small, mobile groups of several hundred men, women, and children. The Sioux fought in such groups against other tribes to defend hunting and trapping areas and to allow their young men to win war honors needed to advance in their societies. Only during the early summer and the winter did they usually come together in larger groups for the sun dance ceremony and for discussions on topics of national importance. In June, buffalo were gathered in large herds for the rut (mating), an opportunity for a large Native American rendezvous. By then, too, there was enough new grass on the plains to support large horse herds. To escape the cold winds of winter, most bands of Sioux sheltered in large groups in river valleys. There, they were close to herds of similarly sheltering buffalo and could keep their horses out of winter's most severe grasp. But for much of the year—spring, most of the summer, and fall—the Sioux lived in the small, mobile groups well-designed to follow migrating buffalo and to engage in raiding and trade.[30]

Numbering about fifteen thousand tribal members by the 1830s and 1840s, the Lakota Sioux, the westernmost division of the Sioux, developed something of an empire on the northern Great Plains. (The other two divisions were the Dakota and the Yankton to the east.) The Lakota empire was similar in many ways to the empire the Comanche maintained at about the same time in the Southwest and on the southern Great Plains. The Lakota engaged in diplomacy, trade, and warfare with other tribes and the United States, developing an increasingly centralized form of governance, but one flexible enough to meet changing circumstances on the plains. Like the Comanche, the Lakota were quick to adopt new members into their ranks, a major source of their continuing strength. Personal property certainly had a place in Sioux life, but not private ownership of land. Like other Native groups in this study, the Sioux believed they had the right to use certain resources, such as hunting areas, but not the right to own them. "Like most Native peoples in the interior," Hämäläinen explains, "Sioux did not understand territory as an exclusive bounded domain of one people." Continuing, he observes, "A border was not a line on the ground that kept out strangers. It was a space . . . where one kinship sphere ended and another began."[31]

The Sioux usually fought against the United States Army in small groups, as was typical of Plains tribes. The large gathering of several thousand Sioux and Cheyenne warriors that defeated Colonel Custer and the Seventh Cavalry at Greasy Grass (Battle of the Little Bighorn) on June 25, 1876, was the exception, not the rule. In only 7 percent of the conflicts between Native Americans and European Americans in the trans–Mississippi West were military units consisting of more than four companies (about 600 men) involved. In all the conflicts on the Great Plains between 1866 and 1890, the army lost 69 officers and 879 enlisted men in battle. Native Americans suffered about 4,371 men, women, and children killed.[32]

The defeat of the Sioux and other mounted Native Americans on the Great Plains came from several sources. For one, diseases to which they had no immunities weakened them. A smallpox epidemic of 1780–81 impaired them, as did another in 1837–38. Although less susceptible than village-dwelling tribes, they were greatly affected. Another source was the commercial hunting of buffalo by American hide hunters, which deprived the Sioux of their major source of food. By the 1870s, the northern buffalo herds were decimated, and by the mid-1880s, they were gone.[33] Then, too, the army was relentless in its pursuit of the Sioux. Supplied from outside the Great Plains, troopers fought many small-scale skirmishes and battles with the Sioux and destroyed, wherever possible, their food supplies and horse herds. Sioux successes in battle—Red Cloud, the leading Sioux war chief of the 1860s forced a rare retreat by army forces in 1868—did not long offset the army's persistent pursuit. Nor did the Lakota victory over Custer. By the mid-1880s, all Sioux bands had accepted reservation life.

EUROPEAN AMERICAN AND AFRICAN AMERICAN FARMING ON THE GREAT PLAINS

European American and African American ranchers and farmers replaced Native Americans on the Great Plains. After the Civil War of the 1860s, liberalized land laws facilitated Euro-American settlement in the trans–Mississippi West. By the tens of thousands, would-be farmers rushed onto the Great Plains, just as they had earlier done in the Ohio Country and the Oregon Country. Once again, Americans were on the move. What occurred in western Kansas—highlighted in the rest of this chapter—typified many aspects of this new migration: the ballyhoo, the optimism, and the stark realities.

After the Civil War, the goal of federal government authorities was to move settlers onto land by disposing of the public domain. The older Preemption Act of 1841 remained active and effective, allowing pioneers to squat on and later buy land once it was surveyed. The Homestead Act of 1862 gave 160 surveyed acres free to family heads (usually, but not always, men), provided they paid certain fees and lived on and improved the land for five years. Perhaps fittingly, a westward-moving Ohioan claimed the first plot of land under the Homestead Act, doing so at a federal government land office in Brownville, Nebraska, on

January 1, 1863.[34] The Timber Culture Act of 1873 allowed homesteaders to claim an additional 160 acres if they planted trees on at least forty of those acres. A modification in 1878 reduced the acreage needed to be planted with trees to ten. The Desert Land Act of 1877 permitted individuals to claim 640 acres with an initial payment of $0.25 per acre and a second payment three years later of $1.00 per acre provided they irrigated some of the land.[35]

Farming under the terms of the Homestead Act of 1862 and its later modifications was especially important in western states. Between 1860 and 1900, nearly two-thirds of the farms created in seventeen western states were formed on land acquired through the Homestead Act. Those farms accounted for about one-third of the growth in western farmland during those years, with 77 million acres of the 231 million acres acquired by western farmers. (While limited to 160 acres under the Homestead Act, farmers could purchase larger tracts of land from railroads, which had been given land grants from the public domain by Congress, and from other sources.)[36]

Still, there were problems with this land system. Some fraud accompanied it, though scholars dispute just how much. In 1970, historian Everett Dick concluded, "After the Civil War, fraud was so general, so little deprecated on the frontier, and the officers so few in number that the [US Land] Commissioner was like a man fighting a prairie fire with the brands flying ahead and setting many little fires."[37] But a careful 2017 examination by three scholars suggested that the frequency of fraud was small, involving between 3.2 percent and 8.5 percent of the land claims made under the Homestead Act.[38] Too, much more land left the public domain to go to railroads, land speculators, and states than found its way directly to pioneers. To encourage railroads to build out west in advance of population needs, Congress gave them 181 million acres in land grants between 1850 and 1871. Railroads then sold their lands to prospective settlers. The Burlington Railroad sold massive holdings in Nebraska for an average of $5.14 per acre. All railroad lands sold in 1880 went for an average price of $4.76 per acre. These were significant prices at a time when an industrial worker, if fully employed, might earn $500–$600 annually. State governments also received 140 million acres of the public domain, which they could sell to support building land-grant universities under the terms of the Morrill Land-Grant Act of 1862. Some 100 million acres were sold directly to speculators, usually land companies, and an additional 100 million acres were sold when Indian reservations were reduced in size and their land was put on the market after 1887.[39]

Some scholars argue that the Homestead Act was fundamentally flawed in not allocating pioneers sufficient land to succeed as ranchers or farmers in the arid West. The 160 acres allowed was plenty of land for those trying to farm in humid, well-watered regions, such as Ohio and western Oregon, but was far from adequate on the almost rainless Great Plains. There, 2,000–50,000 acres might be needed for success as a rancher and 360–640 acres for success as a farmer. The Homestead Act was, as historian Paul Gates explained in 1936, "an incongruous land system." That is, the law did not fit the environment.[40]

Many scholars agree that the nation's land laws were ill-suited to the Great Plains. Environmental historian Richard White labels the nation's late nineteenth-century land system as "dysfunctional." He asserts, "The movement west of the 100th meridian became one of the greatest social and environmental miscalculations in American history, one that would play out far beyond the nineteenth century."[41] David Danbom, a leading historian of rural America, calls the Great Plains "America's most disappointing frontier." Even in the twenty-first century, the Great Plains, he observes, "remains largely colonial, exporting raw materials and importing capital and manufactures." The Great Plains are, Danbom concludes, "a ward of the United States."[42]

In fact, preconceived ideas about farming that had developed in the humid Ohio Country and Oregon Country soon collided with new realities as people moved onto the Great Plains. Many of those moving to Kansas, probably a majority, came from the Midwest, including Ohio. On the Great Plains, unbridled optimism met arid reality. The dry climate of the western Great Plains in places such as western Kansas was new to settlers from Ohio and other humid regions and called for adjustments in living and farming. A 1936 report by the federal government conceded, "Mistaken public policies have been largely responsible for the situation [drought and dust storms]." In fact, "a mistaken homesteading policy," the report explained, "led to over-cropping and over-grazing, and encouragement of a system of agriculture which could not be both permanent and prosperous." Summarizing, the report concluded, "The basic cause of the present Great Plains situation is an attempt to impose on the region a system of agriculture to which the Great Plains are not adapted."[43]

Ohioans moving to western Kansas certainly saw the land new to them as different and perhaps forbidding. The daughter of one settler from southern Ohio, "right on the Ohio river," later recalled missing Ohio terribly, lamenting no longer being able to see the "beautiful country of wooded hills and fruitful valleys." Traveling west in 1879 with her mother to meet her father who had gone ahead to claim land and build a house, she "could not help contrasting the Kansas bunch grass with the blue grass in the meadows of Ohio." She later recalled that in Kansas "there were no roads then, nor trees, nor houses." Another Ohio girl entering western Kansas in the same year, remembered, "The road was a mere trail, and we were in an open wagon and were burned as brown as a penny."[44]

Even so, a majority of homesteaders succeeded in patenting their claims and gaining ownership of land, at least in the nineteenth century, though often only after enduring severe hardships. Historians estimated in 2017 that 56–69 percent of homesteaders proved up their claims and took ownership of their land under the terms of the Homestead Act before 1880, and 55 percent did so on claims filed between 1881 and 1900.[45] Through a combination of perseverance and adaptation to new farming conditions, especially aridity, settlers often had some success on the Great Plains. Human agency was important, as European Americans moving onto the Plains used new sorts of plows drawn by oxen to break the tough prairie sod and built fences made of barbed wire, invented in the mid-1870s, to keep wandering cattle away from growing crops.[46] Indeed, in assessing Euro-American settlement on the Great Plains, some scholars have recently emphasized that the region should be defined more by what it offered settlers than by what it denied them. Historian Julie Courtwright takes this approach. Certainly, she acknowledges, some elements were missing, enough water, for example. However, grass was abundant—that sea of grass—and the earth was fertile. Most settlers stayed, leading to population booms on the Great Plains. The gold rush to the Denver area caused one population explosion in the late 1850s and early 1860s, but others were more agricultural in nature. Between 1870 and 1880, the number of European Americans living in Kansas rose from 365,000 to 996,000, those in Nebraska from 123,000 to 452,000, and the number of people residing in the Dakota Territory from 14,000 to 135,000.

Historian Jon K. Lauck has surveyed the explosive economic development of the Dakota Territory, describing the growth in terms of population increases, rising wheat production, tremendous expansion of railroad mileage, and a burst of land sales. However, more than economic growth was involved. Drawing upon antecedents in New England and the Midwest, settlers in Dakota, Lauck writes, "embraced the republican principles of civic virtue, patriotism, physical work, agrarian fundamentalism, and dedication to the commonwealth, and they abhorred corruption and self-interestedness." Moreover, they supported numerous schools, voted in high numbers, attended many public lectures, established numerous voluntary organizations, and read a wide variety of newspapers. As in Ohio and Oregon, more than a desire for profits motivated European Americans in the Dakota Territory. "Pioneer farmers," Lauck finds, "were not motivated solely by material gain." On the contrary, he asserts, "The settler's market orientation was circumscribed by their attachment to republic notions of virtue, their obligations to their neighbors, their sense of civic duty, their vision of a decentralized agrarian economy, and their religious commitments."[47] Republicanism, important on earlier frontiers, continued as a potent force on the Great Plains.

Some of those moving onto the Great Plains were African Americans, drawn west, in part, just like European Americans, by the promise of good farmlands. Added to the quest for land was a burning desire to escape from violence and discrimination against African Americans in the South after the Civil War. They were pushed out of the South and pulled to the West, especially to what would become the states of Texas, Oklahoma, and Kansas. Called "Exodusters," they took up homesteads and formed Black towns like Nicodemus, Kansas. Indeed, by the early 1900s, there were thirty-two Black towns in Oklahoma alone.[48]

Historian Nell Painter gives the most compelling account of African Americans moving onto the Great Plains as Exodusters.[49] It was the failure of Reconstruction to provide land and physical protection for

African Americans in the South, Painter finds, that led them to move west. Many African Americans had hoped the federal government would award them land, a mule, and supplies with which to begin farm lives for themselves and their families in the South. But they received little or nothing of such aid. On the contrary, White terrorists formed groups like the Ku Klux Klan and the White Camelias, which attacked and killed African Americans trying to make progress, denying them the right to vote and often the ability to own land. Most became renters or sharecroppers on White-owned land and were perennially in debt. Under such circumstances, migrating to Kansas, which unlike Ohio and Oregon had no anti-Black laws, was very appealing. Moreover, Kansas, even western Kansas, was relatively nearby, when compared to possible refuges like Liberia in Africa. One African American woman later recalled, "It seemed as if God had prepared [western Kansas] for the colored people, that they might come out from a land of trouble and live and enjoy it forever."[50]

Land, Painter forcefully argues, lay at the heart of matters: "Whatever the importance of the new race relations of the postwar South, the issue of land remained one of the most crucial, to both Blacks and whites."[51] John Solomon Lewis, who joined the exodus to Kansas in 1879, expressed well the connections many African Americans saw between land ownership and freedom. "I landed on the soil," remembered Lewis upon reaching Kansas, "I looked on the ground, and I says this is free ground. . . . Then I looked within my heart, and I says to myself I wonder why I was never free before." Lewis was hardly alone, as African American settlers moved to Kansas in the late 1860s after hearing favorable reports on farmlands there. By 1870, about 16,250 African Americans lived in Kansas. Ten years later, about 43,110 did, drawn to the possibility of land ownership and repelled by the anti-Black violence of the South.[52]

Painter judges the movement of African Americans to Kansas as a success, "a qualified but real success." African American farmers in Kansas had considerably more prosperous lives than those remaining in the South, and they escaped much of the violence that hurt and killed those staying in southern states. In addition, the work of Exodusters gave Americans "proof that African Americans did not quietly resign themselves to the political or economic order of the Redeemed South."[53]

Still, life as a farmer on the Kansas plains required making difficult adjustments to an environment new to African Americans and European Americans alike. The lack of trees and wood led many American settlers to live in sod houses, called "soddys." Made of plowed-up blocks of sod, dirt held together by the tough roots of prairie grasses, the houses were nearly impossible to keep clean. The sod roofs, supported by wooden rafters, dripped water for days after a heavy rain. A wry joke said that it rained one day on the outside but two or three days on the inside of a soddy. More, the lack of wood meant that farmers' wives had to use buffalo chips, dried cattle dung, and other fuels for fires in their stoves. Dried sunflower stalks were a favorite. One acre produced twelve cords, a year's supply. (Burning dried dung may have caused another problem. Smoke from such fires, even in stoves, generated a large amount of particulate matter and may have contributed to pulmonary diseases.) Without much wood in handy supply, farmers had to use other materials for fencing as well. Barbed wire fences came into common use in the 1870s and 1880s.[54]

Many other physical problems plagued those trying to farm on the Great Plains. Severe weather, such as blizzards and tornadoes, hurt crops and sometimes endangered lives. Summer heat could shrivel crops and make them standing tinder for prairie fires. Grasshoppers spread over much of the Great Plains in 1874–76, eating just about everything in sight, destroying crops, and polluting water supplies. A farmer in western Kansas described the grasshoppers as coming "in untold millions, in clouds upon clouds, until their fluttering wings looked like a sweeping snowstorm in the heavens."[55] Their crushed bodies created grease on railroad tracks that stopped train service at times. In 1874, the situation was so dire the Nebraska legislature passed a law declaring grasshoppers "public enemy number one" and drafting all able-bodied men between the ages of eighteen and forty-five into a posse to fight them. Just how was unclear.

Mental challenges exacerbated physical ones. Early farm life on the Great Plains often seemed drab and monotonous, especially for women, who rarely got into town. There were no mountains and few trees to break the sameness of the plains, and distances between homesteading families were often great. Isolation was common in the early days and was exacerbated by the nearly constant wind, always the wind. An agent for an eastern investment company who visited many plains settlers wrote: "The prairie has a solitude way beyond the mere absence of human beings." He elaborated: "Raise the eyes to the bare prairie and they sweep the horizon. Nothing stops them. They stare, stare—and sometimes the prairie gets to staring back."[56] Eventually, the growth of towns and the construction of better roads alleviated those issues. One observer wrote in 1893: "In all our prairie towns one finds in winter many farmers' families who left their homes and stock in the care of hired men, and are living in rooms over stores, or in parts of dwellings rented for temporary occupancy, in order to give their children opportunity for education and to escape the dreary monotony of isolation."[57]

Most persevered, and over time the Great Plains went through what historian Geoff Cunfer has recently identified as three stages or phases of development. "A pioneer era of cropland expansion and prairie reduction came to a head early in the twentieth century as farmers reached the natural limits of their environment." Between about 1870 and 1930, pioneers learned what would and would not work on the plains. "A transition era of only about a decade," Cunfer further writes, "saw many farmers plow a bit too much marginal land, realize their error, and restore some of it to pasture."[58] Those blunders and the subsequent adjustments occurred during the 1930s. Finally, "once they adjusted to those natural limits, they sustained a remarkably stable land-use pattern for more than half a century."[59]

That stability assumed two major forms. First, most land was kept as pasture. Only about 30 percent of the Great Plains was ever plowed. Most was maintained as grazing land.[60] Second, even as farm technologies changed—with tractors replacing horses, some use of irrigation, and extensive usage of artificial fertilizers—there was basic stability in the crops grown on the plowed lands. Corn, wheat, sorghum, cotton, rye and barley, hay, and oats were produced in varying amounts between 1880 and 1997. Great Plains farmers, Cunfer shows, were usually diversified agriculturalists and rarely raised just one or two major crops. Like farmers in Ohio and Oregon, they spread their risks around several crops and apportioned their scarce labor among crops with somewhat different growing seasons, a situation that changed in the twentieth century, especially after World War II. Then, specialization rapidly increased.[61]

Legal changes accompanied farmers' dealing with the dry environment. Before the federal government became increasingly involved in irrigation with the passage by Congress of the Newlands Act of 1902, farmers, resorting to irrigation to water their crops, either banded together to build the necessary ditches and reservoirs or relied on private companies to do so. As irrigation became more common, localities and states abandoned riparian rights in favor of prior appropriation. Under a water doctrine of prior appropriation, the first user of a source for any use deemed beneficial by residents, such as mining or farming, could claim exclusive use of all the water. No water had to be returned to a stream for others to use. Originating in a number of regions short of water and employed in California's mining camps during the years of the gold rush, this doctrine spread to many parts of the arid West.[62] In fact, eight states west of the Rocky Mountains abandoned riparian-rights concepts for those of prior appropriation.[63] Donald Pisani, a dean of western-water historians, writes, "The triumph of prior appropriation—the legal principle that the first to put water to a 'beneficial use' has the paramount right to the future use of that water—is a complicated but compelling part of the history of the American West."[64]

HENRY AND ROSIE ISE AND DAVID PENNER: EUROPEAN AMERICAN FARMERS IN KANSAS

The efforts of Henry and Rosie Ise illustrate some of the difficulties and rewards of farming on the western Great Plains.[65] Newlyweds, the two traveled two hundred miles by wagon in June 1873 to take up 160 acres in western Kansas that Henry had claimed and already begun working under the terms of the Homestead Act. Like many others, they hoped to build a prosperous life out west. Rosie was seventeen years old, and Henry, who had been a farm laborer in Illinois and Iowa to earn money to buy land, was nearly thirty. It was the perceived richness of the soil that drew the two into semiarid western Kansas, as one of their sons later wrote, "fine, black" soil, "deep and rich."[66] A veteran of the Civil

War for the Union, Henry was eager to strike out on his own. The Ises moved into a region still in its frontier stage of development. There were neighbors, including Rosie's brother and his wife, but not many. There was at first no railroad and only the very small town of Russell nearby.[67]

Rosie was more fortunate in her housing than many women. Henry had already constructed a log cabin of timbers hewed from wood taken from trees growing along a nearby stream. Rosie never had to endure living in a sod house, although her cabin had a sod roof. Spacious by the standards of the day, the cabin measured fifteen feet by eighteen feet. Boasting a cottonwood floor, the cabin had three windows. Furniture consisted of a "bedstead made of cottonwood boards, with a bed tick filled with straw, a table made also of warped cottonwood boards, and a tiny cooking stove." There was more, but not much: "Two empty nail kegs and two boxes served as chairs, and on another nail keg by the door there was a washpan, half full of soapy water." The farm had, as well, a stable "made of wheat straw thrown over a frame of logs and saplings," a sod chicken house, a well "with a wheel and two buckets on a rope," and a small corral. As he broke more land to the plow, an arduous task, Henry enclosed it with a barbed wire fence from 1879 onward, "although it was not yet determined whether horses would be safe with barbed wire fences."[68]

Henry and Rosie engaged in diversified agriculture, with most of their produce going to market but some held back for home consumption. In this sense, they acted very much like their counterparts in Ohio and Oregon. From the start, the fields Henry worked, initially only about ten acres, yielded spring wheat, corn, barley, and oats. Henry planted five acres in sod corn put in with his hatchet. He planted another five acres in wheat. In the home garden, Rosie produced peas, turnips, lettuce, tomatoes, and cucumbers. Chickens that Rosie tended laid eggs. And a cow produced milk, which Rosie churned into butter. Yields from the virgin land were large at first, 200 bushels of wheat from Henry's five-acre field. Fifty bushels sufficed for the family's bread and seed, leaving 150 bushels to take to market in Russell. By 1882, Henry had sixty acres planted in wheat, yielding 30 bushels per acre.[69]

The Ise family faced serious challenges in living and farming. As Rosie began having children, the cabin seemed small; and whenever it rained, "rivulets of muddy water" poured in through the sod roof. Nine years after they began homesteading, Henry was able to afford replacing the cabin with a clapboard house built on stone foundations. In 1874, grasshoppers, which came in a cloud that "obscured the sun," descended on their crops, destroying many of them. Ravenous, the grasshoppers "ate holes in the curtains on the windows, and in the clothes hanging on the wall." Hot winds and rainless summer days sometimes dried up their corn, turning it into tinder for prairie fires, and those fires threatened the Ises' cabin despite the firebreak Henry plowed around it. In the winter, "snow and cold drove wolves to depredations on the poultry and livestock." An "incessant, wearying wind" seemed omnipresent. Accidents occurred, as they might on any American farm then: a man's legs were crushed when logs rolled off a wagon; a rabid wolf bit a neighbor, infecting and killing him; and ants swarmed over an untended baby. A lack of competent medical aid exacerbated these problems, and neighbors died from infections of typhoid and diphtheria. Malaria was also a problem.[70]

Yet Henry and Rosie persisted and were compensated for the difficulties they faced. They soon owned their farm, were free from most debt, and, despite hot summers and grasshoppers, often enjoyed bounteous harvests. Parties with neighbors, featuring oysters brought in from the East by railroad, provided entertainment and sociability. As more people moved into the region and railroads reached it, towns grew and, with them, organizations developed to which the Ises belonged, including a literary society. Circuses, civic celebrations such as the Fourth of July, and religious meetings also broke the monotony of farm life. Above all, Henry and Rosie lived for the future of their family. They reared eleven children on their homestead (one other child died) and sent nine of them through college. Six went on to graduate school, an unusual record in those days or even now.[71]

Just to the east of the Ises, the family of David Penner, a German immigrant from Russia, purchased the 160 acres composing the southeast quarter of Section 27, Township 21 South, Range 4 West near Inman, Kansas, for $1,260. (Russian officials invited Germans to settle in some regions of their nation in the nineteenth century. Later harassed by Russians, many Germans left for the United States.) In

1885, Penner bought the northeast quarter of 160 acres in that section as well.[72] Pushed by czarist impositions in the Ukraine and pulled by reports of fertile farmland in Kansas, Penner was eager to move. He bought the virgin land from the Santa Fe Railroad in 1874, married another Russian immigrant, and started what would become a century-long family farm. Situated in a transition zone between regions of high and low levels of rainfall, the farm was initially covered with mixed prairie grasses. Some of the feelings David might have had toward the land and farming come through in the musings of Mil Penner, his great-grandson, writing in 2002: "I am very grateful that I had the opportunity to enjoy the mystery of the barn, to love a calf, to catch a lamb, to plow the earth, to feed the chickens, and to experience the miracle of growing things."[73]

David soon changed his land by plowing up the grasses with a breaking plow and planting crops. The Russian immigrants brought seeds of a hard, red winter wheat with them to Kansas, called "Turkey Red," and that species of wheat quickly became their main cash crop. Unfortunately, they also inadvertently imported Russian thistle seeds with the wheat seeds and accidentally planted them. That thistle (also called tumbleweed) soon spread across the plains.[74] Diversified farming was the norm on the land of the Penner family through World War II. The farm grew wheat, oats, and barley. Livestock and poultry were raised for home consumption and the market. Gardens near the house produced corn, beets, beans, and tomatoes. An orchard yielded peaches, plums, and apricots, and pastures produced hay and feed crops. As on the Ise farm and as was also typical on farms in Ohio and Oregon, a gender division of labor long persisted on the Penner farm. Women cooked, nurtured children, performed all the housework, and tended chickens. Men cultivated crops and took care of livestock. As Mil recalls, "Working in the fields, from shocking oats to driving tractors, was considered improper for ladies until the 1950s, as were construction and barnyard chores."[75]

In his family history, Mil depicts what the introduction of farming by European Americans meant for the countryside in his part of Kansas. "By the turn of the century [1900], only twenty-six years after the settlers had arrived, the prairie's natural contours were marked by fence rows and hedgerows." Continuing, Penner notes, "Rectilinear fields of grain, straight roads with bridges across streams, neat farmsteads surrounded by shade trees and orchards, and gardens yielding produce from foreign seeds" had come to dominate the landscape.[76]

The joys and hardships of homesteading on the Great Plains have been described by a multitude of writers, with many speaking from experience. Perhaps the most famous writer about late nineteenth-century and early twentieth-century US farm life is Hamlin Garland. Born to parents on a farm in Wisconsin in 1860, Garland moved westward with his family to a new farm venture in Iowa ten years later and finally to a farm in the Dakota Territory during the early 1880s. He graduated from the Cedar Valley Seminary in Osage, Iowa, in 1884 and, eschewing farm life, moved to Boston, where he began a career as a teacher, lecturer, and writer. His best-known piece of literature, *Main-Travelled Roads,* which sketches western farm and small-town life, appeared in 1891, and his incisive autobiography, *A Son of the Middle Border,* was published in 1917.[77]

A realist in his literary endeavors, Garland nonetheless sees beauty in the Great Plains, writing in his autobiography about the Dakota Territory: "Duck and geese rose from every icy pond and resumed their flight into the mystic north, and as we advanced the world broadened before us." In the next sentence, he comments on "the treelessness of the wide swells" and the "crispness of the air." He waxes nostalgic about how plowing the land "prophesied the death of all wild creatures and assured the devastation of the beautiful, the destruction of all the signs and seasons of the sod."[78] Garland soon tires of the Plains, however. In the summer, "winds were hot and dry and the grass, baked on the stem, had become as inflammable as hay." Gardens "withered, and many of the women began to complain bitterly of the loneliness, and lack of shade." Winter turns Garland even more against the Plains. "No man knows what winter means until he has lived through one in a pine-board shanty on the Dakota plain," he exclaims in his autobiography. That experience, he writes, "permanently chilled my enthusiasm for pioneering the plain." Garland decides to "escape the terror and loneliness of the treeless sod" and "began to plan for work in other airs."[79]

Main-Travelled Roads reflects Garland's growing disillusionment with farming, especially on the Great Plains. Naturalism permeates chapter 1, in which Garland writes of "seas of corn," "gleaming fields of barley," and "wheat already mottled with soft gold." So does realism, as he describes harvest scenes accurately and in detail. One of the two protagonists of the chapter is a young wife, Agnes, who "was worn and wasted incredibly" by the demands of farm life. In fact, the farm life of Garland's fictional account bears little to admire. Even the parlor of the farmhouse is "a poor little sitting room, with furniture worn and shapeless" and with "hardly a touch of pleasant color." At the end of the chapter, Agnes escapes her drab life by running away with a former boyfriend, an action that "close[s] the door on [her] sufferings."[80]

There is more to Garland's literary work than realism and naturalism, however. As much as he personally rejected farm life, Garland championed midwestern and Great Plains regionalism in his writing. His is a complex personality. Historian Jon Lauck aptly characterizes Garland's approach: "Finding a place for their region in the mass culture clatter is what animated midwestern regionalists such as Hamlin Garland, who felt his region and its voices were diluted and suppressed by the cultural domination of New York and Hollywood."[81] Even as he moved to Boston and New York City, Garland considered the Midwest and Great Plains to be his homes.

Other writers have also portrayed well what the landscape of the Great Plains was like and how it changed. For many, the Great Plains was a hostile environment. Writing in 1918, novelist Willa Cather described the land of Nebraska: "There seemed to be nothing to see; no fences, no creeks or trees, no hills or fields. . . . There was nothing but land . . . slightly undulating."[82] Pulitzer-Prize-winning poet Theodore Roethke saw Michigan land in 1953 similarly:

> The upland of alder and birchtrees,
> Through the swamp alive with quicksand,
> The way blocked by the fallen fir-tree,
> The thickets darkening,
> The ravines ugly.[83]

For Cather and Roethke, and for many other writers, nearly uncivilized nature hostile to humans dominates their scenes.

For most writers, no cities and few people intrude on the Plains. So it is for O. E. Rolvaag in his now-classic novel *Giants in the Earth,* first published in 1924 and 1925, when Chicago and Cleveland were booming. Focusing on Scandinavian settlers to the northern Great Plains, this work of fiction observes that the region featured a "bright, clear sky over a plain so wide that the rim of the heavens cut down on it around the entire horizon." And "tall grass" is everywhere.[84] Farming on the plains engenders isolation and loneliness, which drives Beret, wife of settler Per Hansa, brooding in her dark sod house in the Dakotas, insane. There is no romantic image of the life on the land here, yet land hunger keeps driving people to endure this life. Nor is there romanticism in a 2018 murder mystery written by Laurie Loewenstein. Set in Oklahoma in mid-1935, a time of dark dust storms and despair, the work describes the plains as overwhelmingly brown. "In Oklahoma, the palette was nothing but brown," writes Loewenstein. "Brown bridal trains of dust billowed behind tractors." The dust and its coloring effects dominate her depiction of life: "Curtains turned from white to strong coffee. Folks spit river mud after a duster. Washes of beige, cinnamon and umber bled into the blue sky depending on which direction the wind blew." In fact, Loewenstein says, "The people, the land, the buildings absorbed the dust. All other colors leached away, while brown and its infinite variations remained."[85]

MEN, WOMEN, AND THE ENVIRONMENT ON THE GREAT PLAINS

Women like Rosie Ise may have felt the harshness of the Plains more than men. It was hard for women to leave behind family and friends to move to the Great Plains. Once there, women dealt with all the challenges Rosie Ise faced in designing new lives for an alien environment. They lived in dugouts (houses built into the sides of hills) and sod houses (it took about one acre of prairie turf to supply the sod for one sod house) and small cabins. Their husbands typically broke the prairie sod with large, heavy "breaking plows" pulled by several yokes of oxen, after which the men planted corn, wheat, oats, and other crops. Gender roles sometimes blurred, with women working in the fields alongside their men as needed. Historian Stratton notes, "The mother and the daughters assisted with the traditionally male tasks of planting and harvesting, tending livestock, hauling water, gathering fuel, and even hunting."[86] However, women still did all the cooking, tending of children, laundry, and sewing. And it was usually expected for women to give care to those struck down by illnesses—cholera, malaria, smallpox, and typhoid fever.[87]

Like Rosie, most Kansas women took pleasure in visiting with neighbors, going to town, and watching their children grow up. But not all came as wives or daughters of homesteaders. In Kansas and throughout the West, perhaps 10–12 percent of homesteaders were women. Under the terms of the Homestead Act of 1862 and its later modifications, single women, widows, and even married women considered family heads (because they were abandoned or had incompetent husbands) could claim land on their own, prove it up, and come to own it.[88] One woman who homesteaded in Kansas later reminisced, "It might seem a cheerless life, but there were many compensations: the thrill of conquering a new country; the wonderful atmosphere; the attraction of the prairie, which simply gets into your blood and makes you dissatisfied away from it; the low-lying hills and the unobstructed view of the horizon."[89]

As they moved out onto the Great Plains, women and men altered the environment. The changes were many. As in other regions of North America, from Ohio to Oregon, Native Americans, weakened by introduced diseases, were defeated in battle and displaced from their lands. Buffalo were nearly extirpated. So were wolves, allowing their prey, rabbits, to multiply. Prairie grasses—there were 470 species in the southern Great Plains alone—were plowed under when the sod was broken, giving way to wheat and other crops.[90] Plowing was generally done in straight lines that did not follow the contours of the land, making the plowed soil more subject to erosion by the wind than it might otherwise have been.[91] Historian Cunfer goes so far as to write, "Plowing is the ecological equivalent of genocide" and that "plowing a grassland is comparable to clear-cutting a forest."[92]

With parts of the Plains disturbed by plowing, dust storms resulted, especially on the southern Great Plains during the drought years of the 1930s. The worst occurred during 1935 and 1936, when dust from the Great Plains fell on midwestern and eastern US cities and as far away as London, England. Perhaps the most catastrophic of the storms took place on Palm Sunday 1935, when dust clouds blackened skies from the Dakotas south to Oklahoma and Texas. Dust covered and killed crops, suffocated livestock, and induced "dust pneumonia" in humans, some of whom later died. Still, too much can be made, some scholars argue, of the role farmers played in bringing on the dust storms of the mid-1930s. Overplowing, incorrect plowing, or plowing up marginal lands probably did not by themselves cause the Dust Bowl of the 1930s, experts assert. High winds, abnormally high temperatures, and a lack of rain—all natural phenomena—were, they conclude, the most likely culprits. It is important to remember that dust storms occurred on the Great Plains before and after the 1930s.[93]

Over time, European American settlers adjusted to the environment of the Great Plains. They wisely gave up on trying to tame and domesticate buffalo and prairie chickens. They planted strains of wheat resistant to heat, cold, and drought, and they downplayed or abandoned corn. They had limited success with irrigating crops and introducing industry to the Great Plains, such as processing sorghum for sugar. None of these steps were accomplished easily, for settlers were stubborn. Historian Miner observes of those coming to western Kansas, "When settlers did not believe in something, they were remarkably slow to see it, and when they did strongly believe, they could conjure it up despite evidence that they were banking on a mirage."[94]

President Franklin D. Roosevelt's New Dealers sought to address weather and climate issues on the Great Plains during the 1930s. Some of their attempted solutions were plowing with the contour of the land, removing land from agricultural production, limiting grazing, and planting shelterbelts of trees. The Prairie States Forestry Project, better known as the Shelterbelt, was strongly pushed by Roosevelt. Begun in 1934 and lasting into the early 1940s, the project was the most ambitious effort to remake the Plains. The project involved planting trees and shrubs as "windbreaks along the borders of croplands and pastures to reduce wind speeds and decrease the evaporation of moisture from the soil." The wide band was to cross the Great Plains from Texas to Canada. Labeled "the most ambitious afforestation project in world history" by historian Douglas Brinkley, Shelterbelt resulted in the planting of 220 million trees and shrubs on thirty thousand farms. Unfortunately, those plants also brought unwanted insects and diseases to the Great Plains: tent caterpillars, cankerworms, and rust disease.[95]

Few of the trees remained a decade or two later, for most were killed by drought and lack of care. Not all the trees died, however. Some were Siberian elms, which survived to serve as local windbreaks. Many of those tough trees were uprooted and removed by farmers in the 2010s in the interests of efficiency and profits, for the trees took up space and water that could be used for crops, and farmers said they no longer needed wind protection.[96]

Plant diversity suffered with farming. The makeup of the soil did too; nitrogen that had accumulated for thousands of years was removed by corn, wheat, cotton, and other crops. Not even the spreading of manure and planting of legumes, like hay, clover, and beans, were able to return enough nitrogen to the soil to offset the losses, causing crop yields to decline over four or five decades. Only the application of massive amounts of fertilizer made from artificially produced nitrogen reversed that trend after World War II.[97] Also, emigrants like the Penners accidentally introduced weeds like Russian thistle (tumbleweed) to their regions. Thistle became an especially noxious problem for farmers on the eastern plains of Montana. Desperate farmers there fed ground, salted thistle to their cattle during the 1930s. A few people even ate it, but horses could not stomach the thistle.[98] Other invasive species caused problems as well. The introduced Russian olive tree sucked up water. Some agronomists estimate that eliminating this species from the Great Plains would increase water availability there by 20 percent. Writing in 2012, naturalist Catherine Raven commented on kochia, yellow sweet clover, and Russian thistle, the alien weeds she encountered while living on the high plains of Montana.[99]

In time, some ranchers, farmers, and others used fire in controlled burnings to keep the plains in good condition. In fact, fire is almost a necessary ingredient in the good health of plains ecosystems. Fire clears away old grass, shrubs, and trees without damaging the roots of grasses. Fall and winter fires can regenerate the plains with new, fresh grass growth in the spring and summer. In the absence of fires, plains may become overgrown with bushes and trees, lose their viability, and slowly disappear. This growth can lead to unexpected consequences. For instance, as trees move onto the Great Plains, they can deplete already scarce water supplies.

In precontact times, Native Americans often used fire to clear the plains of old or unwanted growth, thus encouraging the development of new grasses for herds of buffalo and horses. They also used fire for signaling, hunting, and war. European American settlers were divided in how they saw fire. Most viewed prairie fires romantically, using phrases like "awe-inspiring," "beautiful," "sublime," "magnificent," and "stupendous" to describe them. But in utilitarian, pragmatic approaches they varied. Some ranchers copied Native Americans, adopting fire as a tool to keep the Great Plains healthy for their cattle herds. Nearly all farmers, however, opposed burning and sought to extinguish all fires, which they saw as likely to destroy their houses, barns, fences, haystacks, crops, and livestock. (In fighting fires, the same gender divisions that permeated farming were common. Men fought fires on the front line. Women usually stayed back a bit to care for the children and provide food and drink.) Only in recent decades have controlled burns reemerged as a valuable tool for ecosystem management on the Great Plains. By 2010, for example, ranchers were burning about two million of the four million acres of rangeland in the Flint Hills of Kansas each year. Even farmers are using controlled burns in some regions.[100]

It is important to remember that only about 30 percent of the 380 million acres composing the Great Plains have ever been plowed; the rest remained as grassland. Grazing by the cattle, which replaced the buffalo, led to fewer changes in flora and fauna than did plowed farming. Yet alterations did occur. One major result of cattle grazing was "to shift prairie communities from mid-grass and tall-grass dominants toward short-grass dominants." Little and big bluestem, tall dropseed, side-oats grama, switchgrass, Indian grass, and June grass gave way to buffalo grass, sand dropseed, and blue grama. The shift began with grazing by buffalo 13,000 years ago and has continued with cattle grazing since the late nineteenth century.[101] In semiarid areas, cattle destroyed the tall grasses, and now there is often only sagebrush. Tall grasses have roots that extend twenty feet underground. As those grasses were eaten, their roots got shorter and eventually could not recover. It is, in fact, very difficult to recreate tall-grass prairies.

In the late twentieth century, some of the western Great Plains were partially depopulated as farmers continued to struggle with harsh social and economic environments. Farms were abandoned and small towns became smaller. Despite economic renewal in some areas, those trends continued into the early 2000s, prompting some easterners to declare that the plains should be remade as a great "buffalo commons." That is, people should leave and animals return to a "rewilded" Great Plains. The notion was hotly rejected by most westerners, however.[102]

This idea was decades-old. As early as during the dry years of the 1920s, some people thought the Great Plains should be abandoned. An editorial in the *Farmers' Dispatch* of St. Paul, Minnesota, opined in 1921 that it was a waste of money for the federal government to provide seed aid to drought-stricken farmers in eastern Montana. The editorial asserted that one of the "greatest economic crimes perpetuated in recent years was the breaking up of cattle ranges for agriculture, and that settlers of the district ought to be removed." Replying to that editorial, the son of a Montana homesteader asked, "Where, may I ask, has a new region been developed without meeting difficulties?" He bluntly concluded, "We are not seeking a more comfortable environment. We do not wish to be transported."[103] It would, in fact, be extremely difficult to rewild the Great Plains, given all the changes that have taken place. Few such efforts have been made. Even so, there has been some return of buffalo to the region. By the 1990s, some 250,000 buffalo lived on the Great Plains, some in national parks and reserves, but most on private ranches where they were raised for the market.[104]

Conclusions

Land, Water, and People

More than any other single factor, the lure of farmland drew Americans westward. More than mining, ranching, lumbering, or fishing, it was farming that pulled European Americans westward across the North American continent. For many European Americans and African Americans in Ohio and elsewhere, land was valuable for its use in subsistence farming, for the commercial production of edibles, as a mark of republican values, and as a token of prestige—all at the expense of Native Americans who viewed and used land differently as a source of food and communal strength.

In part, the search for new lands was driven by the increase in the population of the United States, from 3.9 million people in 1790, to 31.5 million in 1860, and to 76.1 million by 1900. Most Americans were farmers and wanted land to cultivate. In addition, older lands "wore out" and declined in fertility. Euro-American farming methods simply did not return enough nitrogen to the soil to offset its constant removal by the cultivation of crops such as corn, wheat, and cotton. An essential building block for the growing of commercial crops, nitrogen was in short supply. European American farmers sought to replenish their lands by spreading manure and planting legumes such as hay, clover, and beans, actions which returned nitrogen to the soil. Those steps, however, were almost always inadequate. The drain of nitrogen from their soils and the consequent substantial drop in crop yields led farmers to be ever on the move seeking lands farther west for themselves and their family members.[1]

Only the massive application of artificial fertilizers on farmlands after World War II seemed to end the need to find new soils. In 1940, American farmers nationwide applied just over ten million tons of synthetic fertilizers, but by 1981, their applications exceeded fifty million tons. The mechanization of farming, development of crop hybrids, and tremendous increase in the usage of chemicals in fertilizers and pesticides revolutionized American agriculture after World War II. In 1940, an American farmer produced enough food to feed ten other people, but by 2000, a farmer produced enough to feed one hundred others. Crop yields soared. United States corn yields, for example, rose from 38 bushels per acre in 1950 to 120 bushels per acre in 1987, and those of wheat from 14 bushels per acre to 39 bushels per acre in the same years.[2] British farmer and ecologist James Rebanks observes, "In the year 2000 the average American farmer produced twelve times as much per hour as his grandfather did in 1950."[3]

Still, there were problems. Synthetic nitrogen production and usage had two major drawbacks. First, it required large inputs of natural gas to heat nitrogen and hydrogen to high temperatures at which they could be combined to make fertilizer.[4] The production of one ton of anhydrous ammonia required 33,000 cubic feet of natural gas. Second, unless applied very carefully, much of the fertilizer ended up in streams, lakes, and oceans as runoff from farm fields. There, the fertilizer polluted water and fed algae blooms in warm summer months. In the summer of 2015, the city of Toledo, Ohio, had to shut down its water system, which drew from Lake Erie, because of algae blooms covering large parts of the lake. Residents had to use expensive bottled water for drinking, cooking, and bathing. By the early 2000s, concerns about the depletion of soil nitrogen reached into novels written about Ohio. In *Ohio: A Novel,* writer Stephen Markley exclaimed in 2018, "Ohio's monoculture farms massacred the soil" and "then pumped in nitrogen fertilizers to keep it alive, zombielike."[5] And additional environmental difficulties abounded. By destroying forests, pioneer actions contributed to global warming. Burning trees released CO2 into the atmosphere, and the lack of trees made the sequestering of the heat-trapping gas difficult. Moreover, farm animals, especially cattle, released large amounts of methane, another planet-warming gas, into the atmosphere.

* * *

Whether acquired from land companies, as was common in the Ohio Country, from railroads, as was typical on the Great Plains, or via direct sales of the public domain by state and federal governments, as often occurred in the Oregon Country, land was the pull in the westward development of the United States. Thus, the Ohio Company advertised fertile lands "far exceeding any lands to the east of the Great Mountains" in the mid-1700s.[6]

However, not just any land would do. European Americans brought with them preconceived ideas of how land that could be made into fertile farmland should look. Coming mainly from Virginia, Kentucky, and Pennsylvania—all well-forested regions, for the most part—early European Americans entering Ohio looked for big hardwood trees, such as white oaks, beeches, hickories, and chestnuts, as indicators of rich and profitable soils. A protagonist in Richard Powers's Pulitzer Prize–winning novel *Overstory*, published in 2018, observes this situation: "The beech told the farmer where to plow, limestone underneath, covered the best, darkest loam a field could want."[7] European Americans moved onto the lands of the Black Swamp in northwestern Ohio only after all other lands in the region had been taken up. Girdling or cutting down trees and then burning them was simply accepted as part of farming. Much of the same sequence of events occurred in the Oregon Country. Again, trees were generally seen as signifying the presence of rich soil for farming. European Americans initially passed over the treeless Great Plains on their way to the forested lands of the Pacific Northwest—not surprising, since a majority of those moving to Oregon came from the Old Northwest of Ohio, Indiana, Illinois, Michigan, and Wisconsin, all well-timbered lands. Only when railroads mounted massive advertising campaigns to change attitudes about the land on the Great Plains did European Americans move onto the prairie.

On most American frontiers, then, trees, especially large ones, were seen as suggesting the existence of rich soil, but forests were also viewed by European Americans as obstacles to be removed for farming to develop. In their assumptions, they were only partially correct. Trees could indeed indicate good soil for farming. However, wet prairies and swamps, once drained, also made excellent farmland. The Black Swamp became (and remains) some of the most productive farmland in the United States. Similarly, parts of the Great Plains, when properly farmed, were (and are) very productive—in fact, it is a breadbasket of wheat and other grains.

Yet trees were also seen as a hindrance by European American settlers, and remove the trees they certainly did. The sound of axes on wood and the smell of smoke in the air permeated most frontiers in the United States, except for the Great Plains. Clearing the land and preparing it for the plow were the first tasks of most European American settlers, often preceding building any but the most rudimentary housing. Families huddled in rude lean-tos while men girdled or felled trees. Usually, only later were log cabins constructed. As they plowed their lands and turned their livestock loose to graze nearby, European Americans altered their environments. In a message to Congress in 1935, President Franklin D. Roosevelt observed, "During the three or four centuries of white men on the American Continent, we find a continuous striving of civilization against Nature." In fact, as we have seen repeatedly, Native Americans had already changed those environments considerably even earlier. By their hunting, use of fire, and agricultural practices, they had created partly managed environments. European Americans and African Americans, however, took the processes of environmental change much further. Moving onto forest and prairie lands, they built new landscapes.

New plants and animals replaced or supplemented old ones. Cattle, horses, sheep, goats, and pigs replaced deer, turkeys, beavers, and wolves in the Ohio Country. Corn and wheat fields covered increasing expanses of land. Soon, little remained of the old. But this situation was not limited to Ohio. As British biologist Chris D. Thomas points out, by the early 2000s "over a third of the world's land surface" was "covered by human-selected crops, pastures and forestry plantations." Many scholars and environmentalists argue that Earth is currently experiencing its sixth great extinction event, comparable to the one in which all dinosaurs, except those that became birds, vanished some sixty-five million years ago. Wild flora and fauna are disappearing, they say, replaced by domesticated ones, all due to human actions. Biodiversity, they claim, has severely suffered.[8]

Water, as well as land, was much on the minds of European Americans. Water was needed for farming, and they sought out humid, well-watered lands. Reliable rainfall was valued, and farmers selected lands with clear springs and streams whenever possible. No one wanted the expense and danger of digging deep wells. Rivers were also prized for their utilitarian value. Rivers and canals could carry produce to markets much more easily and cheaply than could wagons on primitive roads. Yet water was a mixed blessing, for it was often seen as carrying disease and death. No one understood germ theory in the early 1800s, and so no one fully knew how waterborne germs spread cholera and typhoid. However, people did see rotting animal carcasses and decaying plant matter as creating diseases in accord with the miasmic concept of associating diseases and illnesses with unclean water.

The continuing attraction of Americans to fertile, well-watered lands may be seen in the lure exerted by Alaska's Matanuska Valley during the Depression of the 1930s. By this time, Alaska had been home to commercial salmon fisheries, mining, and the fur trade for decades. All had gone through the boom-and-bust cycles typical of frontier industries. Nearly all farmers, however, had been discouraged by the territory's cold climate and long distance from markets. To address this issue, the federal government sponsored the resettlement of several hundred farmers from the northern Great Plains to Matanuska Valley just north of Anchorage as a New Deal project. With considerable federal aid, it was hoped, relocated men and women would become yeoman farmers, even joyous tillers of the soil, living on the land. As self-sufficient agriculturalists, the Alaskans would produce, it was anticipated, bumper crops for markets from this virgin land. The plan did not work. Federal government preparations proved inadequate, farmers were unprepared for the rigors of Alaskan life (such as bears taking their cattle!), and getting crops to market was expensive (for some crops were successfully grown).[9]

* * *

On most frontiers, federal and state governments played active roles by selling land and helping provide the roads, canals, and railroads by which farmers moved their crops to market. Sometimes, in fact, the federal government may have gone too far, as with its perhaps overly generous financing of transcontinental railroads through direct aid and land grants. Importantly, exploration sponsored by the federal government, from the Lewis and Clark expedition of 1804–6 through at least the three expeditions headed by John C. Fremont in the 1840s, provided specific information about the West and, even more significantly, gave Americans a sense that western lands were theirs for the taking. The United States Army cleared away what most European Americans viewed as the Indian "menace" and showed the potential for raising livestock and crops in the West. As important as individuals were, they moved ahead only with plentiful government aid.

Those European Americans were diversified farmers, growing a variety of crops for their own consumption and, very quickly at most locations, for external markets. So were African American settlers. From the first, most farmers were market oriented. Corn—high in carbohydrates and thus a good source of energy, though low in protein—was planted among trees and their stumps almost as soon as they had been girdled or cut down. Wheat, oats, and barley soon followed. Only where it was too cloudy, as in parts of the Oregon Country, or too dry, as on the western Great Plains, did farmers forgo growing corn. Nearly all kept livestock. Pigs turned loose in nearby woods subsisted on mast, which is nuts and other foodstuffs on the forest floor. Some went feral and altered their environments for years to come. Cattle, horses, sheep, and goats added to these changes.

As they moved out of the Ohio Country to American regions new to them, men and women took their ideas about land and its resources with them. In the Ohio Country, European American and African American settlers tried for several years to grow cotton and mulberry trees needed to produce silk, eventually giving up after repeated severe winters destroyed their efforts. The Oregon Trail served as a conduit for farming notions to the Oregon Country, and a bit later various trails and railroads transported people and their ideas to the Great Plains. In both regions, farmers sought to grow corn, a staple crop in the Ohio and Mississippi valleys, but one often unsuited to the cloudy Pacific Northwest or the dry plains. Old ideas died hard, whether they were about what crops to raise or, more generally, how to live. Settlers from the East tried to take their ideas about civilization to the West. Thus it was for Nannie Alderson, the wife of a small-time rancher in Montana during the 1880s. When Native Americans burned Nannie's log cabin, what she missed most was the loss of her mother's silverware, for Nannie, a symbol of eastern civilization on the frontier. Too, Nannie's family's dog was trained to remove the hats of cowboys sitting at the dining table, again, a mark for Nannie of civilized life.[10] Native Americans did not fit into this scene, unless they gave up their cultures and fully assimilated into European American culture. Forced assimilation was, in fact, the major goal of the Indian policy of the United States throughout the nineteenth century.

I pose this important question: Do the experiences of men and women grappling with environments new to them in the Ohio Country, Oregon Country, and Great Plains have anything to teach Americans dealing with climate change today, certainly a rapidly changing environment?[11] Their experiences demonstrate, I think, just how difficult it is to alter established ways of living. It took repeated crop failures for farmers in the Oregon Country and on the Great Plains to reluctantly give up on trying to grow corn, for example. Still, changes did occur. Over time, after enduring many hardships, some European Americans did learn new ways to treat their lands, returning in some places, for example, to no-till agriculture. I say "returning" because many Native Americans had long practiced farming without plowing their lands with bountiful results. Change, though possible, was often difficult to achieve. More generally, success in agriculture came to European Americans and African Americans alike as they learned not to fight nature. Thus, grazing livestock often has proven to be more successful than farming crops on much of the Great Plains.

As they moved to and settled on frontiers, European Americans and African Americans viewed the lands new to them with both utilitarian and romantic eyes. Lands should be put to productive and profitable use, surely, but lands were also "beautiful," "unusual," "awesome," and even "sublime," to repeat some of the terms commonly found in early journals and letters. For all of their familiar trees, the lands were, nonetheless, somewhat different from what pioneers were accustomed to. Coming to understand and manage life on frontiers was thus a complex experience, as can be seen in the often competing utilitarian and romantic ideas Americans harbored about their nation's lands. Underlying pragmatic and romantic thoughts about nature was the ethos of capitalism, especially in the nineteenth century. The thought that investment in capital and labor could bring profitable returns from the exploitation of natural resources, including soil and water, ran through the American experience. It was this capitalism that writer William Dean Howells condemned as "pitiless greed," a lust for land that led European Americans to dispossess Native Americans across the North American continent.

Notes

INTRODUCTION

1. *Christopher Gist's Journals with Historical, Geographic, and Ethnological Notes and Biographies of His Contemporaries,* ed. William Darlington (Pittsburgh: J. R. Weldon, 1893; repr., London: Forgotten Books, 2012), 47, 55; page numbers from 1893 edition. In return for moving at least one hundred settlers into the West, the company was to receive up to five hundred thousand acres of land along the Ohio River, which its officers could then sell. Plans were destroyed, however, by the French and Indian War of 1754–63. The short-lived Ohio Company of the 1750s should not be confused with the Ohio Company of Associates, which was organized in Boston in 1786, bought land at the confluence of the Ohio and Muskingum Rivers in 1787, and founded Marietta in 1788. Marietta was the first permanent American settlement in the Old Northwest (Ohio, Indiana, Illinois, Michigan, and Wisconsin) north of the Ohio River. (There was no standard English language in the 1700s and 1800s. Thus, many quotations used in this work contain idiosyncrasies of spelling, capitalization, and punctuation.)
2. For instance, Indians "sent a clear message" to Gen. Arthur St. Clair after defeating him and his troops in Ohio in 1791 "by filling the mouths of the dead bodies with dirt and leaving them to rot." Joshua Casmir Catalano, "Blue Jacket, Anthony Wayne, and the Psychological and Symbolic War for Ohio, 1790–95," *Ohio History* 126, no. 1 (Spring 2019): 4–34, esp. 6. This Native way of signaling dislike was long-standing. In the early 1600s, Native Americans "stuffed bread into the mouths of dead colonists" in Virginia, historian Pekka Hämäläinen notes, as a "warning not to 'eat up all the land.'" Hämäläinen, *Indigenous Continent: The Epic Contest for North America* (New York: Liveright, 2022), 66.
3. Henry Howe, *Historical Collections of Ohio,* vol. 1 (1848; repr., Cincinnati: C. J. Krehbiel, 1904), 128.
4. William Dean Howells, *Stories of Ohio* (New York: American Book, 1897), re-created as Howells and C. Stephen Badgley, *The Story of Early*

Ohio: Indians, Frontiersmen, Pioneers, Statesmen and Wars (n.p.: Badgley, 2014), 30.

5. Malcolm J. Rohrbough, *The Trans–Appalachian Frontier: People, Societies, and Institutions, 1775–1850*, 2nd ed. (Belmont, CA: Wadsworth, 1990), 7, 15.
6. R. Douglas Hurt, *The Ohio Frontier: Crucible of the Old Northwest, 1720–1830* (Bloomington: Indiana University Press, 1998), 143–78. The scholarly literature on frontier Ohio is extensive. Works dealing with Ohio as part of the Ohio River valley are esp. compelling: Andrew R. L. Cayton and Stuart D. Hobbs, eds., *The Center of a Great Empire: The Ohio Country in the Early Republic* (Athens: Ohio University Press, 2005); and Kim M. Gruenwald, *River of Enterprise: The Commercial Origins of Regional Identity in the Ohio Valley, 1790–1850* (Bloomington: Indiana University Press, 2002). See also Timothy G. Anderson and Brian Schoen, eds., *Settling Ohio: First Peoples and Beyond* (Athens: Ohio University Press, 2023), a valuable collection of eleven essays. For another new look, see Rob Harper, *Unsettling the West: Violence and State Building in the Ohio Valley* (Philadelphia: University of Pennsylvania Press, 2018). Harper emphasizes that most of the violence that occurred in the Ohio Valley was due to state actions, not the work of unruly settlers. Still, a desire for land lay behind state actions, as "the lure of legal title to fertile land persuaded many to move west" (120). On the importance of land hunger in the settlement of the nearby Illinois Country (Illinois and Missouri), see John Reda, *From Furs to Farms: The Transformation of the Mississippi Valley, 1762–1825* (DeKalb: Northern Illinois University Press, 2016). See also Lucy Eldersveld Murphy, *A Gathering of Rivers: Indians, Métis, and Mining in the Western Great Lakes, 1737–1832* (Lincoln: University of Nebraska Press, 2000), esp. 137–66.
7. Frederick Jackson Turner, "The Significance of the Frontier in American History," *Annual Report of the American Historical Association for the Year 1893* (Washington, DC: Government Printing Office, 1894), 199–227, esp. 199. For a valuable look at Turner's ideas and more generally the importance of frontiers in the shaping of American history, see Greg Grandin, *The End of the Myth: From the Frontier to the Border Wall in the Mind of America* (New York: Henry Holt, 2019), esp. 1–3, 112–24, 270. For a provocative, if breezy, account of land issues globally, see Simon Winchester, *Land: How Hunger for Ownership Shaped the Modern World* (New York: Harper Collins, 2021).
8. Walter Prescott Webb, *The Great Plains* (Boston: Ginn, 1931), 8–9.
9. Patricia Nelson Limerick, *The Legacy of Conquest: The Unbroken Past of the American West* (New York: W. W. Norton, 1988), 26. Studies of western American history resonate with those of rural history. On the expansion of rural history as a field of study during the 1980s and early 1990s, see Dean L. May, *Three Frontiers: Family, Land, and Society in the American West, 1850–1900* (Cambridge: Cambridge University Press, 1994), 3–7.

For a survey history of rural America, see David Danbom, *Born in the Country: A History of Rural America,* 3rd ed. (Baltimore: Johns Hopkins University Press, 2017).

10. See, for example, Geoff Cunfer, *On the Great Plains: Agriculture and Environment* (College Station: Texas A&M University Press, 2005). See also Pekka Hämäläinen, *The Comanche Empire* (New Haven, CT: Yale University Press, 2008); and Hämäläinen, *Lakota America: A New History of Indigenous Power* (New Haven, CT: Yale University Press, 2019), both studies that deal with Native Americans and environmental issues. Yet other examples of new directions in frontier history may be found in Anne E. Hyde, *Empires, Nations, and Families: A New History of the North American West, 1800–1860* (Lincoln: University of Nebraska Press, 2011); and Hyde, *Born of Lakes and Plains: Mixed-Descent Peoples and the Making of the American West* (New York: W. W. Norton, 2022). Finally, see Elliott West, *The Contested Plains: Indians, Goldseekers, and the Rush to Colorado* (Lawrence: University Press of Kansas, 1998). West stresses, "We need to recognize the play between the 'natural world' and human minds" (xxiv).
11. Darlington, *Gist's Journals,* 55.
12. Timothy G. Anderson, "Conclusion," in Anderson and Schoen, *Settling Ohio,* 240.
13. On using fiction to understand history, see Richard Cohen, *Making History: The Storytellers Who Shaped the Past* (New York: Simon and Schuster, 2022), 256–91.
14. Historian Grandin has observed that the meaning of frontiers has changed for Americans over time. Originally, Americans conceived of frontiers, he notes, as borders and boundaries. Later, the word *frontier,* became "fuzzier." A frontier "came to suggest a cultural zone or a civilizational struggle, a way of life." See Grandin, *Myth,* 115–16. In James Crawford, *The Edge of the Plain: How Borders Make and Break Our World* (New York: W. W. Norton, 2022), the author posits, "And what is a border, if not a story? It is never simply a line, a marker, and edge. First, it is an idea. An idea that is then presented as a reality" (22).
15. West, *Contested Plains,* 13.
16. In Richard White, *The Middle Ground: Indians, Empires, and Republics in the Great Lakes Region, 1650–1815* (Cambridge: Cambridge University Press, 1991), White writes that the French and Indians in the Great Lakes region worked together in a middle ground based on trade, gift giving, fluid and shared legal concepts, and personal relationships for almost two hundred years, with no one group dominant. Not all historians accept White's findings. In Michael A. McDonnell, *Masters of Empire: Great Lakes Indians and the Making of America* (New York: Hill and Wang, 2015), the author argues that, on the contrary, Native Americans, especially Anishinaabeg groups such as the Odawa, totally dominated European Americans in their large region. In other areas,

European Americans were dominant. Looking at the Oregon Country, historian Gray H. Whaley asserts there was no middle ground between Native Americans and incoming European Americans. By the 1850s, he states, "Conceptions of a single nation-state, citizenship, and absolute land title" were too well established by Americans to include Native peoples. See Whaley, *Oregon and the Collapse of* Illahee: *U.S. Empire and the Transformation of an Indigenous World, 1792–1859* (Chapel Hill: University of North Carolina Press, 2010), 11. Similarly, in his depiction of the Comanche Empire, Hämäläinen finds little in the way of a middle ground, as the Comanche almost completely dominated matters.

17. Stephen Warren, *The Shawnees and Their Neighbors, 1795–1870* (Urbana: University of Illinois Press, 2005); and Warren, *The Worlds the Shawnee Made: Migration and Violence in Early America* (Chapel Hill: University of North Carolina Press, 2014). In their very wide-ranging travels, Shawnees may not have been representative of most Native American groups, though many other groups moved to new areas under pressure from European American colonists.
18. Alexis de Tocqueville, *Democracy in America,* ed. Richard D. Heffner (New York: Mentor, 1956), 216.
19. For a succinct discussion of American exceptionalism in the writing of early American history, see Alan Taylor, *American Colonies: The Settling of North America* (New York: Penguin Books, 2001), x–xi.
20. Mansel G. Blackford, *Politics of Business in California* (Columbus: Ohio State University Press, 1977).
21. Mansel G. Blackford, *The Lost Dream: Businessmen and City Planning on the Pacific Coast, 1890–1920* (Columbus: Ohio State University Press, 1993); Blackford, *Fragile Paradise: The Impact of Tourism on Maui, 1959–2000* (Lawrence: University Press of Kansas, 2001); Blackford, *Pathways to the Present: U.S. Development and Its Consequences in the Pacific* (Honolulu: University of Hawai'i Press, 2007); and Blackford, *Columbus, Ohio: Two Centuries of Business and Environmental Change* (Columbus: Ohio State University Press, 2016).
22. See Mansel G. Blackford, *Pioneering a Modern Small Business: Wakefield Seafoods and the Alaskan Frontier* (Greenwich, CT: Johnson Associates, 1979); and Blackford, *Making Seafood Sustainable: American Experiences in Global Perspective* (Philadelphia: University of Pennsylvania Press, 2012).
23. In 1999, historians Christine Meisner Rosen and Christopher Sellers observed, "Business history has never paid much attention to the environment," and in fact has given "little attention to the effects of resource extraction and use on plants, animals, land, air, or water, much less entire ecosystems and climate." See Christine Meisner Rosen and Christopher C. Sellers, "The Nature of the Firm: Towards an Ecocultural History of Business," *Business History Review* 73, no. 4 (Winter 1999):

577–600, esp. 577. That situation has begun to change. Other articles in this issue of *Business History Review* examine relationships between business and the environment, as do those in *Enterprise and Society* 8, no. 8 (June 2007). See also Rosen, "The Business-Environment Connection," *Environmental History* 10, no. 1 (January 2005): 77–79. For a collection of thirteen essays on this topic, see Hartmut Berghoff and Adam Rome, eds., *Green Capitalism? Business and the Environment in the Twentieth Century* (Philadelphia: University of Pennsylvania Press, 2017). Historians of capitalism, too, have dealt with relationships between business development and environmental changes. See, for example, Sven Beckert, *Empire of Cotton: A Global History* (London: Penguin, 2014); and Bartow J. Elmore, *Citizen Coke: The Making of Coca-Cola Capitalism* (New York: W. W. Norton, 2015).

CHAPTER 1: VIEWING LAND IN THE OHIO COUNTRY

1. Margaret Van Horn Dwight, *A Journey to Ohio in 1810*, ed. Max Farrand (Lincoln: University of Nebraska Press, 1991), 34, 47.
2. Mansel G. Blackford, *The Rise of Modern Business: Great Britain, the United States, Germany, Japan, and China*, 3rd ed. (Chapel Hill: University of North Carolina Press, 2008), 17.
3. On land shortages, see David Danbom, *Born in the Country: A History of Rural America*, 3rd ed. (Baltimore: Johns Hopkins University Press, 2017), 38–39, 48, 51–53. Writing about the Midwest, historian Jon Lauck observes, "Farmers were proud to own their own plots of land, which was rare in the Old World." The Midwest, he notes, "saw a marriage of fertile valleys and the ideology of republican labor and a bounteous progeny." Jon K. Lauck, *The Good Country: A History of the American Midwest, 1800–1900* (Norman: University of Oklahoma Press, 2022), 35.
4. William Cronon, *Changes in the Land: Indians, Colonists, and the Ecology of New England* (New York: Hill and Wang, 1983), 12. Cronon called his study "an ecological history," by which he meant "a history which extends its boundaries beyond human institutions . . . to the natural ecosystems which provide context for those institutions" (xv). While critiqued by recent scholars in several ways, Cronon's work remains valuable as a starting point in understanding how European American settlers changed their environments in North America.
5. Shepard Krech III, *The Ecological Indian: Myth and History* (New York: W. W. Norton, 1999); and Paul A. Delcourt and Hazel R. Delcourt, *Prehistoric Native Americans and Ecological Change: Human Ecosystems in Eastern North America since the Pleistocene* (New York: Cambridge University Press, 2004).
6. Joseph A. Gingerich, "The True Pioneers: Native Americans in Ohio," in *Settling Ohio: First Peoples and Beyond*, ed. Timothy G. Anderson and Brian Schoen (Athens: Ohio University Press, 2023), 13.

7. Jennifer Raff, *Origin: A Genetic History of the Americas* (New York: Twelve, 2022), xviii, xxix. See also Pekka Hämäläinen, *Indigenous Continent: The Epic Contest for North America* (New York: Liveright, 2022), 3–10.
8. Gingerich, "True Pioneers," 17–18.
9. Gingerich, 21. About 4,000–3,000 years ago, Native people in the Ohio Country developed the Eastern Agricultural Complex of domesticated plants: squashes, sunflower, amaranth, sumpweed, maygrass, little barley, and erect knotweed.
10. On developments in Ohio and the Midwest, see James H. O'Donnell III, *Ohio's First Peoples* (Athens: Ohio University Press, 2004), 14–27. For more detail, see Bradley T. Lepper, *Ohio Archaeology* (Wilmington, OH: Orange Frazer, 2005); and George R. Milner, *The Moundbuilders: Ancient Peoples of Eastern North America* (London: Thames and Hudson, 2004).
11. In mid-2022, a new exhibit on people of the Hopewell culture at the Ohio History Connection in Columbus, curated with the involvement of Native leaders, noted: "What these people called themselves, we don't know. Archaeologists use the term Hopewell culture. . . . Culture is used because they weren't a tribe or nation, but rather people who shared a number of things in common, such as earthwork building, making ceremonial objects from unusual raw materials, and burying their dead in particular ways." Author's observation, May 6, 2022. See also *Echoes Magazine* 61 (May–June 2022), 6–7, 46–47.
12. On Fort Ancient people and their possible ties to the later Shawnee and others, see Stephen Warren, *The Worlds the Shawnees Made: Migration and Violence in Early America* (Chapel Hill: University of North Carolina Press, 2014), 12–56. Warren concludes that the Fort Ancient people and some postcontact Native American groups shared many aspects of their material cultures and lifestyles, but he observes that direct linkages between the groups of people are missing.
13. John Mack Faragher, *Sugar Creek: Life on the Illinois Prairie* (New Haven, CT: Yale University Press, 1986), 11–12. For more detail on forest resources available in the Midwest, see Susan Sleeper-Smith, *Indigenous Prosperity and American Conquest: Indian Women of the Ohio River Valley, 1690–1792* (Chapel Hill: University of North Carolina Press, 2018), 13–66.
14. As quoted in Hämäläinen, *Indigenous Continent,* 242.
15. As quoted in Michael N. McConnell, *A Country Between: The Upper Ohio Valley and Its Peoples, 1724–1774* (Lincoln: University of Nebraska Press, 1992), 262.
16. On Tecumseh, see R. David Edmunds, *Tecumseh and the Quest for Indian Leadership* (New York: Longman, 1984); and John Sugden, *Tecumseh: A Life* (New York: Owl Books, 1997).
17. *Black Hawk: An Autobiography,* ed. Donald Jackson (Urbana: University of Illinois Press, 1964), 99.

18. William Hogeland, *Autumn of the Black Snake: The Creation of the U.S. Army and the Invasion That Opened the West* (New York: Farrar, Straus and Giroux, 2017); and Mary Stockwell, *Unlikely General: "Mad" Anthony Wayne and the Battle for America* (New Haven, CT: Yale University Press, 2018). On the 1795 treaty, see Barbara Alice Mann, "The Greenville Treaty of 1795: Pen-and-Ink Witchcraft in the Struggle for the Old Northwest," in *Enduring Legacies: Native American Treaties and Contemporary Controversies,* ed. Bruce Elliott Johansen (Westport, CT: Praeger, 2004), 135–201.
19. As quoted in Rob Harper, *Unsettling the West: Violence and State Building in the Ohio Valley* (Philadelphia: University of Pennsylvania Press, 2018), 9–10.
20. William Dean Howells, *Stories of Ohio* (New York: American Book, 1897), 15.
21. Faragher, *Sugar Creek,* 16.
22. Cronon, *Changes in the Land,* 43–48; and Sleeper-Smith, *Indigenous Prosperity,* 27–28.
23. Sleeper-Smith, *Indigenous Prosperity,* 28–31. On corn and the three sisters, see also Hämäläinen, *Indigenous Continent,* 12–14.
24. Robert Leslie Jones, *History of Agriculture in Ohio to 1880* (Kent, OH: Kent State University Press, 1983), 10–11. As early as the 1600s, invading European Americans used scorched-earth policies against Native Americans in Virginia, burning their fields of corn and their food supplies. See also Hämäläinen, *Indigenous Continent,* 64, 315–16.
25. David Andrew Nichols, *Peoples of the Inland Sea: Native Americans and Newcomers in the Great Lakes Region, 1600–1870* (Athens: Ohio University Press, 2018), 33.
26. Sleeper-Smith, *Indigenous Prosperity,* 4–5, 61, 123–27, 134, 138–40, 163.
27. McConnell, *A Country Between,* 213–23, esp. 217.
28. On this question, see also William H. Hildreth, "Travel Literature of the Ohio River Valley (1794–1832)" (PhD diss., Ohio State University, 1944), ii, 148. On frontier travel literature, see Mary Louise Pratt, *Imperial Eyes: Travel Writing and Transculturation,* 2nd ed. (New York: Routledge, 2008). A valuable question is, To what degree were European American observers affected in their writing by the Native Americans they encountered? Most of those coming into the Ohio Country took notions of land with them (pragmatic, romantic, capitalistic) and imposed those ideas on what they saw, remaining relatively unaffected by Native groups and their ideas. Of the European Americans coming into the Ohio Country discussed in this study, only Christopher Gist and Nicholas Cresswell seem to have been influenced in their ideas by contact with Native people.
29. Kevin F. Kern and Gregory S. Wilson, *Ohio: A History of the Buckeye State* (Chichester, UK: Wiley-Blackwell, 2014), 151. See also Adam R. Nelson, "Public Education in the Old Northwest: Legacies of Ohio's First Land Grant," in Anderson and Schoen, *Settling Ohio,* 219–36. Nelson

concludes, "Schools in this period [years before the Civil War] were still mostly local, private, unregulated, and, consequently, very uneven in their quality" (230).

30. On Gist's life, see *Christopher Gist's Journals with Historical, Geographic, and Ethnological Notes and Biographies of His Contemporaries,* ed. William Darlington (Pittsburgh: J. R. Weldon, 1893; repr., London: Forgotten Books, 2012), 88–89; and McConnell, *A Country Between,* 90. For a biography, see Kenneth P. Bailey, *Christopher Gist: Colonial Frontiersman, Explorer, and Indian Agent* (Hamden, CT: Archon Books, 1976). On Braddock's defeat, see David L. Preston, *Braddock's Defeat: The Battle of the Monongahela and the Road to Revolution* (Oxford: Oxford University Press, 2015).
31. *Gist's Journals,* 42, 34.
32. Michael A. McDonnell, *Masters of Empire: Great Lakes Indians and the Making of America* (New York: Hill and Wang, 2015), 152–57. On Pickawillany, see Cameron Shriver, "Situating Settlement in Ohio: The Eighteenth Century from Local and Atlantic Perspectives," in Anderson and Schoen, *Settling Ohio,* 40, 49.
33. *Gist's Journals,* 38–39, 41, 44.
34. On George Croghan, see Alfred A. Cave, "George Croghan and the Emergence of British Influence on the Ohio Frontier," in *Builders of Ohio: A Biographical History,* ed. Warren Van Tine and Michael Pierce (Columbus: Ohio State University Press, 2003), 1–13.
35. As quoted in Patrick Spero, *Frontier Rebels: The Fight for Independence in the American West, 1765–1776* (New York: W. W. Norton, 2018), 165–66.
36. *Gist's Journals,* 57–58.
37. *The Journal of Nicholas Cresswell, 1774–1777* (New York: Dial, 1924; repr., Port Washington, NY: Kennikat, 1968), 88; citations derived from 1968 edition. On Cresswell, see Harper, *Unsettling the West,* 11, 68.
38. Mark V. Barrow Jr., *Nature's Ghosts: Confronting Extinction from the Age of Jefferson to the Age of Ecology* (Chicago: University of Chicago Press, 2009), 16–19, 28–29. For a succinct look at the character of Thomas Jefferson, see Gordon S. Wood, *Empire of Liberty: A History of the Early Republic, 1789–1815* (Oxford: Oxford University Press, 2009), 277–78.
39. *Journal of Cresswell,* 65, 71.
40. *Journal of Cresswell,* v–viii, 1, 276.
41. *Journal of Cresswell,* 68, 76, 81, 72, 84.
42. Stockwell, *Unlikely General,* 182.
43. "Plowshares and Pruning Hooks for the Miami and Potawatomi: The Journal of Gerald T. Hopkins, 1804," ed. Joseph E. Walker, *Ohio History* 88, no. 4 (Autumn 1979): 361–407, esp. 376.
44. "Touring Ohio in 1811: The Journal of Charity Rotch," ed. Ethel Conrad, *Ohio History* 99 (Summer–Autumn 1990): 135–65, esp. 149, 156.
45. "Nine Letters of Nathaniel Dike on the Western Country, 1816–1818," ed. Dwight L. Smith, *Ohio History* 67 (July 1958): 189–220, esp. 211.

46. *Journal of Cresswell,* 92–93.
47. *Journal of Cresswell,* 106, 108.
48. *Journal of Cresswell,* 117, 120, 122.
49. Francis Baily, *Journal of a Tour in Unsettled Parts of North America in 1796 and 1797* (London: Baily Brothers, 1856; repr., London: Forgotten Books, 2015), 1–5, 49, 152, 159, 166, 186, 202.
50. Baily, *Journal,* 192–93, 211–13, 230.
51. On squatters, see Jessica Choppin Roney, "Ohio, the Northwest Ordinance, and the Constitutional Foundation of the United States," in Anderson and Schoen, *Settling Ohio,* 89–90.
52. William H. Goetzmann, "The West and the American Age of Exploration," *Arizona and the West* 2, no. 3 (Autumn 1960): 265–78, discusses rationalism and romanticism in the thoughts of Americans about the West. For more detail, see Goetzmann, *Exploration and Empire: The Explorer and the Scientist in the Winning of the American West* (New York: W. W. Norton, 1966), 3–35.
53. Baily, *Journal,* 144, 126, 178–82, 187. On Long Reach, see Allan W. Eckert, *That Dark and Bloody River: Chronicles of the Ohio River Valley* (New York: Bantam Books, 1995), 44, 330.
54. On the founding and early years of Marietta, see David McCullough, *The Pioneers: The Heroic Story of the Settlers Who Brought the American Ideal West* (New York: Simon and Schuster, 2019). See also Andrew R. L. Cayton and Paula R. Riggs, *City into Town: The City of Marietta, Ohio, 1788–1988* (Marietta, OH: Marietta College, 1991).
55. *Journal and Letters of Col. John May, of Boston: Relative to Two Journeys to the Ohio Country in 1788 and '89; with a Biographical Sketch by Rev. Richard S. Edes* (Cincinnati, OH: Robert Clarke for the Historical and Philosophical Society of Ohio, 1873: repr., Leopold Classic Library, 2016), 91, 96, 136.
56. As quoted in Howells, *Stories of Ohio,* 137.
57. Howells, 138.
58. Mildred Covey Fry, "Women on the Ohio Frontier: The Marietta Area," *Ohio History* 90, no. 1 (Winter 1981): 54–73, esp. 58. This article deals with women in early Marietta. A disclaimer: Fry began work on this essay as a research paper for a class I taught on the history of the American West at the Ohio State University in the early 1980s. For discussions of mortality in early rural America, see Danbom, *Born in the Country,* 26–29, 33.
59. Leo Marx, *The Machine in the Garden: Technology and the Pastoral Ideal in America* (Oxford: Oxford University Press, 1964), 3, 23.
60. On this enduring trope, see William Barillas, *The Midwestern Pastoral: Place and Landscape in Literature of the American Heartland* (Athens: Ohio University Press, 2006). For an examination of the realities of the diversity, complexity, and heterogeneity of the Midwest, state by state, see the essays by thirteen scholars in James H. Madison, ed., *Heartland:*

Comparative Histories of Midwestern States (Bloomington: Indiana University Press, 1988).

61. Peter G. Boag, *Environment and Experience: Settlement Culture in Nineteenth-Century Oregon* (Berkeley: University of California Press, 1992), 26–27.
62. Baily, *Journal*, 178.
63. Jones, *Agriculture in Ohio*, 24. William Cronon explains that in New England, "hickories, maples, ashes, and beeches generally produced a rich black humus beneath their fallen leaves" and were especially prized by settlers "as indicators of prime agricultural lands." Oaks and chestnuts suggested "thinner soils." Conifers grew in even less desirable "acidic and often sandy soils." Cronon, *Changes in the Land*, 115. For a discussion of the preference most settlers had for the settlement of wooded areas over prairies, see Boag, *Environment*, 31–34; and McCullough, *Pioneers*, 17, 46, 58.
64. Cronon, *Changes in the Land*, 28.
65. Baily, *Journal*, 160.
66. Deborah Fleming, *Resurrection of the Wild: Meditations on Ohio's Natural Landscape* (Kent OH: Kent State University Press, 2019), 11.
67. Baily, *Journal*, 162. On how Americans viewed Indian mounds, see Steven Conn, *History's Shadow: Native Americans and Historical Consciousness in the Nineteenth Century* (Chicago: University of Chicago Press, 2004). For more detail, see Robert Silverberg, *Mound Builders of Ancient America: The Archaeology of a Myth* (Greenwich, CT: New York Graphic Society, 1968). Historian Alicia Puglionesi observed in 2022 that European American settlers "nurtured the widespread belief that North American earthworks were built by an ancient lost civilization. The more science could deduce about this vanished empire, the weaker the argument for Native land rights in the present day." Alicia Puglionesi, *In Whose Ruins: Power, Possession, and the Landscapes of American Empire* (New York: Scribner, 2022), 36. For what seeing the Newark Earthworks meant to one tribal leader, Chief Glenna J. Wallace of the Eastern Shawnee, see Glenna J. Wallace, "Afterword: History Versus Legacy" in Anderson and Schoen, *Settling Ohio*, 242–54. Upon remembering first viewing the earthworks, then in use as a golf course, in 2007, Wallace wrote, "The trip changed my life." Her emotions ran "from pride, to questions, to bewilderment, to anger." She concluded, "I felt as if I had been violated" (250).
68. Thomas Ashe, *Travels in America, Performed in 1806, for the Purpose of Exploring the Rivers Alleghany, Monongahela, Ohio, and Mississippi* [. . .] (London: E. M. Blunt, 1808), preface. Ashe traveled by flatboat down the Ohio River by Marietta and Gallipolis to Maysville and Cincinnati and beyond. He recorded his impressions as a series of letters. Letters 8–22 are about Ohio. William Hildreth finds Ashe's account particularly untrustworthy. See Hildreth, "Travel Literature," 78–82.

69. Howells, *Stories of Ohio,* 3.
70. There is an extensive scholarly literature on Native Americans and their conflicts with European Americans in Ohio. Good places to start are Colin G. Calloway, *The Shawnees and the War for America* (New York: Penguin, 2007); and R. Douglas Hurt, *The Indian Frontier, 1763–1846* (Albuquerque: University of New Mexico Press, 2002).
71. Baily, *Journal,* 220.
72. Baily, 217.
73. Claude-François de Lezay-Marnésia, *Letters Written from the Banks of the Ohio,* ed. Benjamin Hoffmann, trans. Alan J. Singerman (University Park: Pennsylvania State University Press, 2017), 12–21, 25, 28, 158–63.
74. Lezay-Marnésia, *Letters,* 66, 68, 70–71, 73. That Native Americans ever fully accepted any European American, even the French king, as their "father," is doubtful.
75. Lezay-Marnésia, 76.
76. As quoted in Victoria Johnson, *American Eden: David Hosack, Botany, and Medicine in the Garden of the Early Republic* (New York: W. W. Norton, 2018), 121. For a recent look at André Michaux, see Shaun Assael, "The Forgotten French Scientist Who Courted Thomas Jefferson—and Got Pulled into Scandal," *Smithsonian* 52 (July–August, 2021), 64–73.
77. Kern and Wilson, *Ohio,* 112.
78. Morris Birkbeck, *Notes on a Journey in America from the Coast of Virginia to the Territory of Illinois* (London: Severn, 1817; Ann Arbor, MI: University Microfilms, 1966), 50.
79. John Melish, *Travels through the United States of America in the Years 1806 & 1807, and 1809, 1810, & 1811* [. . .] (Philadelphia: Melish, 1818; London: Forgotten Books, 2012), 345–46; citation derived from 2012 edition.
80. Melish, *Travels,* 416–18, 436.
81. Birkbeck, *Notes,* 111.
82. Howells, *Stories of Ohio,* 127.
83. Birkbeck, *Notes,* 126.
84. Conrad Richter, *The Trees* (New York: Alfred Knopf, 1940), 6–7. See also his *The Fields* (New York: Alfred Knopf, 1946), and *The Town* (New York: Alfred Knopf, 1951).
85. Howells, *Stories of Ohio,* 16.
86. Annie Proulx, *Barkskins: A Novel* (New York: Scribner, 2016), 3. Similarly, in her romance set in Upstate New York around 1800, Sara Donati writes, "The forest was constant and endless and patient above all things." Donati, *Lake in the Clouds* (New York: Bantam Books, 2002), 85. Likewise, writing about New England in the late 1600s, novelist Leah Angstman observes in her *Out Front the Following Sea* (Raleigh, NC: Regal, 2022), 87, "It's close to the trees. Absolutely do not go into the woods. . . . The devil be in the forest." Finally, writing about his great-great-grandfather's trip into eastern Ohio from Pennsylvania in the early 1800s, William Maxwell resorted to the well-known trope in

his 1985 family history: "The trees frequently had trunks five or six feet thick, and almost no sunlight penetrated the dense foliage. . . . The virgin forest was gloomy and oppressively silent." Maxwell, *Ancestors: A Family History* (Boston: Nonpareil Books, 1985), 27.

87. Melish, *Travels,* 336, 347.
88. Birkbeck, *Notes,* 89, 93.
89. Melish, *Travels,* 356.
90. Cronon, *Changes in the Land,* 5.
91. Jones, *Agriculture in Ohio,* 22–23.
92. Birkbeck, *Notes,* 69.
93. Melish, *Travels,* 420.
94. Melish, 452.
95. R. Douglas Hurt, *The Ohio Frontier: Crucible of the Old Northwest, 1720–1830* (Bloomington: Indiana University Press, 1998), 269–72.
96. Daniel Walker Howe, *What Hath God Wrought: The Transformation of America, 1815–1848* (Oxford: Oxford University Press, 2007), 37.
97. *Journal of Cresswell,* 195–97.
98. As quoted in Lentz, "Ohio's Farming Roots," *Worthington News,* April 11, 2019.
99. As quoted in McCullough, *Pioneers,* 232.
100. Howells, *Stories of Ohio,* 127.
101. Roy Harvey Pearce, *Savagism and Civilization: A Study of the Indian and the American Mind* (Berkeley: University of California Press, 1988). See also Wood, *Empire of Liberty,* 385–87, 394–99.
102. Smith, "Letters of Nathaniel Dike," 217, 219.
103. On New Englanders' sense of abundance, see Cronon, *Changes in the Land,* 22–25.
104. Barrow, *Nature's Ghosts,* 85–86.
105. Ned Blackhawk, *The Rediscovery of America: Native Peoples and the Unmaking of U.S. History* (New Haven, CT: Yale University Press, 2023), 63.

CHAPTER 2: EUROPEAN AMERICANS IN THE OHIO COUNTRY

1. John Allen Trimble, "Reminiscences," n.d., manuscript collection 249, box 7, John Allen Trimble Papers, Ohio History Connection, Columbus, OH.
2. In looking at early Euro-American farming in Ohio, this study contributes to a revitalization of midwestern history that has taken place since the late 1980s. Geographers, historians, and other scholars have been reassessing the place of the Midwest in American history, stressing the region's importance to the development of the United States. On midwestern history as an important but understudied field, see Andrew R. L. Cayton and Susan E. Gray, eds., *The Identity of the American Midwest: Essays on Regional History* (Bloomington: Indiana University

Press, 2001), a collection of eleven essays. For a statement and survey of the historiography, see Jon K. Lauck, *The Lost Region: Toward a Revival of Midwestern History* (Iowa City: University of Iowa Press, 2012). Now-classic studies include Andrew R. L. Cayton and Peter S. Onuf, *The Midwest and the Nation: Rethinking the History of an American Region* (Bloomington, IN: Indiana University Press, 1990); and James R. Shortridge, *The Middle West: Its Meaning in American Culture* (Lawrence: University Press of Kansas, 1989). See also Kristin L. Hoganson, *The Heartland: An American History* (New York City: Penguin, 2019); Jon K. Lauck, *From Warm Center to Ragged Edge: The Erosion of Midwestern Literary and Historical Regionalism, 1920–1965* (Iowa City: University of Iowa Press, 2017); and Jon K. Lauck, Gleaves Whitney, and Joseph Hogan, eds., *Finding a New Midwestern History* (Lincoln: University of Nebraska Press, 2018), a collection of twenty-one essays.

3. In 2017, historian Harry S. Stout wrote the following of the 1820 land law: "The consequences had no equivalency in the Old World as the dispersal of wealth through the Public Land Survey encouraged the growth of a society of landowners without precedent." Stout, *American Aristocrats: A Family, a Fortune, and the Making of American Capitalism* (New York: Basic Books, 2017), 92. See also Hurt, *The Ohio Frontier: Crucible of the Old Northwest, 1720–1830* (Bloomington: Indiana University Press, 1998), 345–46. The 1820 legislation did require, however, that all land sales be made for cash. Unlike with the 1804 law, no sales were allowed on credit, a response to a national depression of 1819, which had been caused in part by overly exuberant land sales made on credit. For more detail, see Malcolm J. Rohrbough, *The Land Office Business: The Settlement and Administration of American Public Lands, 1789–1837* (New York: Oxford University Press, 1968), 141–44, 150–51, 205.
4. There were about twenty-nine million acres in Ohio. Paul W. Gates, *History of Public Land Development* (Washington DC: Government Printing Office, 1968), is the classic work on the history of the public domain of the United States. The origins of the public domain date to March 1, 1784, "when Congress accepted Virginia's cession of territory northwest of the Ohio [River]." Robert Middlekauff, *The Glorious Cause: The American Revolution, 1763–1789*, 2nd ed., (Oxford: Oxford University Press, 2005), 69. See James R. Skillen, *The Nation's Largest Landlord: The Bureau of Land Management in the American West* (Lawrence: University Press of Kansas, 2008), for twentieth-century developments. See also Erika Allen Wolters and Brent S. Steele, eds., *The Environmental Politics and Policy of Western Public Lands* (Corvallis: Oregon State University Press, 2020), a collection of sixteen essays by scholars and practitioners; and Charles Davis, ed., *Western Public Lands and Environmental Politics*, 2nd ed. (Boulder, CO: Westview Press, 2001).
5. Michael N. McConnell, *A Country Between: The Upper Ohio Valley and Its Peoples, 1724–1774* (Lincoln: University of Nebraska Press, 1992), 158.

6. Sara Dant, *Losing Eden: An Environmental History of the American West* (London: Wiley-Blackwell, 2016), 45–47.
7. As quoted in Sara Dant, *Losing Eden,* 1.
8. See Reginald Horsman, "Westward to Ohio: Crossing the Mountains, 1788–1810," *Timeline* 33 (January/March 2016): 3–15.
9. Horsman, "Westward to Ohio," 15. Some 20,000 European Americans descended the Ohio River in 1789; about 1,500 were killed in Indian attacks between 1782 and 1789. See Allan W. Eckert, *That Dark and Bloody River: Chronicles of the Ohio River Valley* (New York: Bantam Books, 1995), 507.
10. On the Oregon Trail, see David Dary, *The Oregon Trail: An American Saga* (Oxford: Oxford University Press, 2004); John Mack Faragher, *Women and Men on the Overland Trail* (New Haven, CT: Yale University Press, 1979); and John D. Unruh Jr., *The Plains Across: The Overland Emigrants and the Trans–Mississippi West, 1840–60* (Urbana: University of Illinois Press, 1979).
11. R. Douglas Hurt, *Agriculture in the Midwest, 1815–1900* (Lincoln: University of Nebraska Press, 2023), 47.
12. Kevin F. Kern and Gregory S. Wilson, *Ohio: A History of the Buckeye State* (Chichester, UK: Wiley-Blackwell, 2014), 18.
13. Robert Leslie Jones, *History of Agriculture in Ohio to 1880* (Kent, OH: Kent State University Press, 1983), 5.
14. Jones, *Agriculture in Ohio,* 11–13, esp. 11. For more detail, see the nineteen essays composing Michael B. Lafferty, *Ohio's Natural Heritage* (Columbus: Ohio Academy of Science, 1979).
15. Christopher R. Laingen, "The Agrarian Midwest: A Geographical Analysis," in Lauck, Whitney, and Hogan, *Finding a New Midwestern History,* 143–60, esp. 151.
16. For an introduction to the history of agriculture in Ohio, see Robert Leslie Jones, "Ohio Agriculture in History," *Ohio Historical Quarterly* 65, no. 3 (July 1956): 229–58.
17. Hurt, *Agriculture in the Midwest,* 95–136, esp. 95–96. A photograph of the Carey plow is on p. 97.
18. Lee Soltow, "Inequality amidst Abundance: Land Ownership in Early Nineteenth Century Ohio," *Ohio History* 88, no. 2 (Spring 1979): 133–51, esp. 136, 143.
19. See Hurt, *Ohio Frontier,* 175. On the actions of one large landowner, see Jonathan J. Bean, "Marketing 'the Great American Commodity': Nathaniel Massie and Land Speculation on the Ohio Frontier, 1783–1813," *Ohio History* 103 (Summer–Autumn 1994): 152–69. A disclaimer: Bean received his doctorate in history under my direction. More generally on the roles that land speculators played in the opening of frontiers to European Americans, see Michael A. Blaakman, *Speculation Nation: Land Mania in the Revolutionary American Republic* (Philadelphia: University of Pennsylvania Press, 2023). In making land available to European

American settlers in smaller parcels than those sold by the federal government and at reasonable prices, speculators encouraged the westward movement of many. On the negative side, they sometimes corrupted politicians to secure land, and their actions helped dispossess Native Americans of their lands.

20. As quoted in Alfred Byron Sears, *Thomas Worthington: Father of Ohio Statehood* (Columbus: Ohio State University Press, 1958), 10–13.
21. Sears, *Worthington,* 14–18, 24.
22. Sears, 19–22, esp. 22.
23. Sears, 26–28.
24. Sears, 28–33. For a biography of another large landowner, Richard Clough Anderson, and his descendants, see Stout, *American Aristocrats.* Anderson speculated in land, especially in the Virginia Military Tract. For historian Stout, "the protagonist in this story is land and the theme is anxiety over acquiring and holding wealth that land represents" (xi).
25. Mary Howitt, *Our Cousins in Ohio* (New York: Collins, 1849; repr., London: Forgotten Books, 2015), 105, 131.
26. George Dell, *The Earth Abideth* (Columbus: Ohio State University Press, 1986), 19, 38, 281.
27. Soltow, "Inequality Amidst Abundance," 135, 143.
28. Mansel G. Blackford, *A History of Small Business in America* (Chapel Hill: University of North Carolina Press, 2003), 21–22, 64.
29. Clement L. Martzolff, "Reminiscences of a Pioneer," *Ohio Archaeological and Historical Society Publications* 19, nos. 1–2 (January–April 1910): 190–227, esp. 190–91.
30. Martzolff, "Reminiscences," 199, 215.
31. Martzolff, 220, 224, 226.
32. William Dean Howells, *Stories of Ohio* (New York: American Book, 1897), 124.
33. William Cooper Howells, *Recollections of Life in Ohio, from 1813 to 1840* (Cincinnati, OH: Robert Clarke, 1895; repr., Ann Arbor: University of Michigan Library, 2016), 14, 47.
34. Howells, 59, 78, 96.
35. Howells, 110.
36. See William Cronon, *Changes in the Land: Indians, Colonists, and the Ecology of New England* (New York: Hill and Wang, 2003), 116–17. Girdling trees had advantages over felling them, at least in the short term. Above all, it took less labor to simply girdle trees. Then, too, the deadened, rotting trees returned some nutrients to the soil. There were problems, however, resulting from girdling; the process wasted wood, ran the risk of accidents from falling tree limbs, and did not completely remove trees (roots had to be dug out later).
37. Howells, *Recollections,* 159, 161, 188.
38. Stephane Elise Booth, *Buckeye Women: The History of Ohio's Daughters* (Athens: Ohio University Press, 2001), 1–18, esp. 17–18.

39. Emily Foster, ed., *American Grit: A Woman's Letters from the Ohio Frontier* (Lexington: University Press of Kentucky, 2002), 27, 37, 60.
40. Foster, *American Grit,* 160–61.
41. Foster, 40, 47, 55, 63–65, 81, 97, 106–107, 122, 142, 151, 184, 293, 309. See also Bayly Ellen Marks, ed., "Correspondence of Anna Briggs Bentley from Columbiana County, 1826," *Ohio History* 78 (1969): 38–45.
42. Harry N. Scheiber, *Ohio Canal Era: A Case Study of Government and the Economy, 1820–1861* (Athens: Ohio University Press, 1968), xvii.
43. Frank P. Goodwin, "Building a Commercial System," *Ohio Archaeological and Historical Society Publications* 16, no. 3 (July 1907): 316–39. There was also some upstream trade carried by keelboats and barges pulled by teams of men upriver against the current.
44. Daniel Kaufman, *Farm Ledger,* manuscript collection 737, box 1, John Kaufman Papers, Ohio History Connection, Columbus, OH.
45. For an introduction to a vast literature on how American farmers combined market and nonmarket activities, see Richard Lyman Bushman, "Markets and Composite Farms in Early America," *William and Mary Quarterly* 55, no. 3 (July 1998): 351–74.
46. Daniel Walker Howe, *What Hath God Wrought: The Transformation of America, 1815–1848* (Oxford: Oxford University Press, 2007), 33–35, 303.
47. The scholarly literature on the topic of the relationship among farming, markets, and republicanism is immense. For a succinct examination of this issue, see James M. McPherson, *Battle Cry of Freedom: The Civil War Era, 1848–1865* (Oxford: Oxford University Press, 1988), 22–26.
48. Gregory S. Rose, "American and European Immigrant Groups in the Midwest by the Mid-Nineteenth Century," in Lauck, Whitney, and Hogan, *Finding a New Midwestern History,* 73–95, esp. 76.
49. As quoted in David McCullough, *Pioneers: The Heroic Story of the Settlers Who Brought the American Ideal West* (New York: Simon and Schuster, 2019), 126–27.
50. Richard Bushman, *The American Farmer in the Eighteenth Century: A Social and Cultural History* (New Haven, CT: Yale University Press, 2018), 11, 21, 121.
51. As quoted in Gleaves Whitney, "The Upper Midwest as the Second Promised Land," in Lauck, Whitney, and Hogan, *Finding a New Midwestern History,* 281–302, esp. 282.
52. Stephen Middleton, *The Black Laws: Race and the Legal Process in Early Ohio* (Athens: Ohio University Press, 2005), 3–60, 154–55, 258, esp. 3.
53. Middleton, *Black Laws,* 54.
54. There were positive elements in the treatment of African Americans. Some of the Black Laws were rarely enforced. Ohio courts often sided with African Americans, and many Ohioans resisted the kidnapping of African Americans to the South. See Jon K. Lauck, *The Good Country: A History of the Midwest, 1800–1900* (Norman: University of Oklahoma Press, 2022), 134–35, 139–43, 70.

55. Anna-Lisa Cox, *The Bone and Sinew of the Land: America's Forgotten Black Pioneers and the Struggle for Equality* (New York: PublicAffairs, 2018), xi–xvi, 3. See also Cox, "What If Manasseh Cutler Were Black? The History of the Diverse Pioneers Who Created Ohio," in *Settling Ohio: First Peoples and Beyond,* ed. Timothy G. Anderson and Brian Schoen (Athens: Ohio University Press, 2023), 186–201.
56. Cox, *Bone and Sinew,* 90.
57. Cox, 108. For a brief look at the enduring legacy of land to African Americans, see Natalie Baszile, "The Indelible Legacy of Land," *National Geographic* 239 (April 2021): 15–18.
58. As quoted in Andrew R. L. Cayton, *Ohio: The History of a People* (Columbus: Ohio State University Press, 2002), 303–304. For a valuable essay about Bromfield, see Deborah Fleming, *Resurrection of the Wild: Meditations on Ohio's Natural Landscape* (Kent, OH: Kent State University Press, 2019), 126–45. For biographies, see Stephen Heyman, *The Planter of Modern Life: Louis Bromfield and the Seeds of a Food Revolution* (New York: W. W. Norton, 2020), esp. 173–75; and Anneliese Abbott, *Malabar Farm: Louis Bromfield, Friends of the Land, and the Rise of Sustainable Agriculture* (Kent, OH: Kent State University Press, 2021).
59. John J. Horton, *The Jonathan Hale Farm: A Chronicle of the Cuyahoga Valley* (Cleveland OH: Western Reserve Historical Society, 1961), 40–43, 52.
60. As quoted in Horton, *Hale Farm,* 12.
61. Horton, 14.
62. Horton, 75, 79, 91, 95.
63. Geoff Cunfer, *On the Great Plains: Agriculture and the Environment* (College Station: Texas A&M University Press, 2005), 87.
64. On the importance of fruit to European American settlers in the Ohio Country, see William Kerrigan, *Johnny Appleseed and the American Orchard: A Cultural History* (Baltimore, MD: Johns Hopkins University Press, 2012).
65. Horton, *Hale Farm,* 119–31, 171–75.
66. Horton, 132–43, 153.
67. Horton, 88, 153, 176, 178.
68. Susan Sleeper-Smith, *Indigenous Prosperity and American Conquest: Indian Women of the Ohio River Valley, 1690–1792* (Chapel Hill: University of North Carolina Press, 2018), 94.
69. Howard E. Good, *Black Swamp Farm* (Columbus: Ohio State University Press, 1997), 2, 10, 13, 17, 19, 29, 62.
70. Good, *Black Swamp Farm,* 17.
71. Tracy Chevalier, *At the Edge of the Orchard* (New York: Viking, 2016), 15.
72. Good, *Black Swamp Farm,* 23, 27, 30–36.
73. Good, 35–36.
74. Timothy H. H. Thoresen, *River, Reaper, Rail: Agriculture and Identity in Ohio's Mad River Valley, 1795–1885* (Akron, OH: University of Akron Press, 2018), x, 1, 10, 20–21.

75. James E. Davis, "How Nature and Culture Shaped Early Settlement in the Midwest," in Lauck, Whitney, and Hogan, *Finding a New Midwestern History*, 25–38, esp. 30–31.
76. Richard W. Judd, *Common Lands, Common People: The Origins of Conservation in Northern New England* (Cambridge, MA: Harvard University Press, 1997); and Anthony Scott, *The Evolution of Resource Property Rights* (Oxford: Oxford University Press, 2008), 63–125.
77. As quoted in Alfred E. Lee, *History of the City of Columbus: Capital of Ohio* (New York: Munsell, 1892), vol. 1, 717–18.
78. Hurt, *Ohio Frontier*, 371.
79. Birkbeck, *Notes on a Journey in America from the Coast of Virginia to the Territory of Illinois* (London: Severn, 1817; Ann Arbor, MI: University Microfilms, 1966), 66.
80. As quoted in Hurt, *Ohio Frontier*, 271–72.
81. Walter Rumsey Marvin, "Columbus and the Railroads of Central Ohio before the Civil War" (PhD diss., Ohio State University, 1953), 38–39, 49, 137.
82. Jon C. Teaford, *Cities of the Heartland: The Rise and Fall of the Industrial Midwest* (Bloomington: Indiana University Press, 1993), 33–34.
83. Mary Stockwell, *The Other Trail of Tears: The Removal of the Ohio Indians* (Yardley, PA: Westholme, 2014).
84. Jones, *Agriculture in Ohio*, 49–213. See also David Danbom, *Born in the Country: A History of Rural America*, 3rd ed. (Baltimore: Johns Hopkins University Press, 2017), 5–6.
85. Wheeler McMillen, *Ohio Farm* (Columbus: Ohio State University Press, 1974), 10, 62.
86. McMillen, 12–13, 23–25, 55, 131, 194.
87. Hurt, *Agriculture in the Midwest*, 309.
88. John Mack Faragher, *Sugar Creek: Life on the Illinois Prairie* (New Haven, CT: Yale University Press, 1986), xv. Similarly, historian Danbom observes, "The foundation of rural America was the nuclear family." Each family member had important economic and social roles to play on the farm, including children from about age five or six. See Danbom, *Born in the Country*, 79.
89. John L. Shover, *First Majority—Last Minority: The Transforming of Rural Life in America* (DeKalb: Northern Illinois University Press, 1976), 58–81.
90. Lauck, *Good Country*, 3, 193.
91. Andrew R. L. Cayton, *The Frontier Republic: Ideology and Politics in the Ohio Country, 1780–1825* (Kent, OH: Kent State University Press, 1986), x.
92. Howells, *Stories of Ohio*, 19.
93. Native Americans did not disappear from the American scene. On the persistence and revitalization of Native American culture, see Philip J. Deloria, *Indians in Unexpected Places* (Lawrence: University Press of

Kansas, 2004); David Treuer, *The Heartbeat of Wounded Knee: Native America from 1890 to the Present* (New York: Riverhead Books, 2019); and Charles Wilkinson, *Blood Struggle: The Rise of Modern Indian Nations* (New York: W. W. Norton, 2005).

94. Andrew R. L. Cayton, *Ohio: The History of a People* (Columbus: Ohio State University Press, 2002), 16–17.
95. Lauck, *Good Country*, 48, 53.
96. Good, *Black Swamp Farm*, 17.
97. Display at the Ohio History Connection in Columbus, Ohio, April 4, 2018. A few plants believed to have been extirpated from Ohio were rediscovered growing in the northern reaches of the state in 2019: American cuckooflower, water marigold, Vasey's pondweed, and black-stemmed spleenwort. See *Columbus Dispatch*, January 10, 2020, C1.
98. See Howells, *Stories of Ohio*, 170; Carolyn V. Platt, *Creatures of Change: An Album of Ohio Animals* (Kent, OH: Kent State University Press, 1998), 12, 33–34, 68–69; and *Columbus Dispatch*, November 22, 2016, B6. The loss of wildlife was part of a national trend. There were perhaps 60 to 400 million beavers in North America in the early 1600s before most were trapped over the next three centuries. The loss of beavers and their dams left the land drier than before. See Leila Philip, *Beaverland: How One Weird Rodent Made America* (New York: Twelve, 2022).
99. *Columbus Dispatch*, September 5, 2016, A1.
100. Peter G. Boag, *Environment and Experience: Settlement Culture in Nineteenth-Century Oregon* (Berkeley: University of California Press, 1992), esp. 41–73.

CHAPTER 3: EUROPEAN AMERICANS IN THE OREGON COUNTRY

1. Osborne Russell, *Journal of a Trapper, 1834–1843*, ed. Aubrey L. Haines (Lincoln: University of Nebraska Press, 1967), 25–26, 44. Russell called the Lamar River valley the Secluded Valley.
2. John Mack Faragher, *Women and Men on the Overland Trail* (New Haven, CT: Yale University Press, 1979), 16, 189–90; and John D. Unruh Jr., *Plains Across: The Overland Emigrants and the Trans–Mississippi West, 1840–60* (Urbana: University of Illinois Press, 1979), 341–42.
3. William A. Bowen, *The Willamette Valley: Migration and Settlement on the Oregon Frontier* (Seattle: University of Washington Press, 1978), 6. See also Robert Bunting, *The Pacific Raincoast: Environment and Culture in an American Eden, 1778–1900* (Lawrence: University Press of Kansas, 1996). Bunting describes his history as "a book about how natural and human history have interacted to shape a region." At the center of his work is land. Bunting argues, "Land and its seemingly inexhaustible nature forms the heart of American history."
4. Carlos A. Schwantes, *The Pacific Northwest: An Interpretive History* (Lincoln: University of Nebraska Press, 1996), 6, 8 (the source of the

quotation). For a broad look at early western trade and settlement in the Pacific, including Oregon, see Stuart Banner, *Possessing the Pacific: Land, Settlers, and Indigenous People from Australia to Alaska* (Cambridge, MA: Harvard University Press, 2007). Banner observes, "In each of these colonies [throughout the Pacific], white settlers hoped to acquire land, but in each they also met indigenous people living on the land," which led to conflicts. "Colonial settlements thus gave rise to some basic legal questions" (1). This work serves as an excellent introduction to issues of settler colonialism in the Pacific Northwest in global perspective. More on settler colonialism generally and the environment globally, see the fifteen essays composing Tom Griffiths and Libby Robin, eds., *Ecology and Empire: Environmental History of Settler Societies* (Seattle: University of Washington Press, 1997).

5. Schwantes, *Pacific Northwest,* 10–11.
6. Gray H. Whaley, *Oregon and the Collapse of* Illahee: *U.S. Empire and the Transformation of an Indigenous World, 1792–1859* (Chapel Hill: University of North Carolina Press, 2010), 37.
7. Timothy Egan, *The Good Rain: Across Time and Terrain in the Pacific Northwest* (New York: Vintage Books, 1991).
8. Schwantes, *Pacific Northwest,* 19.
9. Linda Hogan, *People of the Whale* (New York: W. W. Norton, 2008). On the Makah, see Joshua L. Reid, *The Sea Is My Country: The Maritime World of the Makahs, an Indigenous Borderlands People* (New Haven, CT: Yale University Press, 2015).
10. Robert Boyd, ed., *Indians, Fire and the Land in the Pacific Northwest* (Corvallis: Oregon State University Press, 1999).
11. Bunting, *Pacific Raincoast,* 13–15, esp. 15.
12. Whaley, *Illahee,* 1–19, 34–35. See also Bunting, *Pacific Raincoast,* 17.
13. As quoted in Anne F. Hyde, *Empires, Nations, and Families: A New History of the North American West, 1800–1860* (Lincoln: University of Nebraska Press, 2011), 286.
14. Gordon S. Wood, *Empire of Liberty: A History of the Early Republic, 1789–1815* (Oxford: Oxford University Press, 2009), 357.
15. Among the many historical accounts of the Lewis and Clark expedition are Kris Fresonke and Mark Spence, eds., *Lewis & Clark: Legacies, Memories, and New Perspectives* (Berkeley: University of California Press, 2004), a collection of twelve essays; Donald Jackson, *Thomas Jefferson and the Stony Mountains: Exploring the West from Monticello* (Urbana: University of Illinois Press, 1981); and Douglas Seefeldt, Jeffrey L. Hantman, and Peter S. Onuf, eds., *Across the Continent: Jefferson, Lewis and Clark, and the Making of America* (Charlottesville: University of Virginia Press, 2005), a collection of six essays.
16. Schwantes, *Pacific Northwest,* 53.
17. *The Journals of Lewis and Clark,* ed. Bernard DeVoto (Cambridge, MA: Houghton Mifflin, 1953), lii. The West was far from American, however.

As historian Hämäläinen shows, most of North America remained an Indigenous continent well into the 1800s. In fact, Lewis and Clark were able to proceed up the Missouri River only with the permission of the Lakota Sioux, who controlled the middle reaches of the stream in the early 1800s. See Pekka Hämäläinen, *Indigenous Continent: The Epic Contest for North America* (New York: Liveright, 2022), 362.

18. *The Journals of Lewis and Clark,* ed. John Bakeless (New York: Mentor Books, 1964), 49, 128, 200, 298. See also Stephen E. Ambrose, *Undaunted Courage: Meriwether Lewis, Thomas Jefferson, and the Opening of the American West* (New York: Simon and Schuster, 1996), 205, 216, 385.
19. *Journals of Lewis and Clark,* 157, 182.
20. *Journals of Lewis and Clark,* 63.
21. On how Lewis and Clark and other explorers viewed the Pacific Northwest, see John Logan Allen, *Passage through the Garden: Lewis and Clark and the Image of the American Northwest* (Urbana: University of Illinois Press, 1975). Allen argues that Lewis and Clark took with them the long-established idea of a Northwest Passage but also the notion that the "West was a place of romance and mystery, where hopes and dreams and ambitions could come true" (xxv). He asserts that their discoveries changed forever how Americans viewed the West by offering "a more rational and objective interpretation of western land quality" (394).
22. James P. Ronda, *Lewis and Clark among the Indians* (Lincoln: University of Nebraska Press, 1984). Ronda praises the explorers as solid ethnographers, if not experienced ethnologists: "Fortunately, their cultural biases did not prevent them from asking the right ethnographic questions. Equally fortunate, they had the good sense to write down most Indian answers, including many that seemed bewildering at the time" (114).
23. *Journals of Lewis and Clark,* 238.
24. *Journals of Lewis and Clark,* 57, 85, 293. For more information on meetings between the Sioux, esp. the Lakota Sioux, and Lewis and Clark, see Hämäläinen, *Lakota America: A New History of Indigenous Power* (New Haven, CT: Yale University Press, 2019), 127–44.
25. Darrell M. Millner, "York of the Corps of Discovery: Interpretations of York's Character and His Role in the Lewis and Clark Expedition," *Oregon Historical Quarterly* 104 (Fall 2003): 302–33, esp. 328.
26. *Journals of Lewis and Clark,* 40, 128, 135.
27. Allen, *Passage through the Garden,* 363–64; Ambrose, *Undaunted Courage,* 397–99.
28. William Goetzmann, "The Mountain Man as Jacksonian Man," *American West* 15 (July/August 1978): 4–17.
29. A. B. Guthrie Jr., *The Big Sky* (Cleveland, OH: World, 1947), 65–66, 81, 84–87, 92, 133, 139–42, 158, 162–64, 177–78, 181, 196–210.
30. Guthrie, 108, 169, 385.
31. A. B. Guthrie Jr., *The Way West* (New York: William Sloane Associates, 1949), 51.

32. A. B. Guthrie Jr., *Fair Land, Fair Land* (Boston: Houghton Mifflin, 1982).
33. Russell, *Journal*, 4, 25, 57–58. Born in 1814, Osborne Russell grew up in Maine but ran away from home at the age of sixteen.
34. Russell, 7, 15, 19, 35–36, 43, 46, 103.
35. See Peter G. Boag, *Environment and Experience: Settlement Culture in Nineteenth-Century Oregon* (Berkeley: University of California Press, 1992), 27; Nathaniel Philbrick, *Sea of Glory: America's Voyage of Discovery; The U.S. Exploring Expedition, 1838–1842* (New York: Macmillan, 1982), 458–66; and Schwantes, *Pacific Northwest*, 116.
36. Ray Allen Billington and Martin Ridge, *Westward Expansion: A History of the American Frontier*, 5th ed. (New York: Macmillan, 1982), 458–66.
37. As quoted in Whaley, *Illahee*, 107.
38. Whaley, 108, 157.
39. Mary Kinney's account of her life, "Some Family History," a handwritten notebook in the author's possession; and "Mr. and Mrs. Robert Crouch Kinney" in *Souvenir of Western Women*, with no place of publication, publisher, or date of publication listed.
40. Kinney, "Some Family History," 14–16. But on cooperation between would-be settlers and Native Americans on the Oregon Trail, see Michael L. Tate, *Indians and Emigrants: Encounters on the Overland Trails* (Norman: University of Oklahoma Press, 2006), which shows collaboration as well as conflict between the two groups, as in matters of trade, for example.
41. Kinney, "Some Family History," 17; "Mr. and Mrs. Robert Crouch Kinney."
42. Mike Blakely, *A Sinister Splendor: A Mexican War Novel* (New York: Tom Doherty Associates, 2019), 147.
43. Estimates of numbers of emigrants using the Oregon Trail vary. For one list of emigrants yearly between 1840 and 1868, see David Dary, *The Oregon Trail An American Saga* (Oxford: Oxford University Press, 2004), 305.
44. Dean L. May, *Three Frontiers: Family, Land, and Society in the American West, 1850–1900* (Cambridge: Cambridge University Press, 1994), 24.
45. As quoted in Rinker Buck, *The Oregon Trail: A New American Journey* (New York: Simon and Schuster, 2015), 3.
46. On interactions between Native Americans and European Americans on the central Great Plains, see Elliott West, *The Contested Plains: Indians, Goldseekers, and the Rush to Colorado* (Lawrence: University Press of Kansas, 1998).
47. As quoted in Buck, *Oregon Trail*, 163.
48. As quoted in Whaley, *Illahee*, 148.
49. Bowen, *Willamette Valley*, 6. This far-reaching study is especially valuable for its geographic and demographic maps.
50. May, *Three Frontiers*, 15.
51. Bowen, *Willamette Valley*, 17–21, esp. 18. On motives, see also Boag, *Environment*, 36–37.

52. Bowen, *Willamette Valley*, 25; and Faragher, *Women and Men*, 165.
53. Dary, *Oregon Trail*, 244.
54. On the route of the Oregon Trail, see Faragher, *Women and Men*, 7–11. For a description of the journey by one Ohio woman turned Missourian in 1844, see Dary, *Oregon Trail*, 115–17.
55. Sarah Keyes, "'Like a Roaring Lion': The Overland Trail as a Sonic Conquest," *Journal of American History* 96, no. 1 (June 2009): 19–43, esp. 43. On the cholera epidemic, see Hämäläinen, *Lakota America*, 214; and Hämäläinen, *Indigenous Continent*, 406. About one-seventh of the Lakota died during the cholera epidemic. On ecological changes occurring along the Platte River portion of the Oregon Trail, see West, *Contested Plains*, 88–89.
56. As quoted in Buck, *Oregon Trail*, 181–82.
57. Schwantes, *Pacific Northwest*, 110–23.
58. Schwantes, 121. See also Boag, *Environment*, 52; Bowen, *Willamette Valley*, 69–72, which reprints verbatim early Oregon land legislation; and Everett Dick, *The Lure of the Land: A Social History of the Public Lands from the Articles of Confederation to the New Deal* (Lincoln: University of Nebraska Press, 1970), 128–29.
59. Schwantes, *Pacific Northwest*, 122, 154.
60. On their experiences, see Shirley Ann Wilson Moore, *Sweet Freedom's Plains: African Americans on the Overland Trails, 1841–1869* (Norman: University of Oklahoma Press, 2016).
61. Schwantes, *Pacific Northwest*, 154–56.
62. Whaley, *Illahee*, 161, 168. See also Bunting, *Pacific Raincoast*, 47.
63. Bunting, *Pacific Raincoast*, 120. Romantic, as well as pragmatic, visions stud their diaries. One discerned a "broad river glowing under the morning sun" when viewing the Platte River, "a sheet of silver." As quoted in H. W. Brands, *Dreams of El Dorado: A History of the American West* (New York: Basic Books, 2019), 174.
64. May, *Three Frontiers*, 2.
65. Bowen, *Willamette Valley*, 61.
66. Wallace Stegner, *Angle of Repose: A Novel* (Garden City, NJ: Doubleday, 1971). See also Stegner's autobiographical account about growing up on the Canadian Great Plains, *Wolf Willow: A History, A Story, and a Memory on the Last Plains Frontier* (Lincoln: University of Nebraska Press, 1980), and his fictional account, *The Big Rock Candy Mountain* (Garden City, NJ: Doubleday, 1943).
67. Bowen, *Willamette Valley*, 74–94.
68. Bunting, *Pacific Raincoast*, 101; and Schwantes, *Pacific Northwest*, 111.
69. Boag, *Environment*, 42; and Bowen, *Willamette Valley*, 68 (the source of the quotation) and 73.
70. Boag, *Environment*, 42; Bowen, *Willamette Valley*, 14–15; and Whaley, *Illahee*, 162.
71. Boag, *Environment*, 41–73.

72. May, *Three Frontiers*, 39, 160–63, 177.
73. On the later agricultural development of the Willamette valley, see Peter A. Kopp, *Hoptopia: A World of Agriculture and Beer in Oregon's Willamette Valley* (Berkeley: University of California Press, 2016).
74. Richard White, *Land Use, Environment, and Social Change: The Shaping of Island County, Washington* (Seattle: University of Washington Press, 1980).
75. White, *Land Use*, 25.
76. White, 32–34.
77. White, 38, 43, 47, 51. See also Alan Taylor, *American Colonies: The Settling of North America* (New York: Penguin Books, 2001), 48.
78. Whaley, *Illahee*, 3–18.
79. White, *Land Use*, 26–27. See also Boag, *Environment*, 19–21; Bowen, *Willamette Valley*, 59; Hyde, *Empires, Nations, and Families*, 333–35; and David Igler, *The Great Ocean: Pacific Worlds from Captain Cook to the Gold Rush* (Oxford: Oxford University Press, 2013), 66–70. For more detail, see Robert Boyd, *The Coming of the Spirit of Pestilence: Introduced Infectious Diseases and Population Decline among Northwest Coast Indians, 1774–1874* (Seattle: University of Washington Press, 1999).
80. Hyde, *Empires, Nations, and Families*, 421–34, esp. 428.
81. Alexandra Harmon, ed., *The Power of Promises: Rethinking Indian Treaties in the Pacific Northwest* (Seattle: University of Washington Press, 2008); and Whaley, *Illahee*, 182–91.
82. B. J. Cummings, *The River that Made Seattle: A Human and Natural History of the Duwamish* (Seattle: University of Washington Press, 2020), 30.
83. Bunting, *Pacific Raincoast*, 57.
84. Coll Thrush, *Native Seattle: Histories from the Crossing-Over Place* (Seattle: University of Washington Press, 2007).
85. Bunting, *Pacific Raincoast*, 108.
86. Thrush, *Native Seattle*, 37. On environmental changes occurring in the Seattle area, see also Matthew Klingle, *Emerald City: An Environmental History of Seattle* (New Haven, CT: Yale University Press, 2007).
87. Arthur Denny, *Pioneer Days on Puget Sound* (Seattle: C. B. Bagley, Printer, 1888), 72.

CHAPTER 4: MOVING ONTO THE GREAT PLAINS

1. Gilbert C. Fite, "Daydreams and Nightmares: The Late Nineteenth-Century Agricultural Frontiers," *Agricultural History* 40, no. 4 (October 1966): 285–93. On false advertising of lands in Nebraska see also, Matthew S. Luckett, "'Nebraska Is, at Least, Not a Desert': Land Sales, False Promises, and Real Estate Borderlands on the Great Plains," in *The Interior Borderlands: Regional Identity in the Midwest and Great Plains*, ed. Jon K. Lauck (Sioux Falls, SD: Augustana University, Center

for Western Studies, 2019), 76–90. However, some scholars argue that settlers understood well what they were getting into when they moved onto the Great Plains. See Lauck, "Finding the Center Line: In Search of the Midwest/Great Plains Border Lands," in Lauck, *Interior Borderlands,* xxiii–lii, esp. xxxviii.

2. The leading historian of rural America observes, "The plains imposed severe hardship on any and all settlers." David B. Danbom, *Sod Busting: How Families Made Farms on the Nineteenth-Century Plains* (Baltimore: Johns Hopkins University Press, 2014), 2.
3. A key study is Craig Miner, *West of Wichita: Settling the High Plains of Kansas, 1865–1890* (Lawrence: University Press of Kansas, 1986). Raised in western Kansas, Miner states, "The initial and strongest continuing motivation for writing this book came not from the documents, but from my strong sense of the High Plains of Kansas as a special and powerful region" (vii). He notes, "Thousands of people helped to conquer the [Kansas] frontier, but thousands more were conquered by it," and asks, "Who were these people? What were the conditions of their success or failure?" (3). It is these questions that his study tries to answer.
4. Fred A. Shannon, *The Farmer's Last Frontier: Agriculture, 1860–1897* (New York: Harper and Row, 1945), 148–96, remains a solid introduction to the history of prairie agriculture; but see also Geoff Cunfer, *On the Great Plains: Agriculture and Environment* (College Station: Texas A&M UniversityPress, 2005). On the importance of droughts affecting lives on the southern Great Plains in the 1800s, see Kevin Z. Sweeney, *Prelude to the Dust Bowl: Drought in the Nineteenth-Century Southern Plains* (Norman: University of Oklahoma Press, 2016). Major droughts occurred in 1819–22, 1854–65, 1885–87, and 1893–97.
5. Joanna L. Stratton, *Pioneer Women: Voices from the Kansas Frontier* (New York: Simon and Schuster, 1981), 24, is based upon a close examination of the memoirs of eight hundred women who moved to Kansas between 1854 and 1890. Other state studies are also valuable: Julie Jones-Eddy, *Homesteading Women: An Oral History of Colorado, 1890–1950* (New York: Twayne, 1992); Sarah Carter, ed., *Montana Women Homesteaders: A Field of One's Own* (Helena, MT: Farcountry, 2009); and Glenda Riley, *Frontierswomen: The Iowa Experience* (Ames: Iowa State University Press, 1981).
6. As quoted in Stratton, *Pioneer Women,* 34, 44–45.
7. Miner, *West of Wichita,* 67.
8. Stratton, *Pioneer Women,* 24.
9. Scholars disagree on exactly where the Midwest ends and the Great Plains begin. In 2019, geographer Christopher R. Laingen spoke for many scholars when he wrote that anyone searching for "exactly where the Midwest ends and the Great Plains begins" must be "prepare[d] for a disappointment." See Laingen, "Geographies of the Borderlands," in Lauck, *Interior Borderlands,* 1–19, esp. 1. Similarly, geologist James S. Aber

and librarian Susan W. Aber claim, "Making a precise Midwest–Great Plains boundary remains an illusionary goal." See J. S. Aber and S. W. Aber, "Aerial Transect of the Central Great Plains/Midwest Borderlands," in Lauck, *Interior Borderlands,* ed., 20–39, esp. 37. Still, many scholars have seen a border at about longitude 98° west. Thus, historian Gleaves Whitney describes the region of longitude 98° to 100° west as a zone of tension, "not 'either-or' but 'both-and'—sharing characteristics of both the Midwest and Great Plains." See Whitney, "The 'There' in 'There Is No There There,'" in Lauck, *Interior Borderlands,* 55–75, esp. 71. Likewise, historian Lauck suggests the existence of a "Center Line, which denotes a division, as on a road, but not a hard line or barrier or concrete median or wall, one easily crossed over without much thought." Lauck posits a "Center Line, roughly the area extending fifty miles or so on either side of the 100th meridian" as dividing the Midwest from the Great Plains. See Lauck, "Finding the Center Line," in Lauck, *Interior Borderlands,* xxiii–xxvi.

10. In 1931, Walter Prescott Webb postulated a dividing line around the 98th meridian. See Webb, *Great Plains* (Boston: Ginn, 1931), 37.
11. Wallace Stegner, *Beyond the Hundredth Meridian: The Exploration of the Grand Canyon and the Second Opening of the West* (Boston: Houghton Mifflin, 1962), 215, and map after xxiii.
12. Sweeney, *Prelude,* 21.
13. As quoted in Lauck, "Finding the Center Line," in Lauck, *Interior Borderlands,* xxxii.
14. Fite, "Daydreams," 285–93.
15. Not all Americans viewed the Great Plains negatively. See Dan Flores, *American Serengeti: The Last Big Animals on the Great Plains* (Lawrence: University Press of Kansas, 2016), 163–66.
16. Miner, *West of Wichita,* 3–4.
17. Much has been written about the history of Plains Indians. A valuable starting place remains Preston Holder, *The Hoe and the Horse on the Plains: A Study of Cultural Development among North American Indians* (Lincoln: University of Nebraska Press, 1970). For a succinct account, see Colin G. Calloway, *One Vast Winter Count: The Native American West before Lewis and Clark* (Lincoln: University of Nebraska Press, 2003), 267–300. In times of drought, the horse Indians migrated temporarily to wetter lands, often to the east.
18. Pekka Hämäläinen, *The Comanche Empire* (New Haven, CT: Yale University Press, 2008), 278.
19. Luther Standing Bear, *Land of the Spotted Eagle* (Boston: Houghton Mifflin, 1933), xix. See also Luther Standing Bear, *My People: The Sioux* (Boston: Houghton Mifflin, 1928).
20. N. Scott Momaday, *The Way to Rainy Mountain* (New York: Ballantine Books, 1972), 8.
21. On the expansionary Sioux, see Richard White, "The Winning of the West: The Expansion of the Western Sioux in the Eighteenth and

Nineteenth Centuries," *Journal of American History* 65, no. 2 (September 1978): 319–43. More generally about Plains Indian life, see Pekka Hämäläinen, "The Rise and Fall of Plains Indian Horse Cultures," *Journal of American History* 90, no. 3 (December 2003): 833–62.

22. This account of the Comanche is derived from Hämäläinen, *Comanche Empire,* esp. 141–292.
23. Hämäläinen, *Comanche Empire,* 276. Hämäläinen calls the Comanche Empire "the pinnacle of Indigenous power in North America." See Pekka Hämäläinen, *Indigenous Continent: The Epic Contest for North America* (New York: Liveright, 2022), 429.
24. Hämäläinen, *Comanche Empire,* 324–25. Just as they differed on the meaning of land ownership, the Comanche and European Americans differed on the meaning of trade. As historian Anne Hyde explains, Comanche "saw trade items as part of creating relationships that began cycles of mutual obligations. Anglo-Americans, in contrast, engaged in trade as part of simply earning a living, a scheme that was personal and individual." See Hyde, *Empires, Nations, and Families: A New History of the North American West, 1800–1860* (Lincoln: University of Nebraska Press, 2011), 164.
25. Elliott West, *The Contested Plains: Indians, Goldseekers, and the Rush to Colorado* (Lawrence: University Press of Kansas, 1998), 68–92.
26. On epidemics, see Pekka Hämäläinen, *Lakota America: A New History of Indigenous Power* (New Haven, CT: Yale University Press, 2019), 20–21, 26, 94–96, 120, 186, 190; and Hyde, *Empires, Nations, and Families,* 336–45.
27. Hämäläinen, *Lakota America,* 100. See also Jeffrey Ostler, *The Plains Sioux and U.S. Colonialism from Lewis and Clark to Wounded Knee* (Cambridge: Cambridge University Press, 2004).
28. *Journals of Lewis and Clark,* ed. John Bakeless (New York: Mentor Books, 1964), 94, 99, 102, 112.
29. Stephen Ambrose, *Undaunted Courage: Meriwether Lewis, Thomas Jefferson, and the Opening of the American West* (New York: Simon and Schuster, 1996), 200.
30. Hämäläinen, *Lakota America,* 171–74.
31. Hämäläinen, 40.
32. Robert Utley, *Frontier Regulars: The United States Army and the Indian, 1866–1891* (New York: Macmillan, 1973), 412.
33. Andrew C. Isenberg, *The Destruction of the Bison: An Environmental History, 1750–1920* (Cambridge: Cambridge University Press, 2000). See also Wayne Gard, *The Great Buffalo Hunt: Its History and Drama, and Its Role in the Opening of the West* (Lincoln: University of Nebraska Press, 1959). Environmental historian Dan Flores posits that a "perfect storm" of factors came together to destroy the buffalo: growing drought on the Great Plains, the opening of overland trails across the plains, diseases brought in by settlers' livestock, the work of hide hunters for the market, and the lack of a government policy to protect the buffalo. See Flores, *American Serengeti,* 124–31, esp. 129.

34. Author's visit to the Homestead National Monument in Homestead, NE, July 10, 2013.
35. Ray Allen Billington and Martin Ridge, *Westward Expansion: A History of the American Frontier,* 5th ed. (New York: Macmillan, 1982), 637–43; and Everett Dick, *The Lure of the Land: A Social History of the Public Lands from the Articles of Confederation to the New Deal* (Lincoln: University of Nebraska Press, 1970), 135–39, 224, 227–28, 309.
36. Richard Edwards, Jacob K. Friefeld, and Rebecca S. Wingo, *Homesteading the Plains: Toward a New History* (Lincoln: University of Nebraska Press, 2017), 30–33, 198.
37. Dick, *Lure of the Land,* 48.
38. Edwards, Friefeld, and Wingo, *Homesteading,* 36, 40, 198.
39. Billington and Ridge, *Westward Expansion,* 641; and Dick, *Lure of the Land,* 176. On railroad land grants, see esp. Richard White, *Railroaded: The Transcontinentals and the Making of Modern America* (New York: W. W. Norton, 2011). White is critical of the grants and concludes that not all the transcontinentals were needed. Still, many settlers chose to buy railroad lands. Railroads usually offered credit terms with reasonable interest rates, and railroad lands were close to a transportation system settlers could use to get their crops to market. Homestead Act lands were often farther away. See also Robert William Fogel, *The Union Pacific Railroad: A Case Study in Premature Enterprise* (Baltimore: Johns Hopkins University Press, 1960); and Lloyd Mercer, "Taxpayers or Investors: Who Paid for the Land-Grant Railroads?," *Business History Review* 46, no. 3 (Autumn 1972): 279–94.
40. Paul Wallace Gates, "The Homestead Act in an Incongruous Land System," *American Historical Review* 41 (July 1936): 652–81. See also Dick, *Lure of the Land,* 158. For a different point of view, see Cunfer, *Great Plains,* 16–36.
41. Richard White, *The Republic for Which It Stands: The United States during Reconstruction and the Gilded Age, 1865–1896* (New York: Oxford University Press, 2017), 121, 435. Not all scholars agree with White. Some see his work as ideologically driven. They point out that the Homestead Act was not initially intended to govern land sales in the semiarid and arid West but in the more humid East, where it worked well.
42. Danbom, *Born in the Country: A History of Rural America,* 3rd ed. (Baltimore: Johns Hopkins University Press, 2017), 136–37. However, in an earlier work, Danbom writes, "The process of plains settlement is an American success story." See Danbom, *Sod Busting,* 107.
43. As quoted in Timothy Egan, *The Worst Hard Time: The Untold Story of Those Who Survived the Great American Dust Bowl* (Boston: Houghton, Mifflin, Harcourt, 2006), 267. Not all nineteenth-century Americans thought that older notions about land and water use would work in the Far West. See Donald Worster, *A River Running West: The Life of John*

Wesley Powell (Oxford: Oxford University Press, 2001), esp. 346–49, 356–59, 500–506. A federal government official, Powell believed that community-based irrigation systems focused on natural watersheds were needed.

44. As quoted in Miner, *West of Wichita,* 135, 137.
45. Edwards, Friefeld, and Wingo, *Homesteading,* 198.
46. Paula Nelson, "Geography Is Not Destiny: Human Agency in the Midwest/Great Plains Transition Zone," and Brad Tenant, "West of the 100th Meridian: Where the Midwest Ends and the Great Plains Begins," in Lauck, *Interior Borderlands,* 188–200, 256–72.
47. On the settlement and early political development of the Dakota Territory, see Jon K. Lauck, *Prairie Republic: The Political Culture of Dakota Territory, 1879–1889* (Norman: University of Oklahoma Press, 2010), 5, 21–22, 24.
48. Kenneth Marvin Hamilton, *Black Towns and Profit: Promotion and Development in the Trans–Appalachian West, 1877–1915* (Urbana: University of Illinois Press, 1991), 153–54.
49. Nell Irvin Painter, *Exodusters: Black Migration to Kansas after Reconstruction* (New York: W. W. Norton, 1976).
50. As quoted in Miner, *West of Wichita,* 85.
51. Painter, *Exodusters,* 6. Similarly, Richard Edwards and Jacob K. Friefeld, *The First Migrants: How Black Homesteaders' Quest for Land and Freedom Heralded America's Great Migration* (Lincoln: University of Nebraska Press, 2023), asserts that African Americans "were looking for opportunity, freedom and land," and "wherever they moved from, African Americans arrived on the Great Plains seeking land" (3, 11).
52. Painter, *Exodusters,* 4, 146–47.
53. Painter, 260. Other scholars have gone further. Edwards and Friefeld, in *First Migrants,* claim that the Exodusters "constituted the opening wave of Black people out of the South known as the Great Migration" (8).
54. Everett Dick, *The Sod-House Frontier, 1854–1890: A Social History of the Northern Plains from the Creation of Kansas and Nebraska to the Admission of the Dakotas* (Lincoln: Johnsen, 1954). See also Danbom, *Sod Busting,* 34–41.
55. As quoted in Miner, *West of Wichita,* 52.
56. As quoted in Dick, *Lure of the Land,* 155.
57. E. V. Smalley, "The Isolation of Life on Prairie Farms," *Atlantic Monthly* 72, no. 431 (1893): 378–82.
58. Smalley, "The Isolation of Life," 28.
59. Cunfer, *Great Plains,* 27.
60. Cunfer, 28.
61. Cunfer, 86, 112.
62. David Schorr, *Golden Rules: The Origins of California Water Law in the Gold Rush* (Chicago: University of Chicago Press, 2015). See also Dick, *Lure of the Land,* 310.

63. Dick, *Lure of the Land,* 311. See also Mansel G. Blackford, *Fragile Paradise: The Impact of Tourism on Maui, 1959–2000* (Lawrence: University Press of Kansas, 2001), 117–18.
64. Donald Pisani, *Water, Land, and Law in the West: The Limits of Public Policy, 1850–1920* (Lawrence: University Press of Kansas, 1996), 1. See also Pisani, *To Reclaim a Divided West: Water, Law, and Public Policy, 1848–1902* (Albuquerque: University of New Mexico Press, 1992); and Donald Worster, *Rivers of Empire: Water, Aridity, and the Growth of the American West* (New York: Pantheon Books, 1985). The Ogallala Aquifer underlay parts of the central and southern Great Plains and was tapped for irrigation in those regions, especially after World War II. Some Great Plains states asserted control and/or ownership of water in streams and aquifers. Colorado and Wyoming had always done so, and other states joined them: Kansas in 1954 and Oklahoma in 1949. Texas water remained in private hands. See John Opie, *Ogallala: Water for a Dry Land* (Lincoln: University of Nebraska Press, 1993); and Cunfer, *Great Plains,* 164–200, esp. 186.
65. John Ise, *Sod and Stubble: The Story of a Kansas Homestead* (Lincoln: University of Nebraska Press, 1967). John Ise was a son of Henry and Rosie. He became a well-known historian of the American West.
66. Ise, *Sod and Stubble,* 21.
67. On the movement to Kansas, see James R. Shortridge, *Peopling the Plains: Who Settled Where in Frontier Kansas* (Lawrence: University Press of Kansas, 1995).
68. Ise, *Sod and Stubble,* 7–8, 112.
69. Ise, 7, 17, 68, 139.
70. Ise, 19, 32, 41, 44, 49, 51, 59, 84, 91, 115, 135, 139.
71. Ise, xi, 22–24, 68, 107, 141.
72. Mil Penner, *Section 27: A Century on a Family Farm* (Lawrence: University Press of Kansas, 2002), 12. The great-grandson of the founders of the family farm, Mil Penner explained his motivation in preparing his history in these words: "It was my original intention to write the story of the land itself unencumbered by personal history, but I soon discovered that one cannot tell the real story of the land without involving its people and their values. In this book, I prefer to use a broad definition of land that includes all of its flora, fauna, and the weather elements" (xi).
73. Penner, *Section 27,* x, 4–5.
74. Penner, 14–15. On Turkey Red wheat and Russian thistle, see also Sweeney, *Prelude,* 161; and Egan, *Worst Hard Time,* 84.
75. Penner, *Section 27,* 24, 63, 62.
76. Penner, 15.
77. Hamlin Garland, *Main-Travelled Roads* (New York: Signet Classics, 1962); and Garland, *A Son of the Middle Border* (St. Paul, MN: Borealis Books, 2007).
78. Garland, *Son,* 237.

79. Garland, 240–41, 243–44.
80. Garland, *Main-Travelled Roads,* 32, 40–41, 52.
81. Jon K. Lauck, *From Warm Center to Ragged Edge: The Erosion of Midwestern Literary and Historical Regionalism, 1920–1965* (Iowa City: University of Iowa Press, 2017), 105. For a biography, see Keith Newlin, *Hamlin Garland: A Life* (Lincoln: University of Nebraska Press, 2008).
82. Willa Cather, *My Antonia* (Boston: Houghton Mifflin, 1954), 7. For more positive views by Cather, see Flores, *American Serengeti,* 165.
83. Theodore Roethke, "Journey to the Interior," in *The Far Field: Last Poems* (Garden City, NJ: Doubleday, 1964), 19.
84. O. E. Rolvaag, *Giants in the Earth* (New York: Harper and Row, 1955), 3.
85. Laurie Loewenstein, *Death of a Rainmaker: A Dust Bowl Mystery* (Brooklyn, NY: Akashic Books, 2018), 91–92. See also Kristin Hannah, *The Four Winds* (New York: St. Martin's Press, 2022). Set in the panhandle of Texas and central California in the 1930s, this novel is permeated by dust which leaves "no houses, no fences, no animals, no windmills. Just endless brown-gold dirt molded into hills and dunes" (81). For a look at recent Great Plains literature, see David Pichaske, "The Great Plains Vision: Horizontal Grandeur," in Lauck, *Interior Borderlands,* 149–62. Rachel Hanel, "Exploring Midwest/Great Plains Borderlands in Modern Women's Memoir," in Lauck, *Interior Borderlands,* 128–39, examines works by women writers. Hanel concludes, "The women writing of the Great Plains leave the area to reinvent themselves; the women writing of the Midwest reinvent themselves in order to stay" (129).
86. Stratton, *Pioneer Women,* 61.
87. Stratton, 71. Making a plains farm was costly. Land might be free, but nothing else was. In the eastern Dakotas during the 1880s, for example, the cost of starting a farm came to about $3,200 for the home and other buildings, fencing, equipment, horses, digging a well, breaking the sod, and planting crops on 160 acres. See Danbom, *Sod Busting,* 51–54.
88. Edwards, Friefeld, and Wingo, *Homesteading,* 137–38.
89. As quoted in Stratton, *Pioneer Women,* 56.
90. Egan, *Worst Hard Time,* 19, 112–13.
91. The classic work is Donald Worster, *Dust Bowl: The Southern Plains in the 1930s* (Oxford: Oxford University Press, 1979). On the Dust Bowl, see also R. Douglas Hurt, *The Dust Bowl: An Agricultural and Social History* (Chicago: Nelson-Hall, 1981).
92. Cunfer, *Great Plains,* 16. See also Flores, *American Serengeti,* 167.
93. Egan, *Worst Hard Time,* 198–221; and Lauck, "Finding the Center Line," xxxix.
94. Miner, *West of Wichita,* 50, 172–88, 235.
95. Douglas Brinkley, *Rightful Heritage: Franklin D. Roosevelt and the Land of America* (New York: Harper Collins, 2016), 287, 289, 444. See also Egan, *Worst Hard Time,* 161, 271, 280, 444.

96. Wilmon H. Droze, *Trees, Prairies, and People: A History of Tree Planting in the Plains States* (Denton: Texas Women's University, 1977). Droze oversaw the tree-planting project. See also Heidi Marttila-Losure, "Shelterbelts, One of the Great Soil Conservation Measures of the 1930s, Are Being Removed," *Dakotafire Media,* February 4, 2013, https://dakotafire.net/.
97. Cunfer, *Great Plains,* 205.
98. For a brief examination of the Great Plains in the late twentieth century stressing environmental issues, see R. Douglas Hurt, "The Great Plains: Agriculture and the Environment in the Late Twentieth Century," *Agricultural History* 75, no. 4 (Autumn 2001): 395–405.
99. Catherine Raven, *Fox and I: An Uncommon Friendship* (New York: Spiegel and Grau, 2021), 39–40.
100. Julie Courtwright, *Prairie Fire: A Great Plains History* (Lawrence: University Press of Kansas, 2011).
101. Cunfer, *Great Plains,* 41. Local losses could be large. In 2001, only 28 percent of North Dakota's virgin prairie land remained, and in Texas, just 20 percent. See Flores, *American Serengeti,* 167.
102. Flores, *American Serengeti,* 167–83, explores the notion of rewilding the Great Plains.
103. As quoted in E. J. Bell Jr., *Homesteading in Montana: Life in the Blue Mountain Country, 1911–1923* (Bozeman, MT: Big Sky Books, 1975), 66.
104. For two firsthand accounts of bison ranching, see Dan O'Brien, *Buffalo for the Broken Heart: Restoring Life to a Black Hills Ranch* (New York: Random House, 2001); and Mary Zeiss Stange, *Hard Grass: Life on the Crazy Woman Bison Ranch* (Albuquerque: University of New Mexico Press, 2010). O'Brien ranched in South Dakota, Stange in eastern Montana.

CONCLUSIONS

1. Historian Geoff Cunfer states, "Over three hundred years Euro-American farmers opened new land, cropped it for several decades as fertility declined, and moved westward to plow richer soil on new frontiers." *On the Great Plains: Agriculture and Environment* (College Station: Texas A&M University Press, 2005), 217–21, esp. 218.
2. David Danbom, *Born in the Country: A History of Rural America,* 3rd ed. (Baltimore: Johns Hopkins University Press, 2017), 220–51. Danbom clearly explains the pros and cons and the winners and losers in the agricultural revolution. Since 1981, the United States has experienced a net loss of 544,000 farms, even as overall farm output has greatly increased. Remaining farms have become larger. *New York Times,* June 3, 2024, B1.
3. James Rebanks, *Pastoral Song: A Farmer's Journey* (New York: Mariner Books, 2020), 173.
4. On the use of chemicals in farming, see Bartow J. Elmore, *Seed Money: Monsanto's Past and Our Food Future* (New York: W. W. Norton, 2021).

5. Stephen Markley, *Ohio: A Novel* (New York: Simon and Schuster, 2018), 147.
6. As quoted in Colin G. Calloway, *The Indian World of George Washington: The First President, the First Americans, and the Birth of the Nation* (New York: Oxford University Press, 2018), 48.
7. Richard Powers, *The Overstory: A Novel* (New York: W. W. Norton, 2018), 115.
8. Chris D. Thomas, *Inheritors of the Earth: How Nature Is Thriving in an Age of Extinction* (New York: PublicAffairs, 2017), 158. Thomas provocatively argues that human actions have increased the variety of flora and fauna globally. Despite some local extinctions, the overall count of types of plants and animals has, he asserts, increased. New flora and fauna have entered regions faster than old ones have disappeared, as environmental changes made by people have created new opportunities and as human activities have sped up evolution and species variation. Thomas goes so far as to state: "We are living through a period of the rapid formation of new populations, races, and species. In the end, the Anthropocene biological revolution will almost certainly represent the sixth mass genesis of new biological diversity. It could be the fastest acceleration of evolutionary diversification in the last half-billion years" (197).
9. On the long-lasting dream of Alaska as home for Jeffersonian yeoman farmers, see James Shortridge, "The Alaskan Agricultural Empire: An American Agrarian Vision, 1898–1929," *Pacific Northwest Quarterly* 69, no. 4 (Oct. 1978): 145–58.
10. Nannie T. Alderson and Helena Smith, *A Bride Goes West* (Lincoln: University of Nebraska Press, 1974). In general, European American settlers, particularly women, sought to recreate cultures and societies they left behind when they moved to western frontiers. Historian David Danbom writes: "Women making homes on the plains might have been in the wilderness, but they had no intention of being of the wilderness." On the contrary, they worked hard at "transferring what they understood to be civilized standards and behaviors from Europe or the East to the Great Plains." *Sod Busting: How Families Made Farms on the Nineteenth-Century Plains* (Baltimore: Johns Hopkins University Press, 2014), 46.
11. Abrahm Lustgarten, *On the Move: The Overheating Earth and the Uprooting of America* (New York: Farrar, Straus and Giroux, 2024), is a comprehensive introduction to the issues of global warming and climate change.

Bibliographic Essay

This study draws on a wide range of primary and secondary sources, as indicated in the endnotes. For primary sources—diaries, memoirs, and collections of letters—and works of fiction, such as novels, see the endnotes for each chapter. This bibliographic essay highlights selected secondary sources that have been most valuable for me and which might lead readers into additional avenues of thought. Much remains to be done on the broad-ranging topic of land and frontier developments.

Particularly important works about Americans, their frontiers, and land include Frederick Jackson Turner, "The Significance of the Frontier in American History," *Annual Report of the American Historical Association for the Year 1893* (Washington, DC: Government Printing Office, 1894), 199–227; Walter Prescott Webb, *The Great Plains* (Boston: Ginn, 1931); and Greg Grandin, *The End of the Myth: From the Frontier to the Border Wall in the Mind of America* (New York: Henry Holt, 2019). These titles examine the significance of frontiers to Americans over several centuries. On the new western history, see Patricia Nelson Limerick, *The Legacy of Conquest: The Unbroken Past of the American West* (New York: W. W. Norton, 1988); Patricia Nelson Limerick, *Something in the Soil: Legacies and Reckonings in the New West* (New York: W. W. Norton, 2001), a collection of sixteen essays; and Richard White, *"It's Your Misfortune and None of My Own": A New History of the American West* (Norman: University of Oklahoma Press, 1991). William Cronon, *Changes in the Land: Indians, Colonists, and the Ecology of New England* (New York: Hill and Wang, 1983); and Anne F. Hyde, *Empires, Nations and Families: A New History of the North American West, 1800–1860* (Lincoln: University of Nebraska Press, 2011) have pointed western American history in important new directions. Sara Dant, *Losing Eden: An Environmental History of the American West* (London: Wiley-Blackwell, 2016) provides a survey of environmental developments west of the 100th meridian.

Paul W. Gates, *History of Public Land Development* (Washington, DC: Government Printing Office, 1968) is the classic work on the history of the public domain of the United States. See also Malcolm J. Rohrbough, *The Land Office Business: The Settlement and Administration of American Public Lands, 1789–1837* (New York: Oxford University Press, 1968); and Everett Dick, *The Lure of the Land: A Social History of the Public Lands from the Articles of Confederation to the New Deal* (Lincoln: University of Nebraska Press, 1970).

On recent developments in the public domain, see James R. Skillen, *The Nation's Largest Landlord: The Bureau of Land Management in the American West* (Lawrence: University Press of Kansas, 2008); and Erika Allen Wolters and Brent S. Steele, eds., *The Environmental Politics and Policy of Western Public Lands* (Corvallis: Oregon State University Press, 2020), a collection of sixteen essays by scholars and practitioners.

Malcolm J. Rohrbough, *The Trans–Appalachian Frontier: People, Societies, and Institutions, 1775–1850,* 2nd ed. (Belmont, CA: Wadsworth, 1990) is a key work on developments in the Ohio and Mississippi valleys. The scholarly literature on frontier Ohio is extensive. R. Douglas Hurt, *The Ohio Frontier: Crucible of the Old Northwest, 1720–1830* (Bloomington: Indiana University Press, 1998) is the place to start. Two works dealing with Ohio as part of the Ohio River valley are especially valuable: Andrew R. L. Cayton and Stuart D. Hobbs, eds., *The Center of a Great Empire: The Ohio Country in the Early Republic* (Athens: Ohio University Press, 2005); and Kim M. Gruenwald, *River of Enterprise: The Commercial Origins of Regional Identity in the Ohio Valley, 1790–1850* (Bloomington: Indiana University Press, 2002). Emily Foster, ed., *The Ohio Frontier: An Anthology of Early Writings* (Lexington: University Press of Kentucky, 1996) reprints primary sources. John Mack Faragher, *Sugar Creek: Life on the Illinois Prairie* (New Haven, CT: Yale University Press, 1986) examines the history of a midwestern farming community. R. Douglas Hurt, *Agriculture in the Midwest, 1815–1900* (Lincoln: University of Nebraska Press, 2023); and David Danbom, *Born in the Country: A History of Rural America,* 3rd ed. (Baltimore: Johns Hopkins University Press, 2017) are superb broad-ranging studies.

Several surveys of Ohio history deal with frontier developments: Andrew R. L. Cayton, *Ohio: The History of a People* (Columbus: Ohio State University Press, 2002); Kevin F. Kern and Gregory S. Wilson, *Ohio: A History of the Buckeye State* (Chichester, UK: Wiley-Blackwell, 2014); and George W. Knepper, *Ohio and Its People,* 3rd ed. (Kent, OH: Kent State University Press, 2003). Timothy G. Anderson and Brian Schoen, eds., *Settling Ohio: First Peoples and Beyond* (Athens: Ohio University Press, 2023) is a valuable collection of essays by scholars in several fields. To explore agriculture, begin with Richard Lyman Bushman, *The American Farmer in the Eighteenth Century: A Social and Cultural History* (New Haven, CT: Yale University Press, 2018). On African Americans in early-day Ohio and the Midwest, see Stephen Middleton, *The Black Laws: Race and the Legal Process in Early Ohio* (Athens: Ohio University Press, 2005); and Anna-Lisa Cox, *The Bone and Sinew of the Land: America's Forgotten Black Pioneers and the Struggle for Equality* (New York: PublicAffairs, 2018). The lives of women on the Ohio frontier may be explored in Mildred Covey Fry, "Women on the Ohio Frontier: The Marietta Area," *Ohio History* 80 (Winter 1981): 54–73; and Stephane Elise Booth, *Buckeye Women: The History of Ohio's Daughters* (Athens: Ohio University Press, 2001), 1–18.

On the recent revitalization of midwestern history, see Andrew R. L. Cayton and Susan E. Gray, eds., *The Identity of the American Midwest: Essays on Regional History* (Bloomington: Indiana University Press, 2001), a collection of eleven essays. For a statement and survey of the region's historiography, see Jon K. Lauck, *The Lost Region: Toward a Revival of Midwestern History* (Iowa City: University of Iowa Press, 2012). Now-classic studies include Andrew R. L. Cayton and Peter S. Onuf, *The Midwest and the Nation: Rethinking the History of an American Region* (Bloomington: Indiana University Press, 1990); and James R. Shortridge, *The Middle West: Its Meaning in American Culture* (Lawrence: University Press of Kansas, 1989). See also Kristin L. Hoganson, *The Heartland: An American History* (New York City: Penguin, 2019); Jon K. Lauck, *From Warm Center to Ragged Edge: The Erosion of Midwestern Literary and Historical Regionalism, 1920–1965* (Iowa City: University of Iowa Press, 2017); and Jon K. Lauck, Gleaves Whitney, and Joseph Hogan, eds., *Finding a New Midwestern History* (Lincoln: University of Nebraska Press, 2018), a collection of twenty-one essays.

The twenty essays composing Jon K. Lauck, ed., *The Interior Borderlands: Regional Identity in the Midwest and Great Plains* (Sioux Falls, SD: Augustana University, Center for Western Studies, 2019) explore both the Midwest and the Great Plains and postulate various dividing lines between the two regions. See also Jon K. Lauck, *The Good Country: A History of the American Midwest, 1800–1900* (Norman: University of Oklahoma Press, 2022).

Colin G. Calloway, *One Vast Winter Count: The Native American West before Lewis and Clark* (Lincoln: University of Nebraska Press, 2003); Pekka Hämäläinen, *Indigenous Continent: The Epic Contest for North America* (New York: Liveright, 2022); and Ned Blackhawk, *The Rediscovery of America: Native Peoples and the Unmaking of U.S. History* (New Haven, CT: Yale University Press, 2023) offer valuable accounts of Native American history. Published too late to be used in this account, but also quite valuable, is Kathleen DuVal, *Native Nations: A Millenium in North America* (New York: Random House, 2024).

On Native Americans in the Ohio Country, see Michael A. McDonnell, *Masters of Empire: Great Lakes Indians and the Making of America* (New York: Hill and Wang, 2015); Colin G. Calloway, *The Shawnees and the War for America* (New York: Penguin, 2007); R. Douglas Hurt, *The Indian Frontier, 1763–1846* (Albuquerque: University of New Mexico Press, 2002); Michael N. McConnell, *A Country Between: The Upper Ohio Valley and Its Peoples, 1724–1774* (Lincoln: University of Nebraska Press, 1992); Stephen Warren, *The Worlds the Shawnee Made: Migration and Violence in Early America* (Chapel Hill: University of North Carolina Press, 2014); David Andrew Nichols, *Peoples of the Inland Sea: Native Americans and Newcomers in the Great Lakes Region, 1600–1870* (Athens: Ohio University Press, 2018); and Susan Sleeper-Smith, *Indigenous Prosperity and American Conquest: Indian Women of the Ohio River Valley, 1690–1792* (Chapel Hill: University of North Carolina Press, 2018).

For travel on the Oregon Trail, see David Dary, *The Oregon Trail: An American Saga* (Oxford: Oxford University Press, 2004); John Mack Faragher, *Women and Men on the Overland Trail* (New Haven, CT: Yale University Press, 1979); and John D. Unruh Jr., *The Plains Across: The Overland Emigrants and the Trans–Mississippi West, 1840–60* (Urbana:

University of Illinois Press, 1979). Rinker Buck, *The Oregon Trail: A New American Journey* (New York: Simon and Schuster, 2015) is an account of traversing the trail by wagon in 2011.

Carlos Arnaldo Schwantes, *The Pacific Northwest: An Interpretive History* (Lincoln: University of Nebraska Press, 1996) is a valuable introduction to the history of the Oregon Country. Earlier comprehensive histories of the region include Dorothy O. Johansen and Charles M. Gates, *Empire of the Columbia: A History of the Pacific Northwest* (New York: Harper and Row, 1957); and Earl Pomeroy, *The Pacific Slope: A History of California, Oregon, Washington, Idaho, Utah, and Nevada* (Seattle: University of Washington Press, 1965). Gray H. Whaley, *Oregon and the Collapse of* Illahee: *U.S. Empire and the Transformation of an Indigenous World, 1792–1859* (Chapel Hill: University of North Carolina Press, 2010) examines interactions among Native Americans, European Americans, and environmental changes. See also Robert Bunting, *The Pacific Raincoast: Environment and Culture in an American Eden, 1778–1900* (Lawrence: University Press of Kansas, 1996); and Robert Boyd, ed., *Indians, Fire and the Land in the Pacific Northwest* (Corvallis: Oregon State University Press, 1999). Peter G. Boag, *Environment and Experience: Settlement Culture in Nineteenth-Century Oregon* (Berkeley: University of California Press, 1992) and William A. Bowen, *The Willamette Valley: Migration and Settlement on the Oregon Frontier* (Seattle: University of Washington Press, 1978) analyze frontier life in the Willamette Valley.

Richard White, *Land Use, Environment, and Social Change: The Shaping of Island County, Washington* (Seattle: University of Washington Press, 1980) examines land use in Puget Sound. B. J. Cummings, *The River That Made Seattle: A Human and Natural History of the Duwamish* (Seattle: University of Washington Press, 2020); Matthew Klingle, *Emerald City: An Environmental History of Seattle* (New Haven, CT: Yale University Press, 2007); and Coll Thrush, *Native Seattle: Histories from the Crossing-Over Place* (Seattle: University of Washington Press, 2007) study changes occurring in the Seattle area.

Regarding the history of Plains Indians, a valuable starting place remains Preston Holder, *The Hoe and the Horse on the Plains: A Study of Cultural Development among North American Indians* (Lincoln:

University of Nebraska Press, 1970). For a succinct account, see Colin G. Calloway, *One Vast Winter Count: The Native American West before Lewis and Clark* (Lincoln: University of Nebraska Press, 2003), 267–300. On the expansionary Sioux, see Richard White, "The Winning of the West: The Expansion of the Western Sioux in the Eighteenth and Nineteenth Centuries," *Journal of American History* 65, no. 2 (September 1978): 319–43. More generally about Plains Indian life, see Pekka Hämäläinen, "The Rise and Fall of Plains Indian Horse Cultures," *Journal of American History* 90, no. 3 (December 2003): 833–62. Elliott West, *The Contested Plains: Indians, Goldseekers, and the Rush to Colorado* (Lawrence: University Press of Kansas, 1998); Pekka Hämäläinen, *The Comanche Empire* (New Haven, CT: Yale University Press, 2008); and Hämäläinen, *Lakota America: A New History of Indigenous Power* (New Haven, CT: Yale University Press, 2019) are pathbreaking. See also Jeffrey Ostler, *The Plains Sioux and U.S. Colonialism from Lewis and Clark to Wounded Knee* (Cambridge: Cambridge University Press, 2004). Robert M. Utley, *Frontier Regulars: The United States Army and the Indian, 1866–1891* (New York: Macmillan, 1973) examines campaigns and battles.

On Euro-American farming on the Great Plains, see Everett Dick, *The Sod-House Frontier, 1854–1890: A Social History of the Northern Plains from the Creation of Kansas and Nebraska to the Admission of the Dakotas* (Lincoln, NE: Johnsen, 1954); Richard Edwards, Jacob K. Friefeld, and Rebecca S. Wingo, *Homesteading the Plains: Toward a New History* (Lincoln: University of Nebraska Press, 2017); Craig Miner, *West of Wichita: Settling the High Plains of Kansas, 1865–1890* (Lawrence: University Press of Kansas, 1986); and David B. Danbom, *Sod Busting: How Families Made Farms on the Nineteenth-Century Plains* (Baltimore: Johns Hopkins University Press, 2014). Nell Irvin Painter, *Exodusters: Black Migration to Kansas after Reconstruction* (New York: W. W. Norton, 1976) remains a notable source on African Americans. See also Richard Edwards and Jacob K. Friefeld, *The First Migrants: How Black Homesteaders' Quest for Land and Freedom Heralded America's Great Migration* (Lincoln: University of Nebraska Press, 2023). Julie Courtwright, *Prairie Fire: A Great Plains History* (Lawrence: University Press of Kansas, 2011) looks at the importance of fire on the Great Plains.

For a work combining frontier, environmental, and agricultural history, see Geoff Cunfer, *On the Great Plains: Agriculture and Environment* (College Station: Texas A&M University Press, 2005). On the Great Plains in the twentieth century, see R. Douglas Hurt, *The Big Empty: The Great Plains in the Twentieth Century* (Tucson: University of Arizona Press, 2011). Dan Flores, *American Serengeti: The Last Big Animals on the Great Plains* (Lawrence: University Press of Kansas, 2016) is an excellent natural history. On western American water issues, see especially Donald J. Pisani, *Water, Land, and Law in the West: The Limits of Public Policy, 1850–1920* (Lawrence: University Press of Kansas, 1996); and Pisani, *To Reclaim a Divided West: Water, Law, and Public Policy, 1848–1902* (Albuquerque: University of New Mexico Press, 1992).

Several important state studies have looked at the roles women played on Great Plains frontiers. Joanna L. Stratton, *Pioneer Women: Voices from the Kansas Frontier* (New York: Simon and Schuster, 1981) is a close examination of the memoirs of eight hundred women who moved to Kansas between 1854 and 1890. Other significant state studies are Julie Jones-Eddy, *Homesteading Women: An Oral History of Colorado, 1890–1950* (New York: Twayne, 1992); Sarah Carter, ed., *Montana Women Homesteaders: A Field of One's Own* (Helena, MT: Farcountry Press, 2009); and Glenda Riley, *Frontierswomen: The Iowa Experience* (Ames: Iowa State University Press, 1981).

On modern-day farming and farm life, see Grace Olmstead, *Uprooted: Recovering the Legacy of the Places We've Left Behind* (New York: Sentinel Books, 2021); Richard Rhodes, *Farm: A Year in the Life of an American Farmer* (New York: Simon and Schuster, 1989); and John L. Shover, *First Majority—Last Minority: The Transforming of Rural Life in America* (DeKalb: Northern Illinois University Press, 1976). James Rebanks, *Pastoral Song: A Farmer's Journey* (New York: Mariner Books, 2020) explores changes occurring in Great Britain and the United States.

On the interchange of germs, flora, and fauna between regions globally, see George W. Cox, *Alien Species in North America and Hawaii: Impacts on Natural Ecosystems* (Washington, DC: Island Press, 1999); Alfred W. Crosby Jr., *The Columbian Exchange: Biological and Cultural Consequences of 1492* (Westport, CT: Greenwood, 1972); Crosby,

Ecological Imperialism: The Biological Expansion of Europe, 900–1900 (Cambridge: Cambridge University Press, 1986); and Yvonne Baskin, *A Plague of Rats and Rubbervines: The Growing Threat of Species Invasion* (Washington, DC: Island Press, 2002). For a provocative examination of issues about alien species, see Chris D. Thomas, *Inheritors of the Earth: How Nature Is Thriving in an Age of Extinction* (New York: PublicAffairs, 2017).

On global settler colonialism and environmental changes, see Stuart Banner, *Possessing the Pacific: Land, Settlers, and Indigenous People from Australia to Alaska* (Cambridge, MA: Harvard University Press, 2007) and the fifteen essays composing Tom Griffiths and Libby Robin, eds., *Ecology and Empire: Environmental History of Settler Societies* (Seattle: University of Washington Press, 1997).

Index

The letter *f* following a page number denotes a figure.